LIBERTY
IN HARMONY

The Story of
Joseph Smith in Pennsylvania

LIBERTY
IN HARMONY

The Story of
Joseph Smith in Pennsylvania

FORREST R. HANSEN

CFI

An imprint of Cedar Fort, Inc.
Springville, Utah

Paperback ISBN 13: 978–1-4621–4507–2
eBook ISBN 13: 978-1-4621-4784-7

Published by CFI, an imprint of Cedar Fort, Inc.
2373 W. 700 S., Suite 100, Springville, UT 84663
Distributed by Cedar Fort, Inc., www.cedarfort.com

Library of Congress Control Number: 2023930788

Cover design by Shawnda T. Craig
Cover design © 2024 Cedar Fort, Inc.
Edited by Liz Kazandzhy

Printed in the United States of America

10 9 8 7 6 5 4 3 2 1

Printed on acid-free paper

Sweet, happy place, called Harmony.

Strangers must say, when they pass by,

The Founder they approve;

Who from a forest wild did raise

A seat where men may spend their days

In friendship, peace, and love.[1]

---

1. Written August 2, 1789, by Samuel Stanton, one of the first settlers of Harmony, Pennsylvania. These few lines of poetry portray Samuel Stanton's vision of building the town of Harmony on the Susquehanna River. Emily C. Blackman, *History of Susquehanna County, Pennsylvania, from a Period Preceding Settlement to Recent Times* (Philadelphia: Claxton, Remsen & Haffelfinger, 1873), 88.

ACKNOWLEDGMENTS

I AM THANKFUL TO THOSE WHO HAVE GUIDED ME IN WRITING AND researching the story of Joseph Smith in Pennsylvania. I must first thank my wife, Shannon, who accompanied me through my historic journey into the life of Joseph Smith in Harmony. She traveled to the Priesthood Restoration Site (several times), Forest City Library, Montrose County Courthouse, Susquehanna Historical Society, Grandin Building, Joseph Smith farm, Hill Cumorah, Joseph Knight farm, Josiah Stowell home, Spanish Silver Mine, Jim McKinny home, and other places, all while watching our then one-year-old boy, Logan. She has endured historical site after site, library after library, and attentively listened to each of my new discoveries. She also read several drafts of the manuscript for this book and gave insightful comments.

This book would not be possible without two historians to whom we are indebted for our profound understanding of Harmony. First, many thanks are due to Larry Porter for his invaluable pioneer research in Harmony, Pennsylvania, and the body of publications that he has authored. His dedication to Harmony is unmatched. Second, I owe deep gratitude to Mark Staker who has poured his resources and time into studying Harmony "from the ground up" for over a decade. Mark's expertise and in-depth knowledge of Harmony has produced several publications and insights on Harmony that are necessary for a complete understanding of Joseph Smith and Harmony. The invaluable research of these two incredible historians has provided the foundation of this book, and both have personally assisted me in prior drafts of it. I also owe a special thanks to Michael MacKay for providing me the inspiration and guidance to get this project to the finish line, and David Ridges for providing insightful encouragement and comments.

Paul Smith also added keen insights and suggestions. I also thank Pam Thacker and Michael Middleton, who carefully read the text and footnotes and pointed out several areas where clarification was required. And I thank my mother and father, Brenda and Greg Hansen, who stopped by several libraries and churches in Pennsylvania and New York while I was living in Jacksonville, Florida and Paris, France. Others who offered assistance and meaningful suggestions include Jack Welch, Mark McConkie, Taylor Hollist, Donald Day, Donald Morgan, Brad Hall, Scott Esplin, Michael Kash, and my mother-in-law, Lorna Thacker. I could not have written this book without the assistance of these remarkable people.

Finally, I am especially grateful to the incredible team at Cedar Fort—Liz Kazandzhy, Dru Huffaker, Shawnda Craig, and Kyle Lund.

TABLE OF CONTENTS

INTRODUCTION

———— ⌒⊙⌒ ————

NESTLED IN THE ENDLESS MOUNTAINS OF NORTHEASTERN Pennsylvania along the banks of the Susquehanna River is a place where heaven once descended upon the earth; a place where holy scripture was translated by the power of God; a place where God's angels ministered to His children; and a place where God bestowed His holy priesthood. Indeed, a holy, hallowed, sacred place called Harmony, Pennsylvania.[1]

The events that transpired in Harmony rendered its grounds forever sacred. Joseph Smith built the foundation of The Church of Jesus Christ of Latter-day Saints in Harmony as he received the priesthood of God, translated the majority of the Book of Mormon, received fifteen significant doctrinal revelations, and met his wife, Emma. A spirit of perseverance and sacrifice remains in Harmony today, which you will notice when walking along the Susquehanna River or pondering in the sugar maple grove of trees. I myself have experienced the spirit of Harmony.[2]

On September 19, 2015, almost two hundred years after Joseph's time in Harmony, President Russell M. Nelson, then President of the Quorum of the Twelve Apostles, dedicated Harmony, Pennsylvania, and acknowledged its significance: "This rural and remote place was the scene of transcendent translation, revelation, and restoration." During his dedicatory prayer, President Nelson continued, "[I] bless the inquiring minds of all who yearn to know more about Thee and

1

Thy eternal and unchanging laws and doctrine. Bless all who enter [the Harmony site], that they may be inspired to emulate the example of Thy Son."[3]

Joseph was not the first religious pioneer to seek refuge in Pennsylvania. Almost one hundred fifty years before Joseph set foot in Harmony, William Penn had founded the colony of Pennsylvania based on religious liberty. William Penn referred to religious liberty as "Liberty of Conscience," meaning the freedom of worship and belief without government interference. Principles of religious liberty were reflected in Pennsylvania's first constitutions and court cases and permeated Pennsylvania's society, culture, and system of government.[4] Pennsylvania's protection of Liberty of Conscience fostered growth not only of well-established religions but also of emerging religions such as The Church of Jesus Christ of Latter-day Saints. In fact, some historians and legal scholars have recognized Pennsylvania as the "most religiously liberal colony" to ratify the United States Constitution.[5]

Joseph arrived in Harmony, Pennsylvania, in November 1825, one year following the Supreme Court of Pennsylvania's landmark decision in *Updegraph v. The Commonwealth*, in which the Supreme Court affirmed Pennsylvania's commitment to "complete" Liberty of Conscience.[6] The Supreme Court relied on the founding documents of Pennsylvania and William Penn's teachings. These included the Charter of the Province of Pennsylvania, the document from Charles II to William Penn conveying the land known today as Pennsylvania, and The Great Law of Pennsylvania, the first law passed by William Penn and the Pennsylvania legislature on December 7, 1682. The Supreme Court further considered the "minds of William Penn and his followers" and attempted to interpret the law as William Penn intended.[7] The Supreme Court boldly declared that "it is irrefragably proved, that the laws and institutions of this state are built on the foundation of reverence for Christianity."[8] In essence, William Penn's laws protecting Liberty of Conscience *prepared the way* for Joseph Smith to translate the Book of Mormon and safeguard the gold plates.

Although Joseph departed Harmony in 1830 because of the contention asserted by members of other faiths, Pennsylvania's protection of Liberty of Conscience enabled Joseph to build the foundation of the Church and safeguard the gold plates without intervention by Pennsylvania state authorities. According to President Nelson, "Harmony provided Joseph with spiritual solitude and protection, allowing him to focus on the translation of the Book of Mormon."[9] Religious liberty prevailed in Harmony.

There is no record that Pennsylvania state authorities arrested or imprisoned Joseph during his stay in Harmony; nor is there any record that Pennsylvania authorities exercised prejudice against Joseph for his religious beliefs or searched his belongings or home. Pennsylvania is distinct from other states where Joseph lived during the early years of the Church. State authorities from New York, Ohio, Missouri, and Illinois arrested and imprisoned Joseph and other Church leaders, or exercised prejudice against them, because of their religious beliefs. In fact, Joseph and his family wrote at length of trials, arrests, and imprisonments in New York during the early years of the Church, but no similar accounts exist in Pennsylvania during the same time period.

Harmony, Pennsylvania, also provided Joseph an environment to mature from an uneducated young man into the Lord's prophet. Indeed, Harmony prepared Joseph to become God's mouthpiece and restore truths and doctrine that had been lost for centuries. God prepared Joseph by teaching him important lessons while there. As stated by President Nelson, Harmony is the place where Joseph "began to exercise his spiritual gifts and perform his prophetic ministry."[10] This book highlights the following lessons and principles:

1. Joseph learned the "Ask Principle"—to inquire of the Lord (see Matthew 7:7; James 1:5). He first asked which church to join while in a grove of trees in Manchester Township, New York, and then he continued often to seek the Lord's guidance while in Harmony.[11]

2. Joseph learned to rely on others. He was not alone in establishing the Church. Many others assisted him, supported him, and even rescued him at key points in the journey. His wife, Emma, was his constant support; Martin Harris served as a scribe and funded the Book of Mormon; Oliver Cowdery devoted his time and talents to transcribing the Book of Mormon; Joseph Knight Sr. contributed provisions and supplies exactly when

Joseph needed them; the Whitmer family gave Joseph a home and supported him; and Isaac Hale provided Joseph a place to stay and protection while in Pennsylvania. I have only named a few of those who assisted Joseph in founding the Church. This heavy burden was carried by many people, with Joseph leading them.

3. Joseph learned to receive official Church revelations as he gained his prophetic voice and dictated the first official revelation of the Church and fourteen other significant revelations in Harmony. He received the first revelation while in the crucible of affliction—he had lost part of the transcribed manuscript, his wife, Emma, was deathly ill, and his first child had died. But Joseph emerged triumphant, gaining his prophetic voice and dictating several significant doctrinal revelations pertaining to subjects such as Christ's Atonement, the nature of God, repentance, life after death, qualifications for missionary work, scripture study, common consent, and the holy sacrament.

4. Joseph overcame weakness, such as desiring monetary wealth and searching for treasure. After several attempts to obtain the gold plates, he overcame his desire to have them for their monetary value and ultimately secured them for their spiritual value. He also eventually fully separated himself from money-digging and the treasure-seeking adventures of his youth. Treasure seeking was an important part of Joseph's development because it likely prepared him to translate the gold plates and was the reason Joseph first set foot in Pennsylvania. Joseph demonstrated that "weak things become strong" (Ether 12:27).

5. Joseph learned to fear God more than man. This lesson is powerfully illustrated by Joseph's agreement with his father-in-law, Isaac Hale, to purchase farmland in Harmony. Because Joseph devoted his time and resources to God's work, he could not adequately earn the respect of his father-in-law and pay for his farm by obtaining full-time, gainful employment. Instead, he borrowed money and paid his father-in-law in installments

and was even late on one payment. Joseph ultimately paid for his farm but moved out of his home only a few days later.[12]

Harmony occupies a significant position in the history of the Church and in Joseph's preparation to become a prophet of God.[13] But many people are unaware of the significance of Harmony. Admittedly, I used to be one of them. I knew that a part of the history of the Church took place in Harmony, but I did not understand what actually happened there. I soon discovered that others—both members of the Church and nonmembers—experienced the same confusion.

An individual who lived in Susquehanna County and passed through Harmony several times a day once said to me, "I know where the Priesthood Restoration Site is, and I pass it often, but I could never figure out why it is so important or what actually happened there. I even walked around the site and still had no idea."[14] Another individual, who lives a mere stone's throw from the Priesthood Restoration Site, said, "I have never quite understood why so many people visit this area. They come by the busload, but why?" A preacher of the Methodist faith even wrote an article about Joseph Smith in Susquehanna County to explain Joseph Smith and dispel any misconceptions about him. He prefaced his article with the following: "Most Methodists today have heard of the Mormon Church, The Church of Jesus Christ of Latter-day Saints (LDS), but few know much about it."[15] While working at the United States Courthouse in Scranton, Pennsylvania, I overheard an individual recount his trip to Temple Square in Salt Lake City, Utah, where he saw a statue of John the Baptist in the woods near the banks of the Susquehanna River. He exclaimed, "Were there Latter-day Saints in Pennsylvania?" My emphatic response: "Yes! In fact, a prominent part of our history took place in Susquehanna County, Pennsylvania." Even some seasoned members of the Church who are generally familiar with its history have trouble recalling the events of Harmony.

The majority of the Book of Mormon was translated in Harmony. Joseph said, "Take away the Book of Mormon, and the revelations, and where is our religion? We have none."[16] The Book of Mormon is the keystone of the Church, and understanding its origin, translation, and doctrine is essential to understanding the beliefs of members of the Church. Certain passages from the Book of Mormon are referenced in this book along with fifteen revelations received by Joseph in Harmony, which are currently contained in the Doctrine and Covenants.[17]

This book relates Joseph's account of the events in Harmony, true to his words and those associated with him. For background and context, I recount events from Joseph's life that occurred in New York, specifically the towns of Palmyra, Colesville, South Bainbridge (now Afton), and Fayette. I have heavily relied on the personal accounts given by Joseph Smith and his mother, Lucy Smith. Their accounts are supplemented by personal accounts of Oliver Cowdery, Joseph Knight Sr., Emma Hale Smith, Martin Harris, David Whitmer, Newel Knight, Isaac Hale, and many others. The whole of these accounts provides the backbone to this book. I have not tried to portray Joseph as a perfect man but as he really was—an adolescent navigating through the challenges of life, a husband caring for his wife, and a prophet seeking guidance from the Almighty to accomplish his mandate. I have attempted to write this book from Joseph's perspective. Initially, I tried to write this book and include Joseph's perspective *and* his opponents' perspectives, but I quickly realized that this is impossible since their perspectives differed on fundamental aspects and elements of the history.[18]

Joseph's message and mission were not well received by everyone. As is the case today, many adamantly fought against him and detested his message. In fact, Joseph's contemporaries did not accept him, and some people today still perceive him in a negative light. During this time, it is said that people called Joseph an "artful seducer" and a "lying imposter."[19] In 1842, a little more than ten years after Joseph left Harmony, John S. Fullmer, a Latter-day Saint missionary sent to preach in Harmony, found great opposition and persecution due to Joseph's alleged deception and dealings.[20] In contrast, others believed Joseph's message and became devoted followers of Jesus Christ. Today The Church of Jesus Christ of Latter-day Saints is worldwide, having over seventeen million members and over 31,000 congregations.[21] Whether one embraces or detests Joseph's message, ultimately one must ask the question articulated by Henry Felton in a Susquehanna newspaper a hundred years after Joseph Smith's time: "Was he a prophet, an apostle, an instrument of divine revelation, or, was he a madman, a fool, a charlatan making innocent people his unsuspecting dupas?"[22] This book demonstrates that Joseph was called as a prophet and matured into a prophet of God while being protected in Harmony. There was religious liberty in Harmony.

Joseph once said in a discourse shortly before his death, "You don't know me; you never will. I don't blame you for not believing my history; had I not experienced it [I] could not have believed it myself."[23] Joseph's story is truly remarkable. Despite his struggles and challenges in Harmony, Joseph triumphed and founded one of the fastest-growing religions in the world today.[24] Joseph fought, sacrificed, and ultimately died for his cause. Not only did he sacrifice everything for his religious beliefs, but his family and friends, in particular his wife Emma, also sacrificed everything. This spirit of sacrifice persists in Harmony today.

Writing and researching this book has enabled me to transcend history on an incredible journey through the early days of the Church in Pennsylvania. I have participated in Church history tours; explored libraries, churches, and courthouse records; explored the hills of Harmony, looking for silver mines and digging holes; spoken to locals and historians; read countless books and articles; and pondered in the woods near the banks of the Susquehanna.

My desire is for everyone to feel the spirit of Harmony by reading this book. May you recognize William Penn's extraordinary sacrifice to establish the colony of Pennsylvania based on religious liberty; experience Joseph's reluctance to give up treasure seeking and his triumph when he does; sense the excitement of uncovering ancient plates with hieroglyphics; witness the contention, persecutions, and mobs that accompanied the plates; contemplate the protections of Liberty of Conscience afforded by the laws of Pennsylvania and William Penn; see the tension as Joseph marries Emma against the wishes of her father; observe Joseph and Oliver Cowdery translate the plates day after day; pray with Joseph and Oliver in the woods near the banks of the Susquehanna; and feel the guiding hand of the Lord and His mercy and love. The surging power and unconquerable spirit of this history will take hold of you and bear testimony of its truthfulness.

Narrative Style and Legal Nature

Unlike many other works of historical nonfiction, this book portrays the events from the lives of William Penn and Joseph Smith in a narrative, story-like style. Many of the disputes and quarrels over technical aspects of the facts are pointed out or analyzed in the footnotes. The reason for relegating these debates to the footnotes or referring readers to other sources to fully explore those debates is to appeal to a broader audience and bring the story to life without significant interruptions. Most readers want to read the story as presented by Joseph and William and their supporters, as opposed to wading through endless pages of scholarly debate. This book alternates between the stories of William and Joseph, mostly focusing on the details of Joseph's life, to demonstrate similarities in their lives, including their inspiration, trials, and successes.

Some chapters in this book are of a legal nature. These chapters analyze and compare constitutions and court cases, which were a large part of the lives of William and Joseph. Any history that does not mention the magnitude of arrests, trials, and imprisonments involving William and Joseph is incomplete. Explanatory introductions to certain chapters are provided to help guide readers and show the relationships between chapters.

Notes

1. On September 19, 2015, President Russell M. Nelson, then President of the Quorum of the Twelve Apostles, dedicated Harmony and declared it "a place of faith, a place of prayer, a place of learning, a place of glory, indeed, a place of holiness." "Transcript: President Russell M. Nelson Remarks and Dedicatory Prayer at Priesthood Restoration Site," *Newsroom of The Church of Jesus Christ of Latter-day Saints*, Sept. 19, 2015, https://newsroom.churchofjesuschrist.org/article/priesthood-restoration-site-dedication-transcript.

2. Historian Michael Hubbard MacKay has provided this keen insight regarding sacred places: "[Members of the Church] today study the history and visit the Restoration sites, which enable individual members to envision their sacred history within the geography where the events took place, as if they had found the Church's Garden of Eden." *Sacred Space: Exploring the Birthplace of Mormonism* (Provo, UT: BYU Religious Studies Center, 2016), 5.

3. "Transcript: President Russell M. Nelson."

4. President Nelson said, "We thank Thee for this land of liberty where we enjoy the freedom to worship in dignity and in faith." "Transcript: President Russell M. Nelson."

5. Jim Wedeking, "Quaker State: Pennsylvania's Guide to Reducing the Friction for Religious Outsiders under the Establishment Clause," *NYU Journal of Law and Liberty* 2, no. 1 (2006): 64; Christie Maloyed, "A Liberal Civil Religion: William Penn's Holy Experiment," *Journal of Church and State* (2012): 2; J. William Frost, *A Perfect Freedom: Religious Liberty in Pennsylvania* (University Park, PA: Pennsylvania State University Press, 1993), 3; Letter from Thomas Jefferson to Thomas Cooper (Nov. 2, 1922), in Andrew A. Lipscomb, ed., *Writings of Thomas Jefferson* (Washington, DC: Thomas Jefferson Memorial Association, 1905), 15:40.

6. 11 Serg. & Rawle 394 (Pa. Sept. 13, 1824), 408.

7. The Supreme Court of Pennsylvania stated, "The minds of William Penn and his followers, would have revolted at the idea of an established church. Liberty to all, preference to none; equal privilege is extended to the mitred Bishop and the unadorned Friend." 11 Serg. & Rawle 394 (Pa. Sept. 13, 1824), 407–408.

8. 11 Serg. & Rawle 394 (Pa. Sept. 13, 1824), 407–408.

9. "Transcript: President Russell M. Nelson." On December 3, 1853, Oakland Township was created from the west part of Harmony Township. Township Incorporations, 1790 to 1853, located at the Susquehanna Historical Society.

10. "Transcript: President Russell M. Nelson." President Nelson further stated, "Through this period [in Harmony], the Lord tutored Joseph in his divine role as prophet, seer, and revelator. Receiving the priesthood empowered Joseph Smith to function fully as the Prophet of this last dispensation. Here he worked during a remarkable and formative season of translation, revelation, and restoration." "Transcript: President Russell M. Nelson."

11. Manchester Township was formerly Farmington Township, Ontario County, New York, in 1820.

12. Joseph received Doctrine and Covenants 3, which is considered the first official revelation of the Church, and was reproved for having "feared men more than God" (verse 7). But Joseph learned and grew from this experience so he could become the prophet of God. Revelation Book 1, 1, josephsmithpapers.org. Doctrine and Covenants 2, received on the evening of September 21, 1823, is also considered an official revelation of the Church, but it was not added to the Doctrine and Covenants until 1876 under the direction of Brigham Young. Stephen E. Robinson and H. Dean Garrett, *A Commentary on the Doctrine and Covenants* (Salt Lake City, UT: Deseret Book, 2000), vol. 1.

13. At the dedication of the Priesthood Restoration Site, President Nelson expressed, "How thankful we are for these historical events." "Transcript: President Russell M. Nelson."

14. This conversation occurred before the Priesthood Restoration Site was restored and dedicated in 2015. Today there is a chapel and visitors' center at the site, and both the Isaac and Elizabeth Hale home and the Joseph and Emma Smith home have been restored.

15. John Goodell, "Joseph Smith in Susquehanna Country: Mormon Beginnings," in *Notes and Sketches from Along the Susquehanna*, ed. John Goodell and John L. Topolewski (Rutland, VT: Academy Books, 1984), 37–46.

16. Minute Book 1, 44, josephsmithpapers.org; Brian Q. Cannon, "Priesthood Restoration Documents," *BYU Studies* 35, no. 4 (1995–96): 177.

17. The Doctrine and Covenants is a collection of revelations pertaining to significant teachings on the nature of God, following inspiration from God, and the organization of the Church.

18. Professor Richard Lyman Bushman emphatically stated, "For a character as controversial as Smith, pure objectivity is impossible." Preface to *Joseph Smith: Rough Stone Rolling* (New York: Alfred A. Knopf, 2005). Another historian noted, "Most people who wrote about Joseph Smith during his lifetime were either faithful Latter-day Saints or carping critics. As one would expect, their respective viewpoints tended to influence that which they wrote." Mark Ashurst-McGee, "The Josiah Stowell Jr.—John S. Fullmer Correspondence," *BYU Studies* 38, no. 3 (1999): 109.

19. Tom Klopfer, *Toponyms & Trivia of Northeastern Pennsylvania* (Olyphant, PA: Dunmore Publishing, 1998), 147.

20. Ashurst-McGee, "Josiah Stowell Jr.—John S. Fullmer," 112–14. In his article, historian Mark Ashurst-McGee analyzes correspondence between Josiah Stowell Jr. (sometimes spelled "Stoal"), a man intimately acquainted with Joseph, and John S. Fullmer, a missionary who had difficulty proselyting in Pennsylvania due to negative rumors about Joseph Smith's youthful activities in New York. Fullmer requested a statement regarding Joseph Smith's character, and Stowell responded in affirming Joseph Smith's good character.

21. "Facts and Statistics," *Newsroom of The Church of Jesus Christ of Latter-day Saints,* accessed Mar. 15, 2024, https://newsroom.churchofjesuschrist.org/facts-and-statistics.

22. Henry W. Felton, "The Pilgrimage to Historically Prominent Places Near Susquehanna: The Historical Data," *Susquehanna Historical Society,* Aug. 9, 1929.

23. Journal, December 1842–June 1844; Book 4, 1 March–22 June 1844, 71, josephsmithpapers.org. Joseph Smith gave this discourse on April 7, 1844, in Nauvoo, Illinois, at a general conference of the Church following the death of an elder named King Follett. This discourse is often referred to as the King Follett sermon or King Follett discourse. Several listeners recorded the discourse. In this text I have quoted the notes of Willard Richards, who

assisted in compiling a personal history of Joseph Smith and served as Church Historian in the early days of the Church.

24. One author has remarked, "The hostility around Harmony belied the name of the town to Joseph [Smith], so he sold what possessions he had there, and took himself to other fields." Richmond E. Myers, *The Long Crooked River: The Susquehanna* (Boston: The Christopher Publishing House, 1949), 342.

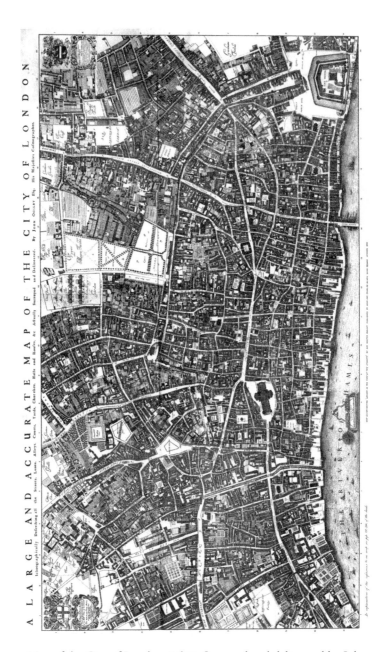

Map of the City of London, 1673. Surveyed and delineated by John Ogilby, His Majesties Cosmographer. The original of this map is 8 feet 5 inches by 4 feet 7 inches, in 20 sheets. In 1894 the British Museum granted permission to the London and Middlesex Archaeological Society to make a reduced copy, of which this is a scanned picture.

TIME LINES

—— ✦ ——

The following time lines provide an overview of the history of William Penn and Joseph Smith in London, New York, and Pennsylvania, as well as the fifteen revelations that Joseph Smith received while in Harmony, Pennsylvania.

TIME LINE: LONDON, NEW YORK, AND PENNSYLVANIA

1656 TO 1701

1656—*Divine Inspiration*—God appears to William Penn at the age of twelve at Chigwell, England, and tells William of his divine mission.

December 1668 to July 1669—*Imprisonment at the Tower of London*—William is imprisoned in the Tower of London for preaching his Quaker faith in the streets of London. William writes his treatise on Jesus Christ entitled *No Cross, No Crown*.

September 1671—*Penn-Mead Trial*—William is arrested, imprisoned, and unfairly tried for preaching his Quaker faith.

February 1671—*Imprisonment at Newgate Prison*—William is imprisoned in Newgate Prison for preaching his Quaker faith in the streets of London. William expands his epistle *The Great Case of Liberty of Conscience*.

March 4, 1681—*Charter Granted*—William successfully obtains a charter granting him proprietorship of Pennsylvania and drafts his first promotional pamphlet, *Some Account of Pennsylvania*.

May 1682—*First Laws of Pennsylvania*—William drafts the first laws governing Pennsylvania, called the Frame of Government of Pennsylvania.

August 30, 1682—*First Visit to Pennsylvania*—William sails on the ship *Welcome* for an eight-week voyage and lands in Pennsylvania for the first time on October 28 or 29, 1682, at a location named Chester.

December 7, 1682—*The Great Law*—The Great Law of Pennsylvania is enacted into law by William and the Pennsylvania legislature. The Great Law invokes the blessings of God and protects Liberty of Conscience.

August 18, 1684—*Back to England*—William stays in Pennsylvania for almost two years and then returns to England on the ship *Endeavor* to protect the Charter of Pennsylvania. William delivers his famous prayer called "Farewell to Pennsylvania."

1692—*Charter Revoked*—The new English government revokes William's charter and places Pennsylvania under the control of the governor of New York. William goes into hiding and is accused of treason.

1693 to 1694—*Charter Restored*—William is acquitted of any charges of treason, reappears in public, and Pennsylvania is restored to him.

September 3, 1699—*Return to Pennsylvania*—William sails to Pennsylvania on a thirteen-week voyage along with his wife, Hannah Penn, and daughter, Laetitia, arriving in Philadelphia on December 2.

1701—*Last Official Act*—As his last official act in Pennsylvania, William approves the Pennsylvania Charter of Privileges, enshrining Liberty of Conscience in Pennsylvania law.

November 1701—*Farewell to Pennsylvania*—William is forced to return to England again to continue the defense of the Charter of Pennsylvania.

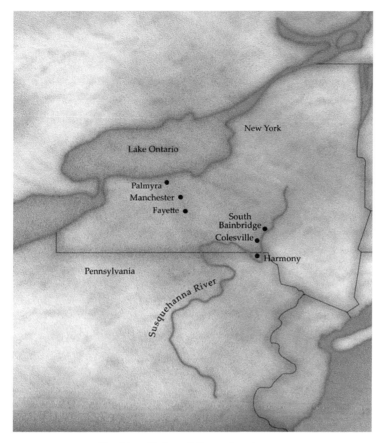

The New York and Pennsylvania area.
© By Intellectual Reserve, Inc.

1820 TO 1826

Spring 1820—*The First Vision*—Joseph Smith sees God the Father
and Jesus Christ in the woods near his family's log home in
Palmyra Township, New York.[1]

September 21, 1823—*First Visit from Moroni*—The angel Moroni
appears to Joseph Smith in the upstairs bedroom of his log cabin.

September 22, 1823—*First Visit to the Hill Cumorah in Manchester
Township*—Joseph visits the Hill Cumorah for the first time to
locate the gold plates and converse with the angel Moroni.

September 22, 1824—*Second Visit to the Hill Cumorah*—Joseph
visits the Hill Cumorah.

September 22, 1825—*Third Visit to the Hill Cumorah*—Joseph visits the Hill Cumorah.

October 1825—*Employment in Susquehanna County, Pennsylvania*—Josiah Stowell hires Joseph to assist him in locating Spanish treasure.

September 22, 1826—*Fourth Visit to the Hill Cumorah*—Joseph visits the Hill Cumorah.

1827

January 18, 1827—*Marriage*—Joseph and Emma are married in South Bainbridge (now Afton), Chenango County, New York.

January 1827—*Move to Manchester Township, New York*—Joseph and Emma move in with Joseph's parents in Manchester Township, New York.

September 22, 1827—*Possession of Plates*—Joseph obtains possession of the plates from the angel Moroni on the Hill Cumorah.

December 1827—*Relocation to Harmony*—Joseph and Emma move to Harmony (now Oakland) and stay with Emma's parents. Shortly after arriving, Joseph and Emma relocate to Jesse Hale's former home.

1828

February 1828—*Martin Harris Departs for New York City by way of Albany, New York*—Martin Harris visits Harmony and then travels to New York City by way of Albany, New York, to display to scholars a transcript of characters taken from the plates.

March 1828—*Martin Returns*—Martin returns to Harmony from New York City and reports to Joseph before traveling to Palmyra.

April 12 to June 14, 1828—*Book of Lehi Translated*—Joseph and Martin complete the dictation and writing of the 116-page manuscript called the Book of Lehi. Martin Harris brings the manuscript to Palmyra, New York, to show it to select family members and friends.

June 15, 1828—*Birth and Death of the Smiths' Firstborn Child*—
Emma gives birth to the Smiths' first child and the child dies that
same day.

Around June 29 or July 1, 1828—*Joseph Seeks out Martin*—Joseph
leaves Harmony in search of Martin and the 116-page manuscript.
Joseph discovers the manuscript is lost.

July 1828—*Joseph Returns to Harmony*—When Joseph arrives in
Harmony, the Lord takes from him the plates, the Urim and
Thummim, and his ability to translate.

1829

Winter 1829—*Joseph's Parents Visit Harmony*—Joseph's parents visit
him in Harmony.

March 1829—*Martin Harris Visits Harmony, and Joseph Knight Sr.
Provides Assistance*—Martin Harris visits Joseph in Harmony.
Joseph Knight Sr. of Colesville Township, New York, provides
money to buy paper for the translation.

April 5, 1829—*Oliver Cowdery Visits Joseph in Harmony*—Oliver
Cowdery travels to Harmony to serve as Joseph's scribe.

April 6, 1829—*Agreement to Purchase a Home*—Joseph enters into
an agreement with Isaac Hale to purchase the property and home
where Joseph and Emma are presently living.

April 7, 1829—*Translation Commences*—Joseph and Oliver commence
the translation of the Book of Mormon.

About May 10, 1829—*Search for More Supplies*—Joseph and Oliver
run out of supplies and travel to the home of Joseph Knight Sr. to
obtain supplies.

About May 14, 1829—*Translation of the Savior's Visit to the
Americas*—3 Nephi 11 of the Book of Mormon is translated.

May 15, 1829—*Restoration of the Aaronic Priesthood*—Joseph and
Oliver receive the Aaronic Priesthood from John the Baptist in
the woods near the banks of the Susquehanna River and baptize
one another.

Between May 16 and 28, 1829—*Restoration of the Melchizedek
Priesthood*—Peter, James, and John confer the Melchizedek
Priesthood upon Joseph and Oliver.

May 31, 1829—*Relocation to Fayette Township, Seneca County, New York*—Joseph and Oliver move to the home of Peter Whitmer Sr. in Fayette, New York, to continue the translation of the Book of Mormon.

Late June 1829—*Witnesses of the Gold Plates*—Three witnesses (Oliver Cowdery, David Whitmer, and Martin Harris) are shown the plates from which the Book of Mormon was translated, in Fayette Township, New York. Eight witnesses see the plates near the Smith log home in Palmyra Township.

About July 1, 1829—*Translation Completed*—Joseph completes the translation of the Book of Mormon while at Fayette.

August 1829—*Arrangements for Publication*—Joseph Smith and Martin Harris complete arrangements with Egbert B. Grandin to publish the Book of Mormon.

October 4, 1829—*Return to Harmony*—Joseph returns home to Harmony.

1830

March 26, 1830—*Publication of the Book of Mormon*—The Book of Mormon is published and made available to the public.

April 6, 1830—*Organization of the Church*—The official organization of The Church of Jesus Christ of Latter-day Saints in Fayette.

June 9, 1830—*General Conference*—The first general conference of the Church is held in Fayette; Joseph travels back to Harmony after the conference.

Around June 28, 1830, to July 1, 1830—*Trials in New York*—Joseph travels from Harmony to Colesville, New York. He is accused of being a "disorderly person," is arrested by a constable of Chenango County, and is later acquitted. Then Joseph is arrested by a constable in Broome County, is acquitted, and returns to Harmony.

August 26, 1830—*Title to Farm*—Joseph receives title to thirteen acres of land previously owned by Isaac Hale.

Early September 1830—*Departure from Harmony*—Joseph and Emma move from Harmony to Fayette and then to Kirtland, Ohio.

REVELATIONS RECEIVED IN HARMONY, PENNSYLVANIA (FIFTEEN IN TOTAL)[2]

1828 (ONE REVELATION)

July 1828—*Doctrine and Covenants 3*—Joseph is called to repentance for repeatedly requesting the Lord to entrust the manuscript to Martin Harris and for fearing man more than God. This is considered the first official revelation of the Church.

1829 (TEN REVELATIONS)

February 1829—*Doctrine and Covenants 4*—Joseph receives a revelation for his father, Joseph Smith Sr., containing the qualifications for missionary service and calling Joseph Smith Sr. to missionary service.

March 1829—*Doctrine and Covenants 5*—At the urging of Martin Harris, Joseph inquires of the Lord for Martin to see the plates. The Lord tells Martin he will see the plates if he is sufficiently humble.

April 1829—*Doctrine and Covenants 6*—Oliver, in doubt of the truthfulness of Joseph's work, is reminded of the witness he received by the Holy Ghost while in Palmyra. He is counseled that if he inquires of the Lord with questions, he will be "enlightened by the Spirit of truth" (verse 15). He is further counseled to lay up treasure in heaven.

Spring 1829 (and/or Summer 1828)—*Doctrine and Covenants 10*—Joseph is advised of the designs of evil men to alter the 116 pages of lost manuscript. The Lord commands Joseph to translate the small plates of Nephi to replace the lost manuscript.

April 1829—*Doctrine and Covenants 8*—Oliver is counseled to ask in faith in order to obtain the knowledge to translate. Knowledge will be conveyed in Oliver's heart and mind.

April 1829—*Doctrine and Covenants 7*—Joseph and Oliver learn that the Lord gave John, Jesus's disciple of the New Testament, power over death so that he might continue to live on the earth and bring souls unto the Lord.

April 1829—*Doctrine and Covenants 9*—Oliver assumed that simply asking the Lord for help would enable him to translate. But he neglected to prepare and study it out in his mind to know if it was right. The Lord directs Oliver to be content with writing for Joseph rather than translating as voice.

May 1829—*Doctrine and Covenants 11*—The Lord counsels Hyrum Smith to put his trust in the Spirit of God, which will enlighten his mind. The time has not yet come for Hyrum to preach, so he must prepare through studying the gospel.

May 1829—*Doctrine and Covenants 12*—Joseph Knight Sr. inquires as to his role in the Lord's work. The Lord tells Joseph Knight Sr. to keep the commandments and "bring forth and establish the cause of Zion."

Summer 1829—*Doctrine and Covenants 19*—The Lord directs Martin Harris to "not covet thine own property, but impart it freely to the printing of the book of Mormon" so Martin would pay the printer E. B. Grandin. The Lord also addresses Church doctrines regarding the nature of God, Christ's Atonement, repentance, and life after death.

1830 (Four Revelations)

July 1830—*Doctrine and Covenants 24*—Under intense persecution, Joseph and Oliver pray to the Lord. The Lord does not take away their afflictions but comforts them, saying, "I am with thee, even unto the end of thy days" (verse 8).

July 1830—*Doctrine and Covenants 26*—The Lord counsels Joseph to study and ponder the scriptures and to conduct official decisions of the Church by common consent.

July 1830—*Doctrine and Covenants 25*—Emma, called an "elect lady" by the Lord, is asked to compile the first hymnbook for the Church, for "the song of the righteous is a prayer unto [the Lord]" (verse 12).

August/September 1830—*Doctrine and Covenants 27*—While Joseph is procuring wine for the sacrament, an angel appears to him and quotes the Lord, saying, "It mattereth not what ye shall eat or what ye shall drink when ye partake of the sacrament, if it so be that ye do it with an eye single to my glory" (verse 2). Later, in September, Joseph receives the other portion of this revelation.[3]

NOTES

1. The vision took place in the woods in Manchester Township, New York. The Smiths' log home was located in Palmyra, New York, but their one-hundred-acre farm was located in Manchester Township.

2. The dates of the revelations Joseph Smith received in Harmony are based on the dates designated by the Joseph Smith Papers, which follows the order of the revelations as composed by John Whitmer and Oliver Cowdery in "Revelation Book 1," a manuscript book of revelations and other items started less than a year after the Church was organized in April 1830. See Revelation Book 1, josephsmithpapers.org.

3. "Historical Introduction," Revelation, circa August 1830 [D&C 27], josephsmithpapers.org.

William Penn in Armor, artist unknown. The Miriam and Ira D. Wallach Division of Art, Prints and Photographs: Print Collection, The New York Public Library.

CHAPTER 1

Visits from Heavenly Messengers

———— ⟨◦⊚◦⟩ ————

The Lord appears to William Penn;
God and Jesus Christ appear to Joseph Smith.

William in Chigwell and Oxford

In London, England, overlooking the Tower of London, sits an ancient Anglican church called All Hallows Barking, which some say is the oldest church in the city of London, built in AD 676.[1] On October 23, 1644, William Penn was baptized as an infant at All Hallows Barking.[2] This would be the start of a spiritual journey that brought William to Pennsylvania along with many others seeking religious liberty.

As a young boy growing up in London, William was particularly sensitive, with an active spirit and mind. He later described himself as a "solitary and spiritual" child.[3] He started school at the age of nine in Chigwell, England, a northeastern suburb of London.[4] In 1656, at the age of twelve, William said that the Lord appeared to him when he was alone in his room at Chigwell. He recalled, "The Lord first appeared to me . . . about the twelfth year of my age" and gave me "divine impressions" of myself.[5] Although William recorded that the Lord "reproved" him for his sins, the heavenly visitation provided William with a "certain sound & testimony of [the Lord's] eternal word," and William knew he was "preserved" for a divine purpose.[6] This experience inspired him to pursue a different course in life than his father and other nobles of England, which would eventually lead him to the colony of Pennsylvania.

For most of William's youth, his father was away from home serving as an officer in the British Navy. Because of his father's elite position and service to England, he was favored in English society and admitted to Oxford University, the college of Christ's Church.[7] But William was introspective and spiritual, which did not fit with the rigid ceremonies and rituals taught at Christ's Church.[8] After two years, he withdrew from Oxford University, which not only disappointed his father but also, according to William, brought upon him "whipping, and beating, and turning out of door."[9]

A few months after William withdrew from Oxford University, his father sent him to live in France, which was standard training ground for a young, noble Englishmen. William's father hoped training in France would set him on the right course. William arrived in France and was introduced to Louis XIV's court at the Palace of Fontainebleau, just south of Paris. He also studied at the Protestant Academy of Saumur, which was about two hundred miles south of Paris.[10] After staying one year in France, William returned to England and enrolled at Lincoln's Inn, one of the most prestigious law schools in England.[11] But his formation in France did not change his search for spirituality and deeper meaning in life, nor did it erase his recollection of the Lord's visit to him and his divine mission. William continued his deeply spiritual path and knew that he had a spiritual purpose to accomplish. He soon graduated from law school at Lincoln's Inn and decided to practice law in Ireland.

The "Burned-Over" District

Like William Penn, Joseph Smith sought spiritual enlightenment at a young age. While living in Palmyra, New York, at the age of twelve to fourteen, Joseph became considerably troubled with the subject of religion.[12] Great excitement over religion persisted among all denominations of Christians; the flames of religious revival burned deep in their hearts, and upstate New York quickly became known as the "burned-over" district.[13] Streams of believers flooded the Methodist, Presbyterian, and Baptists churches.[14] Joseph's mother, Lucy Mack Smith, his brothers Hyrum and Samuel, and his sister Sophronia

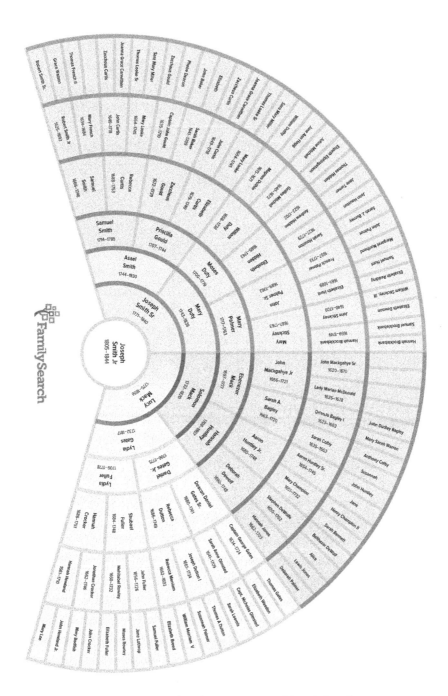

Joseph Smith Jr. fan chart. Courtesy of FamilySearch.
© By Intellectual Reserve, Inc.

espoused the teachings of the Presbyterian faith.[15] His father, Joseph Smith Sr., while a firm believer in God and the Bible, did not affiliate with any one religion. Joseph did not embrace a particular church but often attended the meetings of several churches.[16]

Joseph regularly attended Methodist camp meetings, which were scheduled to coincide with circuit riders, or traveling Methodist preachers, passing through the Palmyra area. Methodist leaders noticed Joseph's passion for religion and asked him to be an "exhorter," or a beginning Methodist preacher, whose task was to bring the circuit rider's general message to local believers in their homes.[17] Proven and experienced exhorters could become local Methodist preachers. Joseph also apparently participated in a local debate club during this time period.[18]

Joseph felt an inclination toward the Methodist Church and may have caught "a spark of Methodism," but the divergent teachings of the local churches prevented him from joining any one church.[19] "So great was the confusion and strife amongst the different denominations that it was impossible for a person [as] young as I was and so unacquainted with men and things to come to any certain conclusion who was right and who was wrong," Joseph lamented. He observed great confusion and contention, "priest contending against priest, and convert against convert so that all their good feelings one for another (if they ever had any), were entirely lost in a strife of words and a contest about opinions."[20]

During this time of religious excitement and confusion, Reverend George Lane, a presiding elder of the Methodist Church, preached in Palmyra and the surrounding towns.[21] It was recorded that "Mr. Lane's manner of communication was peculiarly calculated to awaken the intellect of the hearer, and arouse the sinner to look about him for safety—much good instruction was always drawn from his discourses on the scriptures."[22]

Reverend Lane was a prominent Methodist circuit rider, appointed presiding elder of the Susquehanna District in 1819.[23] He incessantly traveled his territory preaching to congregations; counseling the traveling preachers, local preachers, and exhorters; meeting the official members of the circuit societies; and promoting the interest of the church in every possible way. Reverend Lane also traveled outside his territory to other areas.[24] Possessing profound literary knowledge and deep humility, Reverend Lane was "celebrated throughout the country as a 'great revival preacher.'"[25] It was said that his exhortations were overwhelming, and sinners "quailed under them, and many cried aloud for mercy."[26] Reverend George Peck, a prominent Methodist preacher who knew Reverend Lane, stated that under Reverend Lane's "powerful appeals[,] vast congregations were moved like the trees of the forest before a mighty wind. Many a stout-hearted sinner was broken down, and cried aloud for mercy under his all but irresistible appeals. His language was unstudied, but chaste, correct, simple, and forcible."[27] Reverend Lane appealed to his audience, and his sermons were the result of careful thought and laborious research. He maintained a high standing among his people.[28]

Reverend George Lane from
the *Methodist Magazine*, April 1826.

At a camp meeting in 1819 in Susquehanna County, Reverend Lane delivered a powerful exhortation later described as having a "melting and overwhelming appeal to the unconverted."[29] Many hardened sinners yielded to his call and converted. The meeting was greatly blessed and many joined the Methodist Church.[30] In July 1819 at Vienna, a town not far from Manchester, a conference of about one hundred Methodist ministers was held. This may have been where Joseph caught the "spark" of Methodism.[31]

Joseph Smith Seeks Wisdom from the Bible, by Dale Kilbourn.
© By Intellectual Reserve, Inc.

According to Joseph's younger brother, William Smith, George Lane preached a sermon in Palmyra on "What church shall I join?"[32] The invitation of his discourse was to ask God, as contemplated by James 1:5 in the Bible, which states, "If any of you lack wisdom, let him ask of God, that giveth to all men liberally, and upbraideth not; and it shall be given him." If William Smith is correct, George Lane's message may have awakened Joseph's mind and weighed heavy on his conscience.[33] Joseph read in the book of James and remarked, "Never did any passage of scripture come with more power to the heart of man than this did at this time to mine. It seemed to enter with great force into every feeling of my heart. I reflected on it again and again, knowing that if any person needed wisdom from God, I did."[34] Joseph's mother later recalled Joseph's keen interest in religion: "Joseph never said many words upon any subject but always seemed to reflect more deeply than common persons of his age upon everything of a religious nature."[35]

"Let Him Ask of God"

Joseph concluded that he must do as the book of James directed—pray and inquire of God. One spring morning, in the year 1820, Joseph retired to a grove of trees not far from his home with a humble and burning question: Which church should I join?[36] He knelt down in a previously designated location and began to pray fervently to obtain mercy from the Lord and to receive an answer to his question.[37] Immediately, Joseph was seized upon by some power which entirely overcame him. Thick darkness encircled him, and it seemed that he was doomed to sudden destruction. He exerted all his powers to call upon God to deliver him out of the power of the enemy that had seized him. At the very moment when he was ready to sink into despair and abandon himself to destruction, he saw the forest illuminate. Joseph described the experience in his own words:

> I saw a pillar of light exactly over my head, above the brightness of the sun, which descended gradually until it fell upon me. It no sooner appeared than I found myself delivered from the enemy which held me bound. When the light rested upon me I saw two personages, whose brightness and glory defy all description standing above me in the air. One of them spake unto me, calling me

by name, and said—pointing to the other, this is my beloved Son, hear Him.[38]

Joseph saw and conversed with God the Father and Jesus Christ. He was told that his sins were forgiven.[39] When Joseph asked the heavenly beings which of all the religions he should join, he was directed to join none of them. They told Joseph that some religious ministers were corrupt because they "draw near to me with their lips, but their hearts are far from me; they teach for doctrines the commandments of men: having a form of godliness, but they deny the power thereof."[40] No one was more surprised at the response than Joseph himself. The heavenly visitors left Joseph with the instruction to continue as he was "until further directed."[41]

The First Vision, by Del Parson.

Years passed without visits or direction from the heavenly messengers. Joseph anxiously awaited further direction since he did not know how to use his newfound knowledge. Because he continued to affirm his heavenly vision, both religious and nonreligious men persecuted him.[42] The message that none of the churches were correct caused discord with other preachers and those of other religions, resulting in increased persecution.[43] Joseph stated, "Though I was an obscure boy only between fourteen and fifteen years of age and my circumstances in life such as to make a boy of no consequence in the world, yet men of high standing would take notice sufficient to excite the public mind against me, and create a hot persecution, and this was common among all the sects. All united to persecute me."[44]

When Joseph related his vision to a local Methodist preacher, the preacher reacted with contempt, telling Joseph that his vision had come from the devil, that there were no such things as visions or revelations, and that visions had ceased with the Apostles. Joseph was confused by the adverse reactions to his message. He exclaimed, "Why persecute me for telling the truth? Why does the world think to make me deny what I have actually seen? For I had seen a vision, I knew it, and I knew that God knew it, and I could not deny it, neither dared I do it, at least I knew that by so doing I would offend God, and come under condemnation."[45]

The Company of Money Diggers

Sometimes Joseph associated with members of a neighborhood company organized for the purpose of money digging.[46] Some people thought that Joseph was a "glass-looker," meaning he could discover lost goods, hidden treasures, and mines of gold and silver.[47] It was said that Joseph had "a power to look into the depths of the earth" and find hidden treasure.[48] Though a strange and foreign concept for most people today, many early Americans believed treasures were hidden in the earth by early Spanish explorers and pirates.[49] They dreamed of gold and eventually discovering their own treasure trove. Settlers explored caves, lost mines, hills, and Native American mounds while under the cover of darkness in search of such precious metals. A legend, a treasure map, or a dream of buried treasure inspired their cause. Many consulted witches, wizards, wise men, or conjurors, who were believed to heal with a touch, summon heavenly personages, find lost articles, interpret dreams, and predict the future.[50] These folkways were an integral part of faith and religion at that time.

According to a February 16, 1825, newspaper article in the *Wayne Sentinel*, a local Palmyra newspaper, money digging was common in the area and even considered an honorable and profitable employment. The paper stated, "We could name, if we pleased, at least five hundred respectable men who do in the simplicity and sincerity of their hearts believe that immense treasures lie concealed upon our green mountains, many of whom have been for a number of years industriously and perseveringly engaged in digging it up."[51]

A seer stone belonging to Joseph Smith.
© By Intellectual Reserve, Inc.

Two seer stones supposedly came into Joseph's possession during this time. One stone he discovered some twenty feet below the ground in a well of his neighbor, Mason Chase, in 1822.[52] The other stone may have been from Jack Belcher of Gibson, New York, who obtained it while drawing salt in Salina, New York.[53] One stone was dark striped brown in a form similar to a baby's shoe, and the other stone was white and shaped like a chicken egg.[54] When Joseph participated in money-digging excursions, he would put the stone into a hat and look into the hat at the stone to locate the treasure.[55] The hat created an environment of complete darkness around the stone so Joseph could read its message as a clairvoyant.[56] Martin Harris, a businessman in Palmyra, recalled Joseph finding a small pin in a large pile of shaved straw by looking through the hat with a stone in it.[57]

Joseph Smith Sr. thought highly of his son's "wonderful triumphs as a seer" and described "many instances of his finding hidden and stolen goods."[58] His father did not approve, however, of Joseph's use of this wonderful gift for treasure seeking, believing that God had not miraculously given Joseph this power for the purpose of seeking "filthy lucre, or its equivalent in earthly treasures."[59] Joseph Smith Sr. often prayed that Heavenly Father would manifest His will to Joseph concerning this marvelous power.[60] Joseph later would need to use his gift to further the Lord's work instead of seeking treasure. What may have been perceived by others as a weakness—"seeking treasure"—later became a critical strength to accomplish the Lord's work.

Joseph never denied participating in money-digging adventures but likely regretted his treasure-seeking tendencies.[61] He felt that he had fallen into many foolish errors displaying the weaknesses of youth and the foibles of human nature, which "led [him] into diverse temptations offensive in the sight of God."[62] Joseph was not "guilty of any great or malignant sins" but of "levity" and associating with "jovial company," which Joseph believed "was not consistent with the character which ought to be maintained by one who was called of God."[63] His actions, he said, brought a "wound upon [his] soul."[64]

THE ANGEL MORONI APPEARS TO JOSEPH

Three long years passed with no direction from the heavenly messengers. On the night of September 21, 1823, Joseph knelt in the upstairs room of his Palmyra log home in sincere, humble prayer. Joseph probably lamented his money-digging tendencies and lack of progress in his divine mission. His "mind was unusually wrought up on the subject which had so long agitated his mind . . . and all he desired was to be prepared in heart to commune with some kind of messenger who could communicate to him the desired information of his acceptance with God."[65] Joseph followed the "Ask Principle" by seeking the Lord's guidance as he had done three years earlier in the grove of trees. While imploring God in fervent prayer for hours to forgive him of his weaknesses and mistakes, Joseph discovered a light appearing in his room, which gradually increased until the room was lighter than noonday.[66] A personage appeared and called Joseph by name, saying that he was a messenger from God and that his name was Moroni.[67] The messenger wore a garment that was perfectly white without seam.[68]

The Angel Moroni Appears to Joseph Smith in His Room, by Tom Lovell. © By Intellectual Reserve, Inc.

Moroni informed Joseph that his sins were forgiven and that his prayers were heard.[69] Moroni said that God had a work for Joseph and that his name would be known for good and evil among all nations and people.[70] A book was deposited in the earth, written upon gold plates, that gives an account of the ancient inhabitants of the American continents. The fulness of the everlasting gospel was contained in the book as it was delivered by Jesus Christ to the ancient inhabitants. Moroni quoted passages of scriptures from the Bible to Joseph, including the third and fourth chapters of Malachi, the eleventh chapter of Isaiah, and parts of the third chapter of Acts and second chapter of Joel. As Moroni recited these scriptures, Joseph noted small differences between Moroni's version and the version in Joseph's own scriptures.[71]

Buried with the plates were two stones in silver bows, which when fastened to a breastplate constituted the Urim and Thummim, a deciphering instrument of ancient times prepared by God for the purpose of translating.[72] Joseph was further instructed that after the gold plates were translated, God would restore His holy priesthood. The priesthood would allow saving ordinances to be performed, such as baptism by water and the laying on of hands for the gift of the Holy Ghost.[73] Moroni may have also informed Joseph that the Lord had forgiven him of his sins and counseled him that he must no longer associate with the company of money diggers since there were wicked men among them.[74] Joseph would need to distance himself from the company and treasure seeking, which would be a challenge.

Moroni instructed Joseph to unearth the gold plates from the Hill Cumorah, a hill not far from his home, and to show them to no one unless commanded.[75] Along with this charge, Moroni cautioned him that Satan would try to tempt him to obtain the plates for the purpose of obtaining riches and wealth. To acquire the plates, Joseph could not have any other purpose in mind but to glorify God and build His kingdom on the earth. Through the night and into the morning, Moroni visited Joseph two more times, each time relaying essentially the same message. Joseph recorded that his "interviews" with Moroni "occupied the whole of that night."[76]

Today it is indeed apparent that Moroni's prophecy—that Joseph's name would be had for good and evil—has been fulfilled. For example, Emily Blackman, a prominent historian of Susquehanna, Pennsylvania, dedicated an entire section of her history to Joseph Smith entitled "Joe Smith, the Mormon Prophet. A Madman, or a fool, hath ever set the world agog." She dramatically wrote, "It is a fact, of which we are not particularly proud, that Susquehanna County harbored such a madman as Joe Smith at the period when he was engaged in the compilation, or rather, the translation, of the Book of Mormon."[77] In contrast, Joseph has been listed as one of the hundred most influential Americans, and over 150 million copies of the Book of Mormon have been published in over 100 languages.[78]

Joseph Goes to the Hill Cumorah

The next morning, on September 22, 1823, Joseph attended to the necessary labors of the day, but his strength exhausted him and he could no longer continue. His father noticed something was wrong and sent him home. As Joseph attempted to climb a fence at the edge of a field, his strength entirely failed him, and he fell to the ground unconscious. The first thing Joseph recalled was hearing a voice call him by name. He looked up and saw the angel Moroni, who then delivered the same message as the night before. Moroni commanded Joseph to tell his father of the vision and the commandments he had received. Joseph obeyed and related to his father the occurrences of the previous night and that morning. His father believed him and directed him to follow Moroni's instructions and go to the Hill Cumorah.[79] Joseph obeyed and traveled three miles to the place where the plates were hidden as he had been shown by the angel Moroni. The plates were located on the west side of the Hill Cumorah not far from the top in a stone box covered by a large stone.[80] Joseph removed the stone and the top of the stone box, revealing the plates, the Urim and Thummim, a breastplate, and possibly other items.[81]

As he looked at the plates, temptation beset him and his mind filled with thoughts of the monetary advantages of the plates.[82] His family was poor and in financial distress, with creditors bearing heavily upon them, and the discovery of the plates could relieve his family of such "misfortune and sickness."[83] The plates were made of pure gold, and Joseph knew he could save his family from embarrassment by gaining from the plates financially. But when Joseph reached for the plates, he received a sudden shock, propelling him backward to the ground.[84] He desisted for an instant but quickly regained his composure and made another attempt to secure the plates. The same shock resulted, even more powerful than the first.[85] Joseph made a final third attempt, with increased exertion, when his strength entirely failed him again.[86] His attempts to obtain the plates had failed; his temptation of financial gain had overcome him.[87]

Soon Moroni appeared, and Joseph inquired why he could not obtain possession of the plates.[88] Moroni responded that he had not kept the commandments of the Lord because he had looked upon the plates with their monetary value in mind instead of God's purpose.[89] Joseph later exclaimed, "I had been tempted of the adversary and sought the Plates to obtain riches and kept not the commandment that I should have an eye single to the glory of God."[90] Moroni chastened Joseph for heeding the temptations of the adversary and informed him that he would not obtain the plates for another four years, when he reached the age of twenty-one.[91] Joseph had four years to overcome this weakness. He would need to look upon the plates for their spiritual value instead of their financial value before he could obtain them.

Photograph of the Hill Cumorah,
by George E. Anderson, 1907.

Joseph learned an important lesson in obedience that day and later stated, "Ever afterwards I was willing to keep the commandments of God."[92] He returned home disappointed in his failure. His family cried with him when he told them that he could not obtain the plates.[93] After this experience, on September 22 for the following four years, as Moroni had directed, Joseph returned to the precise spot where the plates were buried. He may not have understood that he would eventually translate the plates himself—he likely only knew that his mission was to have them translated.

Following Joseph's heavenly visits, slanderous rumors concerning him and his family spread through the area. Joseph's younger brother William commented, "It has generally been stated that my father's family were lazy, shiftless and poor: but this was never said by their neighbors, or until after the angel appeared and the story of the golden Bible was told."[94]

Joseph remained under the tutelage of Moroni for the years that followed.[95] In total, Moroni visited Joseph at least twenty times, each time teaching and instructing him.[96] Joseph's mother recalled that Joseph would gather the Smith children together every evening to relate his new discoveries. Joseph described "the ancient inhabitants of this continent, their dress, mode of traveling, and the animals upon which they rode; their cities, their buildings, with every particular; their mode of warfare; and also their religious worship. This he would do with as much ease, seemingly, as if he had spent his whole life among them."[97]

Joseph gained an appreciation for the people described on the plates and progressed in his knowledge of their language and way of life. Many ancient prophets described on the plates visited Joseph, including Nephi, Alma, Mormon, and the twelve disciples who were chosen by the Savior when he appeared to the ancient Americans.[98]

Notes

1. The church survived the Great Fire of London in 1666 but was badly damaged in World War II.

2. "Baptism, 23 October 1644," in *The Papers of William Penn*, ed. Richard S. and Mary Maples Dunn (Philadelphia: University of Pennsylvania Press, 1981–87), 1:30; Andrew R. Murphy, *William Penn: A Life* (New York: Oxford University Press, 2019), 13.

3. "To Mary Pennyman, 22 November 1673," in *Papers of William Penn*, 1:265.

4. Murphy, *William Penn: A Life*, 17.

5. "An Account, 1677," in *Papers of William Penn*, 1:476–77; Murphy, *William Penn: A Life*, 125–126; John A. Moretta, *William Penn and the Quaker Legacy* (New York: Pearson, 2007), 9–10.

6. "An Account, 1677," 1:476–77.

7. Alumni Aedis Christi (Christ Church admissions register), Oct. 26, 1660.

8. Murphy, *William Penn: A Life*, 27.

9. "An Account, 1677," 1:476.

10. Murphy, *William Penn: A Life*, 29.

11. *Records of the Honorable Society of Lincoln's Inn* (London: Lincoln's Inn, 1896), 1:295.

12. Lucy Mack Smith, *Biographical Sketches of Joseph Smith the Prophet and His Progenitors for Many Generations* (Liverpool: S. W. Richards, 1853), 74 (published at the direction of Orson Pratt); Lucy Mack Smith, *Lucy's Book: A Critical Edition of Lucy Mack Smith's Family Memoir*, ed. Lavina Fielding Anderson (Salt Lake City, UT: Signature Books, 2001), 331.

    Versions of Lucy Mack Smith's history are extensively cited throughout this book. The first source cited is either: (1) Lucy Mack Smith's original "rough draft manuscript" of her history, as dictated to Martha Jane Knowlton Coray and her husband, Howard ("Manuscript") in 1844 and 1845 (Lucy Mack Smith, History, 1844–1845, josephsmithpapers.org); or (2) the version of Lucy Mack's history published at the direction of Orson Pratt while he was in England in 1853 ("Pratt") (*Biographical Sketches*). The second source cited is *Lucy's Book*, edited by Lavina Fielding Anderson, which compares the "rough draft manuscript" and "Pratt" versions of Lucy Mack Smith's history using dual columns. The abbreviation "manuscript version" refers to the rough draft manuscript in Anderson's text, and the abbreviation "Pratt version" refers to the Pratt version in Anderson's text.

    This book often cites to Lucy's rough draft manuscript because it is the earliest version of the manuscript, but it also includes citations to Orson Pratt's version when it adds clarity or makes the same statement with modern language. Crossed-out words and editorial notes in the original versions are omitted in this text, and in certain areas I have modernized the language.

    Notably, a third version of Lucy Mack's history also exists, known as the "fair copy" version, as inscribed by the Corays under Lucy's direction in 1845. This version of Lucy's history is not referenced often in this text because it is considered a later version of Lucy Mack Smith's original rough draft manuscript. Lucy Mack Smith, *History, 1844–1845; handwriting of Howard Coray and Martha Jan Knowlton Coray*, Church History Library, Salt Lake City.

    Historians generally consider Lucy Mack's history reliable and authoritative, although at times, but not often, she misstates the date or shows a slight prejudice, which I have noted in this book.

13. Smith, *Biographical Sketches*, 74; Smith, *Lucy's Book*, 330–331 (Pratt version); Goodell, "Joseph Smith in Susquehanna Country," 38.

14. "Oliver Cowdery Letter III," *Latter Day Saints' Messenger and Advocate* (Kirtland, OH), Dec. 1834, 42. The *Latter Day Saints' Messenger and Advocate* was a newspaper published in Kirtland, Ohio, containing eight of Oliver Cowdery's letters concerning Joseph's visions and the rise of the Church. It was the successor newspaper to *The Evening and the Morning Star* and the predecessor to the *Elders' Journal*. Oliver Cowdery was the editor of the *Latter Day Saints' Messenger and Advocate*, and it is believed that William W. Phelps may have assisted him. Oliver Cowdery's letters are widely cited by Church

historians and found to be credible accounts of the events of early Church history.

15. History, circa June 1839–circa 1841 [Draft 2], 2, josephsmithpapers.org; also contained in History, 1838–1856, volume A-1 [23 December 1805–30 August 1834], 2, josephsmithpapers.org. This sixty-one page manuscript was inscribed by James Mulholland and Robert B. Thompson between 1839 to 1841. Joseph Smith preferred this draft of the Church's history (called "Draft 2" by the Joseph Smith Papers project), and it was later included as volume "A-1" in the Church's six-volume history. This manuscript is also included in Davidson et al., *Histories, Volume 1: Joseph Smith Histories, 1832–1844*, ed. Dean C. Jessee, Ronald K. Esplin, and Richard Lyman Bushman (Salt Lake City, UT: Church Historian's Press, 2012). The Church's six-volume history served as the basis for the Church history edited by assistant Church Historian B. H. Roberts in the early 1900s. B. H. Roberts, *A Comprehensive History of the Church of Jesus Christ of Latter-day Saints*, 6 vols. (Salt Lake City, UT: Deseret News, 1948–57).

16. History, circa June 1839–circa 1841 [Draft 2], 2, josephsmithpapers.org.

17. O[rsamus] Turner, *History of the Pioneer Settlement of Phelps and Gorham's Purchase, and Morris' Reserve* (Rochester, NY: William Alling, 1852), 214. Calling Joseph Smith a "cheat and a fraud" with an alleged sole desire for "money-digging" and "notoriety," Turner exhibits an obvious and strong prejudice against Joseph Smith. But when he was working as a printer's apprentice, Turner apparently knew Joseph and participated in a debate club with him; therefore, certain statements of his contain such details that, when corroborated by other evidence and accounts, may be credible. For example, historian Larry Porter gives credence to certain statements by Turner because they correctly note Joseph's interest in Methodism during this period. Larry C. Porter, "Reinventing Mormonism: To Remake or Redo," *Farms Review* 7, no. 2 (1995): 128; Donna Hill, *Joseph Smith: The First Mormon* (Garden City, NY: Double Day & Company, 1977), 50.

18. Turner, *History of the Pioneer Settlement*, 214; Porter, "Reinventing Mormonism," 128.

19. Turner, *History of the Pioneer Settlement*, 214.

20. History, circa June 1839–circa 1841 [Draft 2], 2, josephsmithpapers.org.

21. Methodists held camp meetings in Palmyra in June 1818 and in Oaks Corner (within six miles of Palmyra) in July 1819. E. Latimer, *The Three Brothers: Sketches of the Lives of Rev. Aurora Seager, Rev. Micah Seager, Rev. Schuyler Seager* (New York: Phillips and Hunt, 1880); Larry C. Porter, "Reverend George Lane—Good 'Gifts,' Much 'Grace,' and Marked 'Usefulness,'" *BYU Studies* 9, no. 3. (Spring 1969): 338.

22. "Oliver Cowdery Letter III," 42.

23. Oscar Jewell Harvey, *The Harvey Book: Giving Genealogies of Certain Branches of the American Families of Harvey, Nesbitt, Dixon and Jameson* (unpublished manuscript, 1899), 130.

24. Abel Stevens, *The Centenary of American Methodism: A Sketch of its History, Theology, Practical System, and Success* (New York: Carlton & Porter, 1866), 111.

25. William Smith, *William Smith on Mormonism* (Lamoni, IA: Herald Stream Book and Job Office, 1883), 6–7; "Oliver Cowdery Letter III," 42. The accuracy of William Smith's account of the early history of the Church in *William Smith on Mormonism*, which was given many years following the events and after his excommunication from the Church, has been questioned by some historians. For example, it appears he conflates Joseph's visit from Moroni with the First Vision. But some of William's statements are supported by and consistent with other evidence and statements and thus may be credible. For an insightful collection of personal accounts of Joseph Smith, including that of William Smith, see Mark L. McConkie, *Remembering Joseph: Personal Recollections of Those Who Knew the Prophet Joseph Smith* (Salt Lake City, UT: Deseret Book, 2003).

26. George Peck, *The Life and Times of Rev. George Peck* (New York: Nelson & Phillips, 1874), 109.

27. George Peck, *Early Methodism* (New York: Carlton & Porter, 1860), 494.

28. Harvey, *The Harvey Book*, 132.

29. Peck, *Early Methodism*, 315.

30. Peck, 315.

31. Peck, 502; Turner, *History of the Pioneer Settlement*, 214.

32. *Deseret Evening News*, Jan. 20, 1894, 11; Porter, "Reverend George Lane," 338; Porter, "Reinventing Mormonism," 130; Peck, *Early Methodism*, 502. Orsamus Turner and William Smith both reference Joseph's attraction to Methodism (William Smith mentions George Lane by name), and George Peck places a Methodist conference in Vienna (later Phelps), New York, in 1819. Oliver Cowdery also references George Lane's powerful discourse and his influence on Joseph. "Oliver Cowdery Letter III." Accordingly, William Smith's statement that George Lane preached a sermon that influenced Joseph is corroborated by other statements.

33. "Oliver Cowdery Letter III," 42.

34. History, circa June 1839–circa 1841 [Draft 2], 2, josephsmithpapers.org; Roberts, *History of the Church*, 1:4.

35. Lucy Mack Smith, History, 1844–1845, book 3, 10, josephsmithpapers.org; Smith, *Lucy's Book*, 335 (manuscript version).

36. History, circa June 1839–circa 1841 [Draft 2], 3, josephsmithpapers.org; Roberts, *History of the Church*, 1:6.

37. History, circa Summer 1832, 3, josephsmithpapers.org. In an interview, Joseph said he walked to a location where he had been clearing trees and stumps and where he had left his axe in a stump. *New York Spectator*, Sept. 23, 1843; Michael Hubbard MacKay and Gerrit J. Dirkmaat, *From Darkness unto Light: Joseph Smith's Translation and Publication of the Book of Mormon* (Provo, UT: BYU Religious Studies Center, 2015), 2, fn. 4.

38. History, circa June 1839–circa 1841 [Draft 2], 3, josephsmithpapers.org. This quotation is taken from Joseph Smith's 1838 account, which is the most well-known account of Joseph's visit from God the Father and Jesus Christ. Currently a total of ten accounts of the First Vision have been located, one of which is in Joseph's and Frederick G. William's own handwriting. "Accounts of Joseph Smith's First Vision," Joseph Smith Papers, http://josephsmithpapers.org/site/accounts-of-the-first-vision.

   The Church has issued a Gospel Topics Essay exploring the accounts of the First Vision and explaining that the "various accounts of the First Vision tell a consistent story, though naturally they differ in emphasis and detail." While "some [critics] have mistakenly argued that any variation in the retelling of the story is evidence of fabrication," the fact is that "the rich historical record enables us to learn more about this remarkable event than we could if it were less well documented." Gospel Topics Essays, "First Vision Accounts," Gospel Library.

   For example, Joseph's 1832 account focuses on Joseph seeking "mercy" and forgiveness of his sins, while his 1838 account places the vision in a broader context of founding and building the Church. For a thorough and dynamic discussion of these accounts see Dean C. Jessee, "The Earliest Documented Accounts of Joseph Smith's First Vision," in John W. Welch, ed., *Opening the Heavens: Accounts of Divine Manifestations, 1820–1844* (Provo, UT: Brigham Young University Press, 2005), 1–33. An earlier version of this article appeared in *BYU Studies* 9, no. 3 (Spring 1969): 275–94.

39. History, circa Summer 1832, 3, josephsmithpapers.org. The 1832 account of the First Vision is the only account written in Joseph Smith's own handwriting.

40. History, circa June 1839–circa 1841 [Draft 2], 3, josephsmithpapers.org.

41. History, circa June 1839–circa 1841 [Draft 2], 4, josephsmithpapers.org. Following his vision, Joseph told his mother, "I have learned for myself that Presbyterianism is not true." Willard Richards Journal, Dec. 2. 1842, Church History Library, Salt Lake City. Historians have observed that Joseph largely kept his vision private rather than public for a number of years. MacKay and Dirkmaat, *From Darkness unto Light*, 2.

42. History, circa June 1839–circa 1841 [Draft 2], 4, josephsmithpapers.org; Roberts, *History of the Church*, 1:9; Smith, *Biographical Sketches*, 78; Smith, *Lucy's Book*, 335 (Pratt version).

43. James B. Allen and Glen M. Leonard, *Story of the Latter-day Saints*, 2nd ed. (Salt Lake City, UT: Deseret Book, 1992), 35–36.

44. History, circa June 1839–circa 1841 [Draft 2], 4, josephsmithpapers.org; Roberts, *History of the Church*, 1:7.

45. History, circa June 1839–circa 1841 [Draft 2], 4, josephsmithpapers.org; Roberts, *History of the Church*, 1:6, 8.

46. "Mormonism—No. II," *Tiffany's Monthly* 5 (Aug. 1859): 164–65. Joel Tiffany, a journalist in New York, supposedly interviewed several witnesses about the rise and progress of the Church in Ohio and New York and published a three-part article on Mormonism in 1859, which includes an interview with Martin Harris. Although some of Mr. Tiffany's statements are credible, some of the content in his articles lacks historical detail and is apparently focused on his own concerns as a spiritualist, such as his belief that the Book of Mormon was created by a "band of spirits." "Mormonism," *Tiffany's Monthly* 5 (July 1859): 119.

47. A. W. B., "Mormonites," *Evangelical Magazine and Gospel Advocate* 2, no. 25 (Apr. 9, 1831): 120.

48. John A. Clark, *Gleanings by the Way* (Philadelphia: W. J. and J. K. Simon 1842), 225. John Clark was an Episcopalian pastor in Palmyra who wrote a series of letters in 1840 for the *Episcopal Recorder*, a religious periodical published in Philadelphia. Clark held a strong bias against Mormonism or the so-called "Mormon delusion," calling it a "system of imposture" ran by "trickery and artifice." Clark, *Gleanings By The Way*, 218. Caution is warranted in citing Clark's account due to his obvious prejudice, but certain parts are likely credible as they relate facts that are historically sound and do not emit a bias, such as notes from Clark's interview with Martin Harris.

49. Mark Ashurst-McGee, "Moroni as Angel and as Treasure Guardian," *The Farms Review* 18, no. 1 (2006): 40.

50. Jon Butler, "The Dark Ages of American Occultism, 1760–1848," in *The Occult in America: New Historical Perspectives*, ed. Howard Kerr and Charles Crow (Urbana, IL: University of Illinois Press, 1983), 58–78.

51. "Money Diggers," *Wayne Sentinel* (Palmyra, NY), Feb. 16, 1825, 1.

52. "Testimony of Willard Chase," in E. D. Howe, *Mormonism Unvailed* (Painesville, OH: s.n., 1834), 240–241; Gospel Topics Essays, "Book of Mormon Translation," Gospel Library, fn. 18; Larry E. Morris, "'I Should Have an Eye Single to the Glory of God': Joseph Smith's Account of the Angel and the Plates," *Farms Review* 17, 1 (2005): 75.

Mormonism Unvailed is considered to be the first written anti–Latter day-Saint book. The book contains a number of affidavits and statements related to the character of Joseph Smith and Martin Harris but is based on prejudice and vengeance. Mr. Howe hired Doctor Philastus Hurlbut, an excommunicated member of the Church, to assemble affidavits and statements in an attempt to discredit Joseph Smith and the Book of Mormon, and then published them in *Mormonism Unvailed*. Hurlbut was excommunicated from the Church in June 1833 for sexual immorality, and shortly thereafter he traveled to New York and Pennsylvania to obtain the affidavits. Although severe prejudice is notable from these affidavits and must be considered, close analysis reveals that some statements offer historical value.

53. Rhamanthus M. Stocker, *Centennial History of Susquehanna County, Pennsylvania*, 2nd ed. (Baltimore, MD: Regional Publishing Company, 1974), 555; Myers, *Long Crooked River*, 339. Joseph later showed one of the stones to the Quorum of the Twelve Apostles. Brigham Young, Joseph Smith's successor, wrote, "I met with the Twelve at brother Joseph's. He conversed with us in a familiar manner on a variety of subjects, and explained to us the Urim and Thummim which he found with the plates, called in the Book of Mormon the Interpreters. He said that every man who lived on the earth was entitled to a seer stone, and should have one, but they are kept from them in consequence of their wickedness, and most of those who do find one make an evil use of it; he showed us his seer stone." "History of Brigham Young," *The Latter-Day Saints' Millennial Star* 26 (Feb. 20, 1864): 118–19; Ashurst-McGee, "Moroni as Angel," 42. In 1888 President Wilford Woodruff consecrated a seer stone upon a temple altar in Manti, Utah. He wrote that Joseph had found the stone by revelation some thirty feet under the ground and carried the stone with him throughout his life. *Wilford Woodruff Journals, 1833-1898*, 8:499 (May 17–18, 1888), Church History Library, Salt Lake City.

54. For a detailed discussion of the two seer stones, see MacKay and Dirkmaat, *From Darkness unto Light*, 125. Historians Michael MacKay and Nicholas J. Frederick also exhaustively explore the history and origins of seer stones in *Joseph Smith's Seer Stones* (Provo, UT: BYU Religious Studies Center, 2016). The Church is in possession of two of Joseph's seer stones. For a comprehensive overview of the seer stones, including pictures, see Royal Skousen and Robin Scott Jensen, eds., *The Joseph Smith Papers: Revelations and Translations, Volume 3, Part 1: Printer's Manuscript of the Book of Mormon, 1 Nephi 1-Alma 35* (Salt Lake City, UT: Church Historians's Press, 2015), part 1.

55. Clark, *Gleanings by the Way*, 224.

56. "Mormonism," 119.

57. "Mormonism—No. II," 164–65.

58. William D. Purple, *Historical Reminiscences*, Apr. 28, 1877, 8–9, Moore Memorial Library, Greene, New York. William D. Purple entered the medical practice in 1824 and lived in South Bainbridge, New York. When Joseph Smith's trial was held in 1826, Dr. Purple was present and was invited by his friend Justice Neely to take notes. Dr. Purple's account of Joseph Smith's 1826 trial is considered a valid and reliable source of information and is generally corroborated by Justice Neely's bill (record of the trial).

59. Purple, *Historical Reminiscences*, 8–9.

60. Purple, 8–9. It is believed that Joseph Smith Sr. made this statement at Joseph's trial in 1826. Bushman, *Joseph Smith: Rough Stone Rolling*, 52.

61. Joseph responded affirmatively when asked whether he was a money digger. *Elders' Journal* (Far West, MO), July 1838, 43.

62. History, circa June 1839–circa 1841 [Draft 2], 5, josephsmithpapers.org; Roberts, *History of the Church*, 1:9.

63. History, 1838–1856, volume A-1 [23 December 1805–30 August 1834],133, josephsmithpapers.org; History, circa June 1839–circa 1841 [Draft 2], 5, josephsmithpapers.org; Roberts, *History of the Church*, 1:9. This passage was added as an addendum to Joseph's history by Willard Richards on December 2, 1842.

64. History, circa Summer 1832, 4, josephsmithpapers.org; Dean C. Jessee, comp. and ed., *The Personal Writings of Joseph Smith* (Salt Lake City, UT: Deseret Book, 2002), 12.

65. "Oliver Cowdery Letter IV," *Latter Day Saints' Messenger and Advocate* (Kirtland, OH), Feb. 1835, 78.

66. History, circa Summer 1832, 4, josephsmithpapers.org; "Oliver Cowdery Letter IV," 79.

67. "Oliver Cowdery Letter IV," 79; History, circa June 1839–circa 1841 [Draft 2], 5, josephsmithpapers.org; Roberts, *History of the Church*, 1:11.

68. "Oliver Cowdery Letter IV," 79. In the March edition of the *Latter Day Saints' Messenger and Advocate*, Oliver said he had given an "imperfect description of the angel" in the February edition because his "pen would fail to describe an angel in his glory, or the glory of God." "Oliver Cowdery Letter V," *Latter Day Saints' Messenger and Advocate* (Kirtland, OH), Mar. 1835, 95.

69. "Oliver Cowdery Letter IV," 79.

70. History, circa June 1839–circa 1841 [Draft 2], 5, josephsmithpapers.org; Roberts, *History of the Church*, 1:11–12; Gospel Topics Essays, "Book of Mormon Translation," Gospel Library.

71. History, circa June 1839–circa 1841 [Draft 2], 5–6, josephsmithpapers.org.

72. History, circa June 1839–circa 1841 [Draft 2], 5, josephsmithpapers.org; Roberts, *History of the Church*, 1:12.

73. "Oliver Cowdery Letter VIII," *Latter Day Saints' Messenger and Advocate* (Kirtland, OH), Oct. 1835, 199.

74. History, circa Summer 1832, 4–5; "Mormonism—II," 168; Morris, "'I Should Have an Eye Single,'" 40.

75. History, circa June 1839–circa 1841 [Draft 2], 6, josephsmithpapers.org; Roberts, *History of the Church*, 1:13.

76. History, circa June 1839–circa 1841 [Draft 2], 6–7, josephsmithpapers.org; Roberts, *History of the Church*, 1:14; "Oliver Cowdery Letter VII," *Latter Day Saints' Messenger and Advocate* (Kirtland, OH), July, 1835, 156.

77. Emily C. Blackman, *History of Susquehanna County, Pennsylvania* (Philadelphia: Claxton, Remsen & Haffelfinger, 1873), 577.

78. "The 100 Most Influential Figures in American History," *The Atlantic*, Dec. 2006, https://www.theatlantic.com/magazine/archive/2006/12/the-100-most-influential-figures-in-american-history/305384/; "Book of Mormon Reaches 150 Million Copies," *Church News*, Apr. 20, 2011, https://www.churchofjesuschrist.org/church/news/book-of-mormon-reaches-150-million-copies; David Schneider, "Book of Mormon translations: See maps of where the 115 languages are spoken," *Church News*, Feb. 27, 2022, https://www.thechurchnews.com/2022/2/27/23216723/book-of-mormon-translations-maps-where-115-languages-spoken/.

79. Allen and Leonard, *Story of the Latter-day Saints*, 38. Joseph's father said: "My son, be not disobedient to this heavenly vision!" Orson Pratt, in *Journal of Discourses*, 15:184; Ivan J. Barrett, *Joseph Smith and the Restoration* (Provo, UT: Brigham Young University Press, 1970), 43.

80. The Hill Cumorah is mentioned twice in the Book of Mormon regarding two different groups of people. The prophet Mormon recounted the last battle of his people, who were camped around the Hill Cumorah. Another group of people in the Book of Mormon, the Jaredites, called the hill "Ramah" and were destroyed in a battle on the hill. Oliver Cowdery commented, "In this same spot, in full view from the top of this same hill, one may gaze with astonishment upon the ground which was twice covered with dead and dying of our fellowmen. Here may be seen where once sunk to naught the pride and strength of two mighty nations." "Oliver Cowdery Letter VII," 159.

81. History, circa June 1839–circa 1841 [Draft 2], 7, josephsmithpapers.org; Roberts, *History of the Church*, 1:14–16; *Elders' Journal* (Far West, MO), July 1838, 43. According to some accounts, Joseph also uncovered the sword of Laban and the Liahona. "An Angel Told Him," *Kansas City Times*, Apr. 11, 1895, cited in Kyle R. Walker, "Katharine Smith Salisbury's Recollections of Joseph's Meetings with Moroni," *BYU Studies* 41, no. 3 (2002): 4–17.

82. Lucy Mack Smith, History, 1844–1845, book 4, 2, josephsmithpapers.org; Smith, *Lucy's Book*, 346 (manuscript version); History, circa Summer 1832, 4–5, josephsmithpapers.org.

83. "Oliver Cowdery Letter VII," 157.

84. Lucy Mack Smith, History, 1844–1845, book 4, 3, josephsmithpapers.org; Smith, *Lucy's Book*, 347 (manuscript version).

85. "Oliver Cowdery Letter VIII," 197–98.

86. History, circa Summer 1832, 4, josephsmithpapers.org; "Oliver Cowdery Letter VIII," 197–98.

87. Many years later, the *Chicago Times* newspaper printed the following account of the event: "Overpowered by the discovery he rested for a few moments, and then visions of worldly emolument flitted through his overwrought brain. He

had been singled out as the discoverer of this secret of the infinite! Should he neglect this golden opportunity to amass a fortune? No! . . . While these worldly thoughts occupied Joseph's mind, the angel of the Lord again suddenly stood before him, told him that he had approached this sacred spot in [an] irreverent mood, that the secrets of the casket could never be his until he sought them in the proper spirit." "The Golden Tablets," *Chicago Times*, Aug. 7, 1875; Ashurst-McGee, "Moroni as Angel," 3.

88. Oliver Cowdery recounted this event as follows: "[Joseph] exclaimed, 'Why can I not obtain this book?' 'Because you have not kept the commandments of the Lord,' answered a voice, within a seeming short distance." "Oliver Cowdery Letter VIII," 198.

89. "Oliver Cowdery Letter VIII," 197–98; John Corrill, *A Brief History of the Church of Christ of Latter Day Saints*, 1839, 12, josephsmithpapers.org; Joseph Fielding Smith, *Essentials in Church History*, 23rd ed. (Salt Lake City, UT: Deseret Book, 1969), 4.

90. History, circa Summer 1832, 5, josephsmithpapers.org; Morris, "'I Should Have an Eye Single,'" 78.

91. History, circa Summer 1832, 5, josephsmithpapers.org; Jessee, *Personal Writings of Joseph Smith*, 13; History, circa June 1839–circa 1841 [Draft 2], 7, josephsmithpapers.org; Roberts, *History of the Church*, 1:16; Corrill, *Brief History*, 12. The accounts of Joseph and his mother diverge in this instance. Lucy seems to suggest that Joseph was beset by temptation on his *second* visit with Moroni at the Hill Cumorah, and Joseph says it was on his *first* visit with Moroni at the Hill Cumorah. Lucy Mack Smith, History, 1844–1845, book 4, 2–3, josephsmithpapers.org; Smith, *Lucy's Book*, 346 (manuscript version). I have accepted Joseph's account since Joseph likely desired the plates for their monetary advantage during his first visit because his family was in poor condition at that time, and it is unlikely that Joseph looked on the plates for their monetary value during only his second visit.

92. Lucy Mack Smith, History, 1844–1845, book 4, 2, josephsmithpapers.org; Smith, *Lucy's Book*, 341 (manuscript version); Joseph Fielding Smith, *Essentials in Church History*, 50.

93. William Smith, "The Old Soldier's Testimony," *The Saints' Herald*, Oct. 4, 1884, 643–44; McConkie, *Remembering Joseph*, 1472.

94. Smith, "The Old Soldier's Testimony," 643–44; McConkie, 1472–73.

95. "Wentworth Letter," *Times and Seasons* (Nauvoo, IL), Mar. 1, 1842, vol. 3, no. 9, 707. The *Times and Seasons* was the Church-owned newspaper printed by Joseph Smith in Nauvoo, Illinois, from 1839 to 1846. The "Wentworth letter," one of the more well-known writings in the *Times and Seasons*, was a letter written in 1842 by Joseph Smith to "Long" John Wentworth, editor and proprietor of the *Chicago Democrat*. It summarized the history of the Church and included the Articles of Faith and the Standard of Truth.

96. History, circa June 1839–circa 1841 [Draft 2], josephsmithpapers.org; Roberts, *History of the Church*, 1:18; "Visions of Joseph Smith," *Encyclopedia of Mormonism*, ed. Daniel H. Ludlow (New York: Macmillan, 1992), 4:1512.

97. Smith, *Biographical Sketches*, 85; Smith, *Lucy's Book*, 344–45 (Pratt version). At this time, Joseph could not decipher the engravings on the gold plates, so everything he learned probably came directly from Moroni.

98. John Taylor, in *Journal of Discourses*, 17:374; Ivan J. Barrett, *Joseph Smith and the Restoration*, 82.

CHAPTER 2

Faiths in Foreign Lands

———— ⟨⟩ ————

William Penn converts to Quakerism in Ireland;
Joseph Smith finds Methodism in Harmony, Pennsylvania.

IN THE FALL OF 1666, WILLIAM PENN BEGAN HIS PRACTICE OF LAW IN
Ireland. But he did not practice long and soon returned to his home
country, England. In the summer of 1667, William's father asked him
to return to Ireland to handle some of his father's real estate holdings
there. It was during this visit to Ireland that William encountered
the Quakers and caught the spark of Quakerism. Impressed by the
hospitality of the Quakers, which he learned was called the "Quaker
way," William began to attend Quaker meetings.[1] Quakers were a
unique people who generally refused to accept any restraints on their
God-given freedoms and called each other "Friends."[2]

William's Conversion

William eventually followed his heart and converted to Quakerism
at the age of twenty-three.[3] He likely felt that the Quaker faith was
part of his divine mission. At one Quaker meeting that William attended, likely in the fall of 1667 near Cork, Ireland, a soldier entered the meeting and caused a great disturbance. William swiftly
reacted, moving toward the soldier and grabbing him by the collar.
William would have thrown the soldier down the stairs if he had not
been stopped by a Friend who asked him to let the man go because
Quakers were a "peaceable people."[4] He obviously had not yet learned

the "Quaker way." He released the soldier, who then reported William and other Friends to the local magistrates. William and several others were made "prisoners" for their actions. He was brought before the magistrate, but "the magistrate . . . knowing [William,] told him he did not think him a Quaker so would not send him to jail." The magistrate knew of his prominent family and father. William told the magistrate that "whether he thought him [a Quaker] or not . . . he was one and if he sent his friends to prison he was willing to go with them."[5] William, despite his prominence and the option to avoid prison, elected to stay with the other prisoners. He stayed one or two days in Cork jail with the other Friends.

In England during William's time, Quakers often used the terms "thee" and "thou" instead of "you" and "your," regardless of the addressee's rank, which showed the Quaker belief in the equality of all people. Quakers also opposed the swearing of judicial oaths and oaths of allegiance. Their opposition to oaths was based on Matthew 5:33–37, in which Jesus said, "Swear not at all . . . but let your communication be, Yea, yea; Nay, nay: for whatsoever is more than these cometh of evil." Quakers would not participate in the military because they were a peaceful people.

While in Cork jail, on November 4, 1667, William wrote his first statement in defense of religious freedom, or Liberty of Conscience. He composed a letter to the Earl of Orrery, Lord President of Munster, Ireland, stating that "religion . . . is at once my crime & my Innocence makes me a prisoner to a . . . malice."[6] William advocated that it did not "improve or advantage this Country to dispense with freedom in things relating to Conscience." He concluded his letter, writing, "My humble supplication therefore to you is that, so malicious and injurious a practice to innocent English men may not receive any continuance or encouragement from your Lordship."[7]

William's father, Sir William Penn, was not pleased with his son's conversion to Quakerism or imprisonment at Cork jail. William's expulsion from Oxford University likely remained a source of contention between him and his father,[8] and his conversion to Quakerism directly opposed his wealthy, upper-class upbringing. William used the terms "thee" and "thou" toward his father and other nobles instead of acknowledging that social ranks deserve a certain type of deference.

He also embraced the Quaker belief of inner spirituality and a personal search for God instead of the idea that religious worship could only occur in established religious institutions.[9]

William was released from prison in Ireland and immediately left for London to face his father. When he met with his father, the issue of William using "thee" and "thou" became the main point of the discussion, among other things. William explained to his father that "'twas in obedience to God and not any disrespect to him" that he used the language "thee" and "thou." But his father likely saw this as a sign of disrespect and offered him a compromise—that William "might thee and thou those who he pleased" as long as he used respectful terms to address the king, the Duke of York, and his own father.[10] William would not compromise and the conversation ended.

The next day, Sir William Penn took his son out for a ride in his coach and expressed his deep disappointment and grief over his son's conversion to Quakerism. Sir William Penn was concerned about how others would view him as a parent "after he had trained [William] up in learning and other accomplishments for a courtier—as for an ambassador or other minister that he should become a Quaker." William was giving up fame, wealth, and influence in "obedience to the manifestation of God in his own conscience."[11] The two men soon arrived at a tavern, and after entering, Sir William Penn kneeled down and prayed to God that William might not be a Quaker nor go to any more of their meetings. William would not compromise, and he threatened to throw himself out of a window if his father did not stop the conversation. About that time, a nobleman had passed by the tavern, saw Sir William Penn's coach, and decided to stop in and say hello. The nobleman praised William, saying that "he might think himself happy in a son that could despise the grandeur of the world and refrain from the many vices they were running after."[12] This discord between William and his father would continue to divide them.

JOSEPH'S EMPLOYMENT OPPORTUNITY
IN HARMONY, PENNSYLVANIA

William discovered Quakerism during his travels to Ireland, and Joseph Smith encountered the Hales and other faithful Methodists in Harmony, Pennsylvania. Had it not been for the Smith family's financial struggles, Joseph may have never set foot in Harmony, Pennsylvania. In 1823 the Smiths began building a new frame house a few hundred yards away from their log home.[13] But tragedy struck the Smiths in November of that year when Joseph's older brother Alvin died of bilious colic at the age of twenty-five.[14] Alvin's parting words to Joseph were as follows: "I want you to be a good boy, and do everything that lies in your power to obtain the Record. Be faithful in receiving instruction, and in keeping every commandment that is given you."[15]

By 1824, although the Smiths had completed their new frame home, they found themselves in debt with at least two payments remaining on the frame home and no help from Alvin.[16] As the farm was in danger of imminent foreclosure, Joseph and his father canvassed the countryside in search of any type of employment. Finances were a concern for the Smiths, and Joseph felt a responsibility to assist.

In October 1825 a man by the name of Josiah Stowell (often spelled Stoal) traveled from Chenango County, New York, to the Palmyra area. He and his friend Joseph Knight Sr. had conceived the idea of searching for Spanish treasure. Mr. Stowell claimed to have in his possession an old Spanish treasure map and had heard something about an old Spanish silver mine in Susquehanna, Pennsylvania, in the Onaquago Mountains. He had been digging in Susquehanna County for some time without success and sought out Joseph for assistance.[17]

Mr. Stowell did not contact nineteen-year-old Joseph by chance; he already knew of Joseph's skill with seer stones and treasure hunting—that Joseph "possessed certain keys, by which he could discern things invisible to the natural eye."[18] While visiting his relative Simpson Stowell in Palmyra, Mr. Stowell was told of Joseph and the Smith family.[19] When asked about joining the venture, Joseph at first hesitated and discouraged Mr. Stowell from the pursuit. But at Mr. Stowell's insistence, and in part due to the high wages offered, he eventually agreed to participate in the venture.[20]

On November 1, 1825, Joseph and his father hired on with Mr. Stowell and signed a contract of employment.[21] The contract apparently stipulated that Joseph and his father would take two elevenths of all the property obtained and guaranteed them a fixed wage of fourteen dollars a month, an excellent wage at that time. Isaac Hale, a prominent member of the Harmony community, is believed to have witnessed the signing of the agreement. Joseph may have believed that his gift of interpreting stones to find treasure would financially benefit him and his family. Joseph's divine gift ultimately brought him to Pennsylvania.[22]

THE AMERICAN FRONTIER

Joseph and his father, along with other men, traveled in a wagon the arduous 128 miles from Manchester to Harmony, arriving in early November 1825.[23] Harmony sat at the edge of the American Frontier and was much "wilder" than Palmyra.[24] The settlement of Harmony had began only about 150 years earlier, on March 4, 1681, when King Charles II of England bestowed upon William Penn and his religious followers an unsurveyed tract of land, stretching from the Delaware River northward and westward around 300 miles to the shores of the Great Lakes of America. The land included the present-day states of Pennsylvania and New York. William at once made a treaty with the powerful Delaware Indian tribes and secured hunting and fishing rights for "The Commonwealth of Pennsylvania." The Commonwealth became the center of personal, political, and religious freedoms for America.[25]

The banks of the Susquehanna proved to be a popular location for the establishment of settlements in Pennsylvania and New York.[26] Many people wanted to live near the Susquehanna, seeing in its waters a promise of good living, prosperity, and economic opportunity.[27] People were drawn by the rich stocks of fish. Others believed the Susquehanna and its tributaries were wondrous natural highways to transport valuable commodities hundreds of miles through the rugged terrain of Pennsylvania. And others saw the Susquehanna as a channel of communication and travel.[28]

Moses Comstock and his family were the first to settle in the Harmony area.[29] In 1787 they traveled from Rhode Island to a vast and unexplored wilderness and built a simple log home on the land.[30] Soon thereafter, Henry Drinker, a wealthy landowner and banker in Philadelphia, purchased a large tract of land from the state of Pennsylvania and settled on the east bank of the river.[31] In 1789 he built a road, a house, a store, and a blacksmith shop. John Hilborn and his family, of the Quaker faith, were hired by Mr. Drinker to manage his affairs, with assistance from a man named Samuel Stanton.[32]

Mr. Drinker was impressed by the peaceful and harmonious characteristics of the faithful and honest Hilborn family. They used agreeable methods for handling the village affairs, and they welcomed and helped newcomers. As a tribute of respect to the Hilborns, Mr.

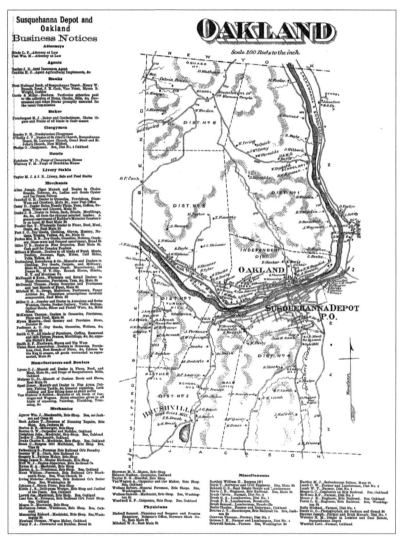

Map of Oakland, Pennsylvania. By Frederick W. Beers, Atlas of Susquehanna County, Pennsylvania, 1872. In 1853, Oakland was created from the west part of Harmony.

Drinker named the settlement Harmony,[33] and in 1809 the township of Harmony was organized.[34]

From 1820 to 1830, the population of Harmony grew from 173 to 341 people.[35] In 1830 families in Harmony Township numbered forty-seven.[36] The prominent families and persons with farms in Harmony at the time were the Hales, Lewises, McKunes, Comstocks, Bennetts, Adams, and Reverend George Peck. Associations between families were critical for survival in frontier communities such as Harmony. A farmer had to depend on neighbors for help and support, especially in times of sickness and during the harvest season.[37]

When settlers first arrived in Harmony, they encountered a dense growth of trees, principally beech, birch, maple, cherry, ash, chestnut, basswood, hemlock, and pine, with hickory and oak.[38] Naturally, trees were converted into lumber and floated downriver.[39] Trees provided for the production of maple sugar, which could be traded anywhere and was transported from the area in great quantities.[40] As the trees were cleared, the land was used for farming.[41] Early settlers grew a variety of crops, including buckwheat, oats, rye, corn, beans, pumpkins, cucumbers, potatoes, carrots, and turnips.[42]

Trout, the native fish to the region, inhabited the Susquehanna, while animals in great number and variety occupied the dense forests. With only a few clearings scattered throughout the area, panthers, bears, wolves, and wildcats thrived in the woods. Deer were numerous along with foxes, skunks, minks, and weasels, who often raided farmers' poultry at night.[43]

Rattlesnakes were prevalent in large numbers in the northern part of Susquehanna County and a nuisance to the people.[44] A story was told of a preacher, Dan Buck, and his brother and their families who celebrated one August by picking huckleberries at a place called Red Rock, just above the Susquehanna River. After filling their pails with berries, they spent the rest of the day killing four hundred and eleven rattlesnakes.[45]

RELIGION AND LIFE IN HARMONY

The immigrants who came to the colonies of Pennsylvania were deeply and sincerely religious. Many of them had left their homelands because they were not permitted to worship God according to the dictates of their conscience.[46] William Penn had established the colony of Pennsylvania based on Liberty of Conscience, religious toleration, and opposition to religious persecution. No state church was permitted and freedom of worship was guaranteed.[47] For these early settlers, including the Hales, the church was the center of social and spiritual life.[48] Regular church attendance was common.[49]

For many years, Presbyterianism was the only denomination present in the Susquehanna Valley. In 1787 Daniel Buck settled in the Great Bend area and became a local pastor for the Congregational Church.[50] The Hale and Lewis families took their one-year-old sons, Alva Hale and Levi Lewis, to Daniel Buck to be baptized.[51] When John Hilborn and his family arrived in Harmony, they brought with them their Quaker faith and beliefs and apparently held the first religious meetings in Harmony for "Friends," or members, at their house.[52]

Then the early 1800s brought the wave of Methodism—"Everybody espoused Methodism, men, women, and children. They frequently walked six miles to be present at prayer meetings."[53] Missionary zeal prospered among the settlers of all faiths; they greeted each lost sheep with rejoicing and fellowship.[54] To the religiously devoted, the church was an instrument of social order. Church discipline, or Christian ethics, governed conduct and provided a substitute where civil authority was weak. Church trials were held to settle disputes between members or to determine the guilt or innocence of members accused of violating the religious code. The churches effectively enforced decisions.[55]

Next to early settlers' reverence for God was their desire for knowledge.[56] Education held an important place in society, and as soon as a community could bear the expense, a school was opened and public funding provided. School teachers emphasized reading and trained students for a higher status in life than that of their parents. The communities built public libraries to extend reading to communities.[57] An individual with the necessary ability and motivation could climb to the higher levels of society. Upon completing school, students trained in a particular vocation through the apprenticeship system.[58]

The school buildings were crude and simple in style, similar to a log cabin. Students sat on slab benches with their faces toward the writing tables and their backs toward the center of the room. The fireplace occupied one end of the building, and logs were used for fuel to warm the school room.[59] The first school in Harmony Township opened in 1813.[60] Twenty-seven years later, a public school house was built.[61] Schools were open for three to six months a year.[62] During the early years of Harmony, however, books were scarce and were generally only available through Mr. Hilborn.[63]

For sports and entertainment, early settlers engaged in target shooting and wrestling as well as hunting and fishing. Men participated in athletics, while women generally engaged in less physical endeavors. All participated in sleigh rides, parties, and dances.[64] Frolics were also common—social gatherings for dancing, eating, and socializing while raising a barn, husking corn, or making a quilt.[65] Most settlers in Harmony were on the same economic level and fully embraced the belief of equality. Some visitors to Harmony observed that the settlers were unrefined and uncultivated, but the early settlers were unified and God-fearing.[66] The task of converting the natural forests into civilized communities and surviving the rigors of the frontier united them in one common purpose.[67]

Methodism in Harmony

Methodism was an aggressive missionary faith, adapted for frontier conditions like Harmony where members lived in widely scattered and thinly populated communities.[68] When settlers arrived in a region, local preachers were found and, as soon as cabins were built and a few acres cleared for a crop the next year, the local preacher invited his neighbors to his cabin for religious service.[69] When a regular circuit preacher arrived in the area, Methodism was often already established and thriving.[70]

A typical Methodist itinerant, or circuit rider, was responsible for predominantly rural areas of 200 to 500 miles in circumference. He was expected to visit all the communities and villages within his circuit every two to six weeks, with the standard being a four-week circuit.[71] After traveling from cabin to cabin and becoming acquainted with the families in the area, Methodist preachers would gather together those who were willing and offer prayers.[72] The preachers emphasized individual responsibility and equality of all men in the sight of God.[73]

A Methodist preacher's career followed a progression from class leader, to exhorter, to local preacher, to itinerant preacher, and, more often than not, back to local preacher when he married or his health failed. Local preachers commonly preached on Sundays and often led prayer and class meetings during the week. The task of nurturing members between visits by the itinerant preacher almost always fell on the local preacher.[74]

Methodist circuit riders ate their meals with Methodist families, slept in cabins or out in a barn with animals, and then rode their horses during the day to the next appointment.[75] They traveled light, carrying their belongings and books in their saddlebags. The willingness of the circuit riders to go any place, any time, led to the saying, "It's weather fit only for crows and Methodist preachers."[76] Probably the greatest danger for circuit riders was recurring and severe illness. The fatigue of constant riding, exposure to wind and rain, and often spoiled food caused illnesses for which there was no treatment except the home remedies of the people.[77] Not everyone welcomed the circuit riders. One circuit rider described his meeting with an angry crowd as follows: "I was pursued by the wicked, knocked down, and left almost dead on the highway."[78]

Methodism in northeastern Pennsylvania experienced remarkable growth in 1818 and 1819.[79] As the number of Methodists in cities and larger towns grew, circuit riders in the Broome County circuit were assigned to "stations" in these communities.[80] By 1820 the Methodist Church had approximately the same numerical strength as the Baptists and by 1825 had swelled to nearly 350,000 in the United States, with more than 1,300 preachers.[81] Forty years of circuit riding had firmly established societies and classes of Methodists in small frontier communities such as Harmony.[82]

In Pennsylvania, the number of Methodists increased more than 570 percent between 1790 and 1810, while the overall state population less than doubled during the same interval.[83] Revivals, or protracted prayer meetings, played an essential part in the growth of Methodism and were traditionally held in the forest. They frequently continued for several days and sometimes one session would last all day and into the night.[84] The meetings were filled with heartfelt singing, impassioned prayers, and forthright preaching.[85] Reverend George Peck, a renowned Methodist preacher, described revivals as follows: "One incessant tide of prayer and praise rolled on for many hours . . . interrupted at twelve o'clock for a midnight cry, and then resumed and continued until sunrise."[86] The massive revivals of the 1800s brought hundreds of people in the Susquehanna area to join the Methodist faith.[87]

Another important factor that contributed to the rise and success of early Methodism was the emphasis on singing. Religion sang its way into the hearts of the people. Methodists sang hymns in their homes, at work, with their family, and at formal religious services.[88] The hymnbook was a practical manual for the teaching of Christian truth.[89] In the Susquehanna Valley, hymn writing became popular as settlers published hymns in local newspapers.[90]

Methodism started in the Great Bend area in 1805.[91] A certain style of Methodism, called "Shouting Methodism," became popular as worshippers would seek inspiration from God by secluding themselves deep in the woods and praying out loud. They believed they would receive direct answers to their prayers from God.[92] The first Methodist meetings in Susquehanna were held in barns in the summer and private houses in winter until a log schoolhouse was built. The schoolhouse then served as the place of worship on Sundays until a chapel was built.[93]

Harmony was assigned to the "Genesee Conference, Broome Circuit" of the Methodist Church in 1812, which included Broome County, New York, and extended across the Susquehanna River at Great Bend.[94] There was not a church on the Broome Circuit from which the preachers could preach to the 366 members, so they taught in the peoples' homes or the school house.[95] George Peck recorded, "The congregations were good, often crowding the places of assemblage. The spirit of the people was excellent, and their cordiality and warm hospitality greatly encouraged me."[96]

TRAVEL

Traveling to Harmony was not easy for Joseph and his father and often proved dangerous and hazardous for settlers of frontier communities. Before the construction of roads, many of the settlers followed streams, found their way by marked trees, or walked along rough trails built by Indians.[97] Construction of roads commenced in the early nineteenth century, permitting settlers to travel by more advanced means such as horseback, wagon, or stagecoach.[98]

Crossing the Susquehanna River presented an extraordinary challenge for wagons. Travel time increased significantly because the wheels had to be removed and the base of the wagon placed on canoes.[99] It was not until 1837 that a bridge to cross the Susquehanna was erected near Harmony, but it was destroyed soon thereafter.[100] Inclement weather also inhibited travel. Winters in Susquehanna County brought severe storms with heavy snow, making the roads impassable, and the spring brought torrential downpours and thick mud.[101] Settlers of Harmony apparently constructed a foot bridge across the Susquehanna River to increase access to the other side.

The construction of roads in Harmony commenced in 1798, with the opening of a road stretching from Great Bend to the nearby town of Tunkhannock. Around that time, another road was constructed connecting Great Bend to Harmony. Almost twenty years later, in 1819, Henry Drinker built the first turnpike road into the Lackawanna Valley, named the Philadelphia–Great Bend turnpike.[102] Daily mail-coaches drawn by four horses ran up and down the main roads.[103]

Treasure Hunting

Joseph was not alone in seeking treasure. Money digging, or treasure hunting, was widespread among the rural areas of New York and New England and extended into the Great Bend area of Pennsylvania.[104] It was a popular myth among all classes of society in Pennsylvania in the 1800s.[105]

Pennsylvania local legend told of a company of Spanish explorers who, when the country was uninhabited by white settlers, traveled up the Susquehanna River, lured by glittering metal in northern streams.[106] It was said that they excavated ore from the bowels of the earth and coined a large quantity of money. Then they located a cavity in the rock and departed, leaving a part of their treasure there with the intention of retrieving it at some later time.[107] It was also believed that Spanish sailors, lost at sea or fleeing English ships, navigated through the Chesapeake Bay and up the Susquehanna River in order to hide gold and silver until they could return and claim it.[108] It was even speculated that pirates had buried silver at the mouth of the Susquehanna River.[109]

A silver mine left by the Spaniards was supposedly located somewhere in the hills near Harmony.[110] Just south of Susquehanna County, in the Lackawanna Valley, local tradition told of another silver mine only known by Indian tribes, located two miles north of the mouth of the Lackawanna River. It was described as being "on the northeast side of the Lackawanna above a high ledge or mountain, half an hour's walk from the River Susquehanna, twelve miles above Wyoming."[111] Rumors of a gold mine in the Wyoming Valley also circulated among the people, "at a point where a rock of the height of an Indian covered a spring."[112] Today a hill ninety miles down the Susquehanna from Harmony, near Athens, Pennsylvania, bears the name "Old Spanish Hill," a sign of the influence left behind by the Spaniards.[113]

Rumored silver mine in Harmony, Pennsylvania.
Left: Outside the mine. Right: Inside the mine.
Photographs by the author.

Mr. Stowell and his crew were operating two excavation sites in the area, one near the McKune farm and the other on Jacob Skinner's farm.[114] Jacob Skinner lived one and a half miles west of Susquehanna Depot in Oakland Borough, on the hill above the McKune Cemetery.[115] Neither excavation site was far from the Hales' home.[116]

On November 17, 1825, after digging for three weeks without success, Joseph persuaded Mr. Stowell to cease the expedition for treasure.[117] The men had found no treasure, or even any sign of treasure, and the expedition was consuming valuable time and resources. By convincing Mr. Stowell to cease the expedition, Joseph acted against his own financial interest. Had Mr. Stowell continued, even if no treasure were found, Joseph and his father would have continued to be paid under the contract. Forgoing a certain wage is an indication of Joseph's good character and his progress of overcoming his desire for financial gain. Although he and his family surely needed the money, Joseph put the interests of Mr. Stowell over his own financial interests.

Joseph's brief episode of money digging did not go unnoticed, for rumors and stories of his participation spread throughout Harmony. Joseph later stated, "Hence arose the very prevalent story of my having been a money digger."[118]

THE HALE HOMESTEAD

While employed with Mr. Stowell, Joseph and his father boarded with the Hale family, either in the large frame home or log cabin on their property.[119] The Hale family was one of the first families to settle the frontier community of Harmony. In the fall of 1787, Isaac Hale traveled from Wells, Vermont, down the Susquehanna River to settle in the Great Bend area.[120] He stayed a couple of winters, and in 1790 he returned to Vermont to marry Elizabeth Lewis. Together with Elizabeth's brother, Nathaniel Lewis, and his wife, Sarah Cole, along with Sarah's mother and sister, they traveled over 200 miles to take up permanent residence in Harmony, Pennsylvania.[121] The Lewis family occupied the neighboring property to the west of the Hales' property.[122]

Mr. Hale was a mighty hunter and established his homestead in the woods of Harmony where wildlife was in abundance.[123] He lived on approximately 620 acres and slaughtered about one hundred deer annually, most of which he sent downriver to the Philadelphia Market.[124] Mr. Hale often killed bears and elk as well as smaller animals. To preserve the meat, he constructed troughs of birch or maple wood to hold the cut-up meat, salted the meat, and covered it with bark. Heavy stones were then placed on the bark to hold the meat down. He would either give away the meat or offer it in exchange for work on the farm.[125]

Others in Harmony spoke of Isaac as a generous man with forethought who would unselfishly give meat to others in the community. The fruit of his labors often found its way to the tables of neighbors and friends.[126] Through his generosity and skill as a hunter, Isaac became a prominent citizen of Harmony and lived comfortably with his family.[127]

Mr. Hale originally was a deist—he believed in God but not in "prophecy, miracles, or a divine role in the production of scriptures"—but he later converted to Methodism.[128] He also apparently adopted Quaker beliefs because he refused to swear the required oath each time he was appointed to public office, served on a jury, or testified in court.[129]

Most of Mr. Hale's neighbors viewed him as a devoted husband and father, a faithful Christian, and an independent backwoodsman.[130] Sometime between 1805 and 1813, the Hales built a frame home on the foundation of their log cabin and moved their log cabin to a nearby location on their property. [131] The frame home was likely used as a church and a civic center for local meetings and business.[132]

Isaac Hale and his wife, Elizabeth, had nine children. Emma, his daughter, was the seventh of nine, born on July 10, 1804, and raised on the banks of the Susquehanna.[133] Emma, often called Emmy by her friends, attended school and took her education seriously.[134] It was told that she "never used slang and was very particular about her grammar and choice of words."[135] Emma attended an academy for girls where she received training in social behavior.[136] According to William Blair, Mr. Hale's son-in-law, Isaac converted from his faith of deism to Methodism when he happened upon Emma while she was praying out loud in the woods: "Mr. Hale always claimed that he was converted from deism to faith in Christ as the Savior, by a secret prayer of Emma's, when she was but seven or eight years old, which he accidentally overheard when just entering into the woods to hunt. In the course of her prayer she besought the Lord on behalf of her father, and the force and efficacy of that prayer entered into his heart with such power as to lead him to faith in Christ the Lord."[137]

The members of the Hale family were faithful Methodists.[138] According to a local historian, Mrs. Hale "was for fifty years a consistent member of the Methodist church."[139] Traveling Methodist preachers always found a warm welcome at the Hales' home, a place to refresh from their rigorous journeying.[140] Reverend Peck once preached a sermon in the Hales' home based on Isaiah 12:6, which encourages believers to "cry out and shout"—an indication of the Hales' exposure to "Shouting Methodism."[141]

The Lewis and Hale families were members of the first Methodist class in Susquehanna County.[142] In 1811 David Hale (seventeen years old) and Emma (seven years old) joined the Methodist congregation.[143] In 1816 Reverend Peck visited Jesse and Isaac Hale. In the morning, Reverend Peck "rode to Jesse Hale's some six miles above the Great Bend." Afterward, he visited Isaac Hale and recorded, "Mr. Hale gave me a cordial reception, and in the afternoon I preached in a little log schoolhouse to a small but earnest congregation." While preaching at the schoolhouse, Reverend Peck had a startling experience that he personally recorded: "When I was in the midst of my subject, and perhaps, waxing warm therein, a young woman made a leap in the air and uttered an unearthly scream, which startled me, and came near scattering my thoughts and bringing my sermon to a premature end."[144] Reverend Peck found out later that the woman's family was antagonistic toward the Methodist faith.[145]

The Hale family was closely involved in local politics in Harmony.[146] David Hale, one of Isaac's sons, was elected as Harmony Township's "Schoolman" in May 1826 and was responsible for overseeing three schools in the township. Jesse, Isaac's oldest son, served in several political offices, including Tax Assessor, Overseer of the Poor, Supervisor, and Schoolman. The number of taxable persons in Harmony (including Oakland) in 1820, when Jesse served as a tax collector, was twenty-eight.[147] And Alva Hale, another of Isaac's sons, served as town constable for most of the time that Joseph and Emma lived in Harmony. Town constables often served as law enforcement officers.

NATHANIEL LEWIS

Nathaniel Lewis resided down the river on the edge of Harmony Township, on a property neighboring the Hales.[148] He was known as an industrious, shrewd, witty, and intelligent man—"rough as a mountain crag, but deeply pious." He read the Bible and was a devoted Methodist.[149] To Emma and the Hale children, he was "Uncle Nat."[150]

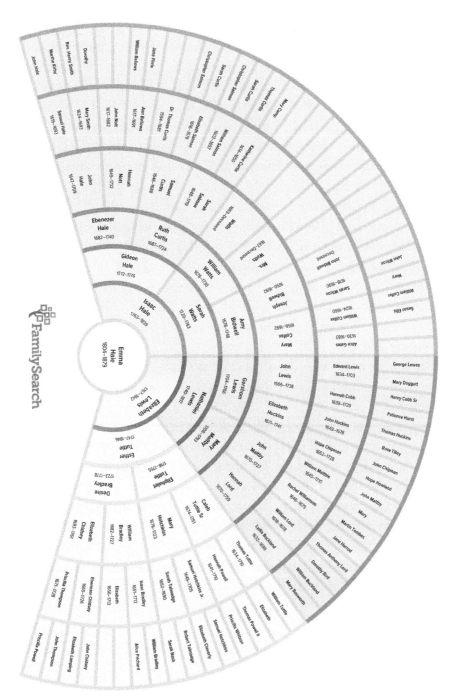

Emma Hale fan chart. Courtesy of FamilySearch.
© By Intellectual Reserve, Inc.

Mr. Lewis was the pioneer Methodist of Harmony. He was ordained a deacon in the church in 1807 and became a powerful leader of the Methodist Church in the area as the settlers in Harmony Township converted to Methodism.[151] People thought of him as talented and hardworking and the reason for the growth of Methodism in Harmony. In fact, Mr. Lewis led a congregation on the east bend of the river, which contended with other religions in the community.[152] The wealthiest member of the local Methodist group to which Lewis belonged was Isaac Hale.[153]

Several interesting stories were told concerning Mr. Lewis. One time he received information of a place, some distance from his home, where there was no religious worship. He traveled to the place and went from door to door inviting people to a meeting. He preached to the people, proclaiming, "Ye uncircumcised in heart and ear, ye do always resist the Holy Ghost." Many were touched by his sermon and a great religious revival followed. As a result of Mr. Lewis's sermon, seventy people were happily converted to God.[154]

On another occasion, a Sabbath morning in the year 1812 when food and provisions were scarce, Mr. Lewis sat reading his Bible in preparation for a sermon. He looked up from his Bible and discovered a deer near his house. He took his gun, shot the deer, and, after dressing it, delivered portions to his neighbors. He was later called to account before the church for breaking the Sabbath day. He said he was not guilty and that the Lord had sent the deer into the field for him. His accusers asked, "What do you suppose the Lord sent the deer into my field for?" Lewis responded, 'Well, I suppose the Lord sent that deer into my field for me," to which an accuser responded, "Well, I suppose the Lord sent you a test." Lewis responded emphatically, "'No, it wasn't, for the Lord knows that when he sends blessings to me I don't wait until the next day before I take them." Mr. Lewis was acquitted.[155]

At another time, Mr. Lewis was disturbed by some disorderly persons while preaching during a service. After patiently waiting for them to stop, he reproved them, calling them "a hogmatical set." After the service, a local preacher, who was present and heard the rebuke, hinted to Mr. Lewis that he had made use of the wrong word.

"What do you mean?" Mr. Lewis asked.

"Why, *hogmatical* is not a proper word," replied the local preacher.

"Yes, it is," replied Mr. Lewis. "You have heard of dogmatical, I suppose."

"O yes, but—"

"Well," interrupted Mr. Lewis, "you can shame a *dog*, but *hog* you can't." This explanation ended the discussion.[156]

Mr. Lewis did not shy from controversy or hesitate to share his strong religious convictions with others. He is quoted as saying, "Send the mind of the people up the river down to me, and the people down the river [the Presbyterians] may go to hell, and I care not."[157] Mr. Lewis's preaching did not linger or embellish but was straight to the point: "Whatever his text might be, after a short introduction, to fight *fatalism* was always the subject and object of his discourse."[158]

Joseph and His Father Board with the Hales

Mr. Hale willing and graciously accepted Methodist circuit riders but was at first hesitant to host Joseph and his father, for he had heard rumors of them participating in money digging.[159] But eventually he relented and allowed them to stay with him. Mr. Stowell's entire company could not fit in Mr. Hale's frame home, so they likely either rented a log cabin on his property, which was built in 1788, or rented a small frame home on the southeast end of his property, which was recently vacated by his son Jesse, daughter-in-law Mary, and their eight children.[160] Isaac Hale recorded his first impressions of Joseph: "His appearance at this time was that of a careless young man, not very well educated, and very saucy and insolent to his father."[161] Isaac Hale did not take fondly to Joseph, nor was he encouraged by Joseph's association with the money diggers. He further commented, "Smith, and his father, with several other 'money diggers' boarded at my house while they were employed in digging for a mine that they supposed had been opened and worked by the Spaniards. . . . This took place about the 17th of November, 1825; and one of the company gave me his note for $12.68 for his board, which is still unpaid."[162]

Mr. Hale himself had participated in money-digging excursions before Joseph's arrival.[163] He had been approached by a relative, William Hale, who told him of concealed treasure in a hill just northeast of Mr. Hale's house.[164] Josiah Stowell eventually agreed to join the effort.

Joseph Meets Emma of Harmony

Not long after his arrival at the Hales' homestead, Joseph took a special liking to Mr. Hale's twenty-one-year old daughter, Emma Hale.[165] According to Joseph's mother, Joseph "immediately commenced paying his addresses to her."[166] Emma was a stately, beautiful, dark-haired woman who religiously attended school, completing a year beyond the common grammar school education of her siblings. Emma often went canoeing along the Susquehanna River and excelled in singing.[167] She was described as "a fair scholar for the common schools of the time, and a good singer and possessed of a fine voice. . . . Her general intelligence and fearless integrity, united with her kindness of heart and splendid physical developments commanded both admiration and respect."[168] All the Hale children were considered bright, but Emma was exceptional.

Those in Harmony appeared to hold Emma in high esteem and harbored prejudices against Joseph. Joseph was described by one local historian as "having been a tall and strong man, light complexioned, quite fond of ardent liquors, not infrequently drunk, by no means intelligent in feature nor prepossessing in appearance, and in education quite limited," while Emma was described as "quite tall, of comely form and feature, well educated, a fine singer and very social."[169] Despite their prejudices, many of the Hales' neighbors admitted that Joseph was "a good, kind neighbor."[170]

Joseph shared his visions and some settlers reacted with hostility. As word spread that Joseph was in the neighborhood, attempts by settlers in Harmony were made to drive him away.[171] Apparently even the Hales were not accepting of Joseph's message.[172] From Joseph's short stay in Harmony in 1825 and 1826, folklore and rumors about him arose that still persist today.[173]

Employment at the Stowell and Knight Farms in Southern New York

After the digging expedition ended, Joseph returned with his father to their home in Manchester for a short period and then was hired to work on the farm of Mr. Stowell.[174] Mr. Stowell operated saw mills on a creek that ran through his farm, which covered hundreds of acres.[175] The farm was situated about two miles south of the town of South Bainbridge, New York, and twenty-six miles northeast of the Hale family residence in Harmony.[176] Mr. Stowell paid Joseph fourteen dollars a month plus room and board.[177]

In March 1826 Peter G. Bridgeman, Mr. Stowell's nephew, accused Joseph of stealing money from his uncle.[178] He claimed Joseph was a "disorderly person," a misdemeanor under New York state law at the time.[179] Joseph was taken into custody by the New York constable and remained under guard for two days and one night.[180] At the hearing held on March 20, 1826, Joseph Smith was examined before Justice of the Peace Albert Neely Jr.[181] According to one account, Joseph testified that he had the ability to locate hidden treasure.[182] He added that he was giving up seeking treasure, did not solicit the business, and would prefer to have nothing to do with it.[183] Most accounts of the trial agree that Mr. Stowell testified at the hearing, stating that Joseph had never deceived him or stolen money from him. Mr. Stowell's testimony was convincing, and Justice Neely purportedly found a lack of evidence against Joseph and acquitted him.[184] Enduring one night and two days in custody and facing the charge of being a disorderly person may have affirmed Moroni's previous rebuking of treasure seeking and could have contributed to Joseph ceasing the practice.[185] Joseph may not have understood that his gift for treasure seeking would serve a much greater purpose in bringing forth the Lord's work. To fulfill that purpose, however, he had to learn to use his gift properly and overcome his weakness.

When the harvest season ended in November 1826, Joseph started working for Joseph Knight Sr., a business partner of Mr. Stowell who lived twenty miles above Great Bend.[186] Mr. Knight operated a farm, gristmill, and carding machine along the Susquehanna River, three and a half miles south of the Stowells' farm.[187] Joseph's work ethic impressed the Knights, as recorded by Joseph Knight Jr.: "My father said Joseph was the best hand he ever hired, we found him a boy of truth, he was about 21 years of age."[188] Joseph worked at the Knight farm until January 1827 and also attended school at a school house not far from the Stowell farm.[189]

While working at the Knights' home, Joseph told them about his vision and the gold plates. Joseph Knight and his son Joseph Knight Jr. believed Joseph and were the first in their family to do so.[190] Later, after getting to know Joseph and seeing his work ethic, Newel Knight immediately liked Joseph. Newel said, "[Joseph's] noble deportment, his faithfulness, his kind address, could not fail to gain the esteem of those who had the pleasure of his acquaintance. . . . So honest and plain was he in all his statements that there was no room for any misgivings with me, no place for any."[191]

NOTES

1. John A. Moretta, *William Penn and the Quaker Legacy* (New York: Pearson, 2007), 33.

2. Moretta, *William Penn*, 9.

3. Andrew R. Murphy, *William Penn: A Life* (New York: Oxford University Press, 2019), 5; Arlin M. Adams and Charles J. Emmerich, "William Penn and the American Heritage of Religious Liberty," *Journal of Law and Religion* 8, no. 1/2 (1990): 59–60.

4. "The Convincement of William Penn," *Journal of the Friends' Historical Society* 32 (1935): 22–23.

5. "The Convincement of William Penn," 22–23.

6. "To the Earl of Orrery, 4 November 1667," in *The Papers of William Penn*, ed. Richard S. and Mary Maples Dunn (Philadelphia: University of Pennsylvania Press, 1981–1987), 1:51–52 (spelling modernized).

7. "To the Earl of Orrery," in *Papers of William Penn*, 1:51–52 (spelling modernized).

8. Murphy, *William Penn: A Life*, 51.

9. "The Convincement of William Penn," 24.

10. "The Convincement of William Penn," 24.

11. "The Convincement of William Penn," 24.

12. "The Convincement of William Penn," 24–25.

13. The Smiths' new frame house was located in Manchester, New York, even though it was only a few hundred yards away from their former log home. The boundary between Manchester, New York, and Palmyra, New York, runs between the two homes.

14. History, circa June 1839–circa 1841 [Draft 2], 7–8, josephsmithpapers.org; B. H. Roberts, *A Comprehensive History of the Church of Jesus Christ of Latter-day Saints* (Salt Lake City, UT: Deseret News, 1948–57), 1:16–17. Alvin died unbaptized, so Hyrum Smith was vicariously baptized for Alvin in 1840 and again in 1841 in Nauvoo. Larry C. Porter, "Alvin Smith: Reminder of the Fairness of God," *Ensign*, Sept. 1978, 65.

15. Lucy Mack Smith, *Biographical Sketches of Joseph Smith the Prophet and His Progenitors for Many Generations* (Liverpool: S. W. Richards, 1853), 88; Lucy Mack Smith, *Lucy's Book: A Critical Edition of Lucy Mack Smith's Family Memoir*, ed. Lavina Fielding Anderson (Salt Lake City, UT: Signature Books, 2001), 352 (Pratt version).

16. Lucy Mack Smith, History, 1844–1845, book 4, 9, josephsmithpapers.org; Smith, *Lucy's Book*, 361 (manuscript version); Richard Lyman Bushman, *Joseph Smith: Rough Stone Rolling* (New York: Alfred A. Knopf, 2005), 47. In 1825 the Smith family moved out of their log home into their larger frame home. They moved back into the log home in the beginning of 1829. Larry E. Morris, "The Conversion of Oliver Cowdery," *Journal of Book of Mormon Studies* 16, no. 1 (2007): 12.

17. Smith, *Biographical Sketches*, 91; Smith, *Lucy's Book*, 359–360 (Pratt version).

18. Smith, *Biographical Sketches*, 91–92; Smith, *Lucy's Book*, 360 (Pratt version); Mark Ashurst-McGee, "Moroni as Angel and as Treasure Guardian," *The Farms Review* 18, no. 1 (2006): 41. Stowell was in search of a substantial quantity of coins minted by Spaniards from ore they had mined in the vicinity. "Oliver Cowdery Letter VIII," *Latter-day Saints' Messenger and Advocate* (Kirtland, OH), Oct. 1835, 201.

19. "Oliver Cowdery Letter VIII," 201; Larry C. Porter, "The Colesville Branch and the Coming Forth of the Book of Mormon," *BYU Studies* 10, no. 3 (1970): 1.

20. Smith, *Biographical Sketches*, 92; Smith, *Lucy's Book*, 360–61 (Pratt version); Joseph Smith, "Editorial," *Elders' Journal*, July 1838, 42–44.

21. History, circa June 1839–circa 1841 [Draft 2], 7–8, josephsmithpapers.org; Roberts, *History of the Church*, 1:17; William G. Hartley, *Stand by My Servant Joseph: The Story of the Joseph Knight Family and the Restoration* (Salt Lake City, UT: Deseret Book, 2003), 7.

22. Appendix 1: Agreement of Josiah Stowell and Others, 1 November 1825, 4, josephsmithpapers.org; Larry C. Porter, *A Study of the Origins of the Church of Jesus Christ of Latter-day Saints in the States of New York and Pennsylvania, 1816–1831* (Provo, UT: BYU Studies, 2000), 49. The original of the Josiah Stowell agreement, or even the apparent printing of the agreement in the

March 20, 1880, edition of the *Susquehanna Journal*, cannot be located. Thus, there are some concerns regarding the authenticity of the agreement, but there is also substantial corroborating evidence of its existence. For a more complete analysis of the agreement, see Michael Hubbard MacKay et al., eds., *Documents, Volume 1: July 1828–June 1831* (Salt Lake City, UT: Church Historian's Press, 2013); "Historical Introduction," Appendix 1: Agreement of Josiah Stowell and Others, 1 November 1825, josephsmithpapers.org.

23. History, circa June 1839–circa 1841 [Draft 2], 8, josephsmithpapers.org; Roberts, *History of the Church*, 1:17; Hartley, *Stand by My Servant Joseph*, 7; Mark Lyman Staker, "Isaac and Elizabeth Hale in Their Endless Mountain Home," *Mormon Historical Studies* 15, no. 2 (2014): 1.

24. Frederic G. Mather, "The Early Days of Mormonism," *Lippincott's Magazine of Popular Literature and Science* 26 (Aug. 1880): 198–211.

25. Grant E. Carter, "Along the Susquehanna," *Improvement Era*, May 1960, 3.

26. Henry Reed VanDeusen, *Elm Park Historical Sketches* (Scranton, Pennsylvania: The Haddon Craftsmen, 1955), 8.

27. Peter C. Mancall, *Valley of Opportunity: Economic Culture along the Upper Susquehanna, 1700–1800* (Ithaca and London: Cornell University Press, 1991), 11.

28. James Arthur Frost, *Life on the Upper Susquehanna 1783–1860* (New York: King's Crown Press, 1951), 122; R. G. Rincliffe, *"Conowingo!" The History of a Great Development on the Susquehanna* (New York, San Francisco, and Montreal: The Newcomen Society in North America, 1953), 9.

29. Emily C. Blackman, "According to Miss Emily C. Blackman," *Susquehanna County Historical Society Journal of Genealogy and Local History* 20, no. 1 (Spring/Summer 2009): 6.

30. *Abner and Hazel Baird Papers, 1956–57*, 942, Church History Library, Salt Lake City; Susquehanna Branch History, March 2006, containing the *Lanesboro Methodist-Episcopal Church, Centennial Celebration*, March 3–5, 1912.

31. Carter, "Along the Susquehanna," 3. Henry Drinker was the cashier of the Bank of North America, which was headquartered in Philadelphia.

32. Samuel Stanton is credited with authoring the lines of poetry on the title page of this book. Many settlers, including Jonathan Bennett, the Smiths, the Greeks, Isaac Hale, and Nathaniel Lewis, purchased land in the Harmony area under Connecticut's claim of the land. After conducting a survey of the land, and subsequent litigation, it was determined that Pennsylvania held title to the land and that Pennsylvania landowners Henry Drinker, Timothy Pickering, Tench Coxe, and Hodgdon were the rightful owners. Some of the settlers moved away, while others, such as the Hale and Lewis families, purchased their claims. The Comstocks decided not to buy the land from

Pennsylvania and were ejected by the Pickering family in 1801. *Abner and Hazel Baird Papers*, 944.

33. *Abner and Hazel Baird Papers*, 944.

34. Rhamanthus M. Stocker, *Centennial History of Susquehanna County, Pennsylvania*, 2nd ed. (Baltimore, MD: Regional Publishing Company, 1974), 63. Harmony, Pennsylvania, in Susquehanna County should not be confused with the hamlet of Harmony in Butler County, located in western Pennsylvania more than two hundred miles away. Arthur I. Steward and Loran W. Veith, *Harmony, Commemorating the Sesquicentennial of Harmony Pennsylvania*, 2nd ed. (Harmony, Pennsylvania: Jan. 1956); John D. Giles, "Restoration of the Melchizedek Priesthood," *Improvement Era*, 1945. On February 21, 1810, the Pennsylvania Legislature set off Susquehanna County from Luzerne County. Township is another word for town. Townships are units of local government common in states in the northeast. "Within 'towns' (townships) are cities, incorporated villages (boroughs in Pennsylvania), and settlements or hamlets." Giles, "Restoration of the Melchizedek Priesthood," 2.

35. Emily C. Blackman, *History of Susquehanna County, Pennsylvania* (Philadelphia: Claxton, Remsen & Haffelfinger, 1873), 573–74.

36. Giles, "Restoration of the Melchizedek Priesthood," 2.

37. Stevenson Whitcomb Fletcher, *Pennsylvania Agriculture and Country Life, 1640–1840*, 2nd ed. (Harrisburg, PA: Pennsylvania Historical and Museum Commission, 1971), 438.

38. Stocker, *Centennial History of Susquehanna County*, 40.

39. Garford F. Williams, "Susquehanna County, Pennsylvania," *Susquehanna County Historical Society Journal of Genealogy and Local History* 19, no. 2 (Fall/Winter 2008): 54–57. The virgin pines in Lathrop, Pennsylvania, were floated downstream to Washington, DC, and used in the original building of the Smithsonian Institution. Williams, "Susquehanna County, Pennsylvania," 57. Lumbering stimulated the economy of Susquehanna County. Stocker, *Centennial History of Susquehanna County*, 554.

40. Williams, "Susquehanna County, Pennsylvania," 57.

41. Williams, "Susquehanna County, Pennsylvania," 58. Today flag stone quarries operate in Susquehanna County, producing Pennsylvania Blue Stone of exceptional quality. Williams, "Susquehanna County, Pennsylvania," 59. The chapel and visitors' center at the Priesthood Restoration Site in Harmony, Pennsylvania, are constructed with Pennsylvania Blue Stone.

42. Blackman, *History of Susquehanna County*, 21.

43. Stocker, *Centennial History of Susquehanna County*, 42.

44. Blackman, *History of Susquehanna County*, 78.

45. Carl Carmer, *The Susquehanna* (New York and Toronto: Rinehart & Co., 1955), 336.

46. Fletcher, *Pennsylvania Agriculture*, 509.

47. "The frame of the government of the province of Pennsylvania in America: together with certain laws agreed upon in England by the governor and divers free-men of the aforesaid province (1682)," Historical Society of Pennsylvania; cited in James B. Allen and Glen M. Leonard, *Story of the Latter-day Saints*, 2nd ed. (Salt Lake City, UT: Deseret Book, 1992), 16.

48. J. William Frost, *A Perfect Freedom: Religious Liberty in Pennsylvania* (University Park, PA: Pennsylvania State University Press, 1993), 32.

49. Frost, *A Perfect Freedom*, 32; Fletcher, *Pennsylvania Agriculture*, 453.

50. J. B. Wilkinson, *The Annals of Binghamton, and of the Country Connected with it, from the Earliest Settlement* (Binghamton, NY: Cooke & Davis, Printers, 1840), 107–08; Staker, "Isaac and Elizabeth Hale," 10. The Congregational Church eventually became part of the Presbyterian Church. Staker, 10.

51. Staker, "Isaac and Elizabeth Hale," 32.

52. Blackman, *History of Susquehanna County,* 92; Staker, "Isaac and Elizabeth Hale," 33.

53. Blackman, *History of Susquehanna County,* 80; A. F. Chafee, *History of the Wyoming Conference of the Methodist Episcopal Church* (New York: Eaton & Mains, 1904), 484.

54. Frost, *A Perfect Freedom*, 34.

55. Frost, 34.

56. Stocker, *Centennial History of Susquehanna County*, 189.

57. Frost, *A Perfect Freedom*, 38.

58. Frost, 36–37.

59. Stocker, *Centennial History of Susquehanna County*, 189.

60. George A. Stearns, *The Schools of Susquehanna County Pennsylvania 1795–1945* (Montrose, PA: Montrose Publishing Company, 1947), 21; Stocker, *Centennial History of Susquehanna County*, 587.

61. Stocker, *Centennial History of Susquehanna County*, 564.

62. Stocker, 190.

63. Staker, "Isaac and Elizabeth Hale," 34, citing Nancy Mess, "Historical Scraps from Susquehanna," on file at Lanesboro Town Hall, Susquehanna Depot, Pennsylvania.

64. Frost, *A Perfect Freedom*, 35.

65. Staker, "Isaac and Elizabeth Hale," 29.

66. Staker, 37–40.

67. Frost, *A Perfect Freedom*, 36.

68. Leroy E. Bugbee, *He Holds the Stars in His Hands: The Centennial History of the Wyoming Annual Conference of the Methodist Church* (Scranton, PA: The Wyoming Annual Conference of the Methodist Church, 1952), 14.

69. William Warren Sweet, *Methodism in American History* (New York, Cincinnati, and Chicago: The Methodist Book Concern, 1933), 147.

70. Sweet, *Methodism in American History*, 148.

71. John H. Wigger, *Taking Heaven by Storm: Methodism and the Rise of Popular Christianity in America* (New York: Oxford University Press, 1998), 35.

72. Halford E. Luccock, Paul Hutchinson and Robert W. Goodloe, *The Story of Methodism* (New York and Nashville: Abingdon Press, 1949), 221.

73. Sweet, *Methodism in American History*, 149.

74. Wigger, *Taking Heaven by Storm*, 31.

75. Edgar F. Singer, "George Peck," in *Notes and Sketches from Along the Susquehanna*, ed. John Goodell and John L. Topolewski (Rutland, VA: Academy Books, 1984), 29.

76. Keith Beasley-Topliffe, "From Traveling Preacher to Settled Pastor: Changes in the Itinerant Ministry," in *Notes and Sketches*, 49. "Preachers were urged to spend from six to twelve every morning in prayerful study, in addition to an hour of prayer and scripture reading on rising and before bedtime." Beasley-Topliffe, 49.

77. Singer, "George Peck," 29.

78. "The Hard Road of a Methodist Circuit Rider," The United Methodist Church, Mar. 21, 2018, https://www.umc.org/en/content/the-hard-road-of-a-methodist-circuit-rider.

79. Louis DeForest Palmer, *Heroism and Romance: Early Methodism in Northeastern Pennsylvania* (Saylorsburg, PA: Engel-Truitt Press, 1950), 199. From 1817 to 1820, the Broome Circuit saw an increase of 202 members. George Peck, *Early Methodism* (New York: Carlton & Porter, 1860), 334.

80. Wigger, *Taking Heaven by Storm*, 35.

81. Abel Stevens, *The Centenary of American Methodism: A Sketch of its History, Theology, Practical System, and Success* (New York: Carlton & Porter, 1866), 106. In 1850 in the four Middle states—New York, Pennsylvania, New Jersey, and Delaware—there were 2,556 Methodist churches, while Baptists, Congregationalists, Episcopalians, and Presbyterians had an aggregate of 3,600. This was due to the missionary spirit and system embraced by Methodism. Stevens, *Centenary of American Methodism*, 107, 191.

82. Bugbee, *He Holds the Stars*, 28.

83. Wigger, *Taking Heaven by Storm*, 5.

84. Frost, *A Perfect Freedom*, 33; Milton V. Backman, *Joseph Smith's First Vision* (Salt Lake City, UT: Bookcraft, 1980), 10; Russell E. Richey, *Early American*

Methodism (Bloomington and Indianapolis, IL: Indiana University Press, 1991), 23.

85. Singer, "George Peck," 28.

86. Charles H. Lippy, "Revival Beginnings," in *Notes and Sketches*, 16. Reverend Peck likely was not one of the preachers who was more interested in preparing formal, well-polished sermons rather than serving the poor and ministering to the communities. Letter from John Comfort to Silas Comfort, Dec. 24, 1836 Staker, cited in Staker, "Isaac and Elizabeth Hale," 35–36.

87. Lippy, "Revival Beginnings," 14.

88. Sweet, *Methodism in American History*, 151–52.

89. Sweet, 151–52. "Methodist singing thus became an important factor in spreading the Methodist gospel on the frontier." Sweet, 152.

90. "Sacred Music," *The Centinel*, vol. 1 (Dec. 1, 1816), 3, cited in Staker, "Isaac and Elizabeth Hale," 36. Emma's upbringing as a Methodist in the hymn-writing culture of Harmony likely prepared her to later compile the first hymnbook of the Church.

91. Peck, *Early Methodism*, 455; Goodell and Topolewski, *Notes and Sketches*, 38; Staker, "Isaac and Elizabeth Hale," 36.

92. Blackman, *History of Susquehanna County*, 138; Staker, "Isaac and Elizabeth Hale," 35–36.

93. Chafee, *History of the Wyoming Conference*, 721. Circuit riders gathered their loyal followers anywhere available—taverns, private homes, town halls, county poorhouses, courtrooms, schools, street corners, clearings in the woods, barns, or, if available, small churches or chapels. Luccock, Hutchinson, and Goodloe, *The Story of Methodism*, 218.

94. VanDeusen, *Elm Park Historical Sketches*, 9; Bugbee, *He Holds the Stars*, 27.

95. Bugbee, *He Holds the Stars*, 17.

96. Chafee, *History of the Wyoming Conference*, 48.

97. Susquehanna Branch History, March 2006, containing the *Lanesboro Methodist-Episcopal Church, Centennial Celebration*, March 3–5, 1912; Frost, *A Perfect Freedom*, 32; Fletcher, *Pennsylvania Agriculture*, 243. Most of the trails created by the Indians were along rivers. Fletcher, 243–44.

98. Fletcher, *Pennsylvania Agriculture*, 253.

99. Blackman, *History of Susquehanna County*, 96.

100. Blackman, *History of Susquehanna County*, 97.

101. Fletcher, *Pennsylvania Agriculture*, 469.

102. Stocker, *Centennial History of Susquehanna County*, 56. By 1821, the state of Pennsylvania had chartered 146 turnpike companies, mostly in southeastern Pennsylvania. Fletcher, *Pennsylvania Agriculture*, 255.

103. Stocker, 46.

104. Staker, "Isaac and Elizabeth Hale," 17–18.

105. Richmond E. Myers, *The Long Crooked River: The Susquehanna* (Boston: The Christopher Publishing House, 1949), 338.

106. J. Taylor Hollist, "Walking-on-Water Stories and Other Susquehanna River Folk Tales about Joseph Smith," *Mormon Historical Studies* 6, no. 1 (2005): 45.

107. "Oliver Cowdery Letter VIII," 201; Porter, *Origins of the Church*, 48.

108. Hartley, *Stand by My Servant Joseph*, 6–7.

109. David Cordingly, *Under the Black Flag: The Romance and the Reality of Life Among the Pirates* (New York: Random House, 1995), 178–79, cited in Staker, "Isaac and Elizabeth Hale," 12.

110. "Oliver Cowdery VIII," 200–201; Inez Smith Davis, *The Story of the Church* (Independence, MO: Herald House, 1948), 40; Raymond T. Bailey, "Emma Hale, Wife of the Prophet Joseph Smith" (master's thesis, Brigham Young University, 1952), 14. The silver mine was located somewhere in "Big Bend" county. Myers, *Long Crooked River*, 338.

111. H. Hollister, *History of the Lackawanna Valley*, 5th ed. (Philadelphia: J. B. Lippincott Co., 1885), 63–64.

112. Hollister, *History of the Lackawanna Valley*, 64.

113. Carl Carmer, *The Susquehanna* (New York and Toronto: Rinehart & Co., 1955), 16–19.

114. Isaac Hale et al., Agreement, Harmony, PA, Nov. 1, 1825, in "An Interesting Document," *Salt Lake Daily Tribune*, Apr. 23, 1880, 4, citing the *Susquehanna Journal*, Mar. 21, 1880; Porter, *Origins of the Church*, 49.

115. Stocker, *Centennial History of Susquehanna County*, 556. According to Emily Blackman, Joseph participated in other diggings on Joseph McKune's land, which is situated directly north of the historic restoration site. Blackman, *History of Susquehanna County*, 580–81. Almost no sign of these excavation sites is present today. Joseph also is said to have dug holes on Jacob J. Skinner's farm. It is reported that for a number of years, Mr. Skinner had to fill the holes with stone to protect his cattle, and his boys used them as swimming holes in the summer. The *Scranton Tribune*, a newspaper circulated in the city of Scranton, Pennsylvania, described one of the digging holes as follows: "The largest digging was about 150 feet in circumference and twenty feet deep. . . . Smaller pits in the same locality were also dug." "Relics of Mormonism," *Scranton Tribune*, July 14, 1896.

According to Rex B. Hawes of Oakland, Pennsylvania, there were three separate excavations on the north hillside about half a mile above the McKune cemetery when Joseph was employed by Josiah Stowell. One of the holes was large enough to hold two good-sized homes. They were being filled with rocks that were being cleared from the land but were still plainly discernible as of October 1957. *Abner and Hazel Baird Papers*, 950. The author visited this area and climbed through the brush and trees to locate the digging sites. No recognizable sign of these diggings exists today.

116. Henry W. Felton, "The Pilgrimage to Historically Prominent Places Near Susquehanna: The Historical Data," *Susquehanna Historical Society*, Aug. 9, 1929, 6.

117. History, circa June 1839–circa 1841 [Draft 2], 8, josephsmithpapers.org; Roberts, *History of the Church*, 1:17.

118. History, circa June 1839–circa 1841 [Draft 2], 8, josephsmithpapers.org; Roberts, *History of the Church*, 1:17. Rhamanthus Stocker, a prominent historian of Susquehanna County, commented that those who were living in Harmony during Joseph's expedition for treasure said that he could point out places where treasure could be found. Stocker, *Centennial History of Susquehanna County*, 556. Money digging in the area—in particular Locust Hill, a hill near Harmony—continued into the late 1800s with some success. Blackman, *History of Susquehanna County,* 580.

119. Statement of Isaac Hale, Mar. 20, 1834, published in *The Susquehanna Register* (Montrose, PA), May 1, 1834.

120. Blackman, *History of Susquehanna County,* 102–03; Porter, *Origins of the Church*, 46. At age 17, Isaac Hale's father served in the Revolutionary War. On October 11, 1730, he marched in Captain Abel Merriman's company for its tour to Castleton to prevent Sir John Johnson's threatened raids from Canada into the Mohawk Valley. Susan Easton Black, "Isaac Hale: Antagonist of Joseph Smith," in *Regional Studies in Latter-day Saint Church History: New York* (Provo, UT: BYU Department of Church History and Doctrine, 1992), 6.

121. Blackman, *History of Susquehanna County,* 103–04; Staker, "Isaac and Elizabeth Hale," 16.

122. Blackman, *History of Susquehanna County,* 102; Staker, "Isaac and Elizabeth Hale," 24, citing Willingborough Township, Direct Tax Lists 1798, 3–4. Around 1810 the Lewis family moved into a new home south of the Susquehanna River. Staker, "Isaac and Elizabeth Hale," 44.

123. George Peck, *The Life and Times of Rev. George Peck* (New York: Nelson & Phillips, 1874), 67–68. According to David Hale, Isaac Hale's son, his father settled in the Susquehanna Valley because of the abundance of animals to hunt. Blackman, *History of Susquehanna County,* 103–4.

124. Peck, *Life and Times,* 67–68.

125. Peck, 67–68.

126. Blackman, *History of Susquehanna County,* 103–4.

127. Stocker, *Centennial History of Susquehanna County,* 554; Porter, *Origins of the Church*, 47; Staker, "Isaac and Elizabeth Hale," 23.

128. Mark L. Staker, "A Comfort unto My Servant, Joseph," in *Women of Faith in the Latter Days: Volume 1, 1775–1820*, ed. Richard E. Turley Jr. and Brittany A. Chapman (Salt Lake City, UT: Deseret Book, 2011), 345.

129. Mark Lyman Staker, "Joseph and Emma Smith's Susquehanna Home: Expanding Mormonism's First Headquarters," *Mormon Historical Studies* 16, no. 2 (Fall 2015): 90. Historian Mark Staker analyzed the Quarter Sessions Docket of Susquehanna County and perceived that court clerks wrote "affirmed" next to Isaac Hale's name, while the court clerks wrote "sworn" next to other names.

130. Peck, *Life and Times*, 67–68; Staker, "Isaac and Elizabeth Hale," 3.

131. Mark Lyman Staker and Robin Scott Jensen, "New Details about Joseph and Emma Smith, the Hale Family, and the Book of Mormon," *BYU Studies Quarterly* 53, no. 3 (2014): 4 (expanded web version).

132. Staker, "Isaac and Elizabeth Hale," 47.

133. "Obituary for Emma Bidamon," *Saints' Herald*, June 1, 1879, 17. Emma's mother, Elizabeth, was a faithful Methodist. Blackman, *History of Susquehanna County*, 103. Historian Jennifer Reeder has produced a compelling and comprehensive work explaining the story of Emma and her role in the founding of the Church. See Jennifer Reeder, *First: The Life and Faith of Emma Smith* (Salt Lake City, UT: Deseret Book, 2021).

134. For a list of sources that mention Emma's nickname and the various spellings, see Staker, "Isaac and Elizabeth Hale," 4, fn. 16.

135. Bailey, "Emma Hale, Wife of the Prophet Joseph Smith," 13, citing unpublished notes on Emma Smith collected by Vesta Pierce Crawford, 21, Special Collections, University of Utah.

136. Ivan J. Barrett, *Joseph Smith and the Restoration* (Provo, UT: Brigham Young University Press, 1970), 47. Emma may also have attended the Female Seminary in Great Bend Township, located about two miles west of Emma's home. Mark L. Staker, "A Comfort unto My Servant," 343–362.

137. William W. Blair to Editors, May 22, 1879, *Saints' Herald* 26 (June 15, 1897): 191 (spelling modernized). Historian Mark Staker notes that Hiel Lewis, Emma's cousin, stated that Isaac Hale was converted by a Methodist circuit rider before Emma was born, in contrast to William Blair's account. Staker, "A Comfort unto My Servant," 345, 22. Thus it is unclear when and how Mr. Hale converted to Methodism, although one possible reconciliation of both accounts is that Mr. Hale's dedication to Methodism ebbed and flowed through the years.

138. Goodell and Topolewski, *Notes and Sketches*, 40.

139. Blackman, *History of Susquehanna County*, 103.

140. Rev. Albert Clarke, *Methodist Episcopal Church, Lanesboro, Pennsylvania 1812–1912* (Lanesboro, PA: 1912), 11; Larry C. Porter, "Reverend George Lane—Good 'Gifts,' Much 'Grace,' and Marked 'Usefulness,'" *BYU Studies*

9, no. 3. (Spring 1969): 331. After the murder of Oliver Harper on May 11, 1824, which was the first recorded murder in Susquehanna County, Mr. Hale entertained Jason Treadwell, the man eventually convicted of the murder, at his house for breakfast. Mark Lyman Staker and Paul Thomas Smith, *The Trial of Jason Treadwell for the Murder of Oliver Harper on May 11, 1824: Transcripts of Official Court Documents*, July 7, 2008.

141. Staker, "Isaac and Elizabeth Hale," 42.

142. Chafee, *History of the Wyoming Conference*, 721; Staker and Jensen, "New Details," 4. In 1811 David Hale joined his uncle Nathaniel Lewis's congregation and Emma, at the age of seven, joined that same year. Staker and Jensen, "New Details," 4, citing Inez A. Kennedy, *Recollections of the Pioneers of Lee County* (Dixon, IL: by the author, 1893). The first Catholic church in Susquehanna County was built in 1831 in Friendsville. Garford F. Williams, "Susquehanna County, Pennsylvania," *Susquehanna County Historical Society Journal of Genealogy and Local History* 19, no. 2 (Fall/Winter 2008): 56; Stocker, *Centennial History of Susquehanna County*, 587.

143. Mark H. Forscutt, "Commemorative Discourse on the Death of Mrs. Emma Bidamon," *The Saints' Herald* (July 15, 1879), 209–217; Staker, "Isaac and Emma Hale," 40.

144. Chafee, *History of the Wyoming Conference*, 46.

145. Peck, *Life and Times*, 67–68.

146. Staker and Jensen, "New Details," 7, fn. 20.

147. Blackman, *History of Susquehanna County*, 96. Not all individuals were subject to taxes in the 1800s, so the number twenty-eight is not reflective of the population of Harmony.

148. Chafee, *History of the Wyoming Conference*, 484.

149. Chafee, 48; *Modified Register for Nathaniel Lewis: First Generation*, Descendants of Nathaniel Lewis, Aug. 6, 2005, 1, Susquehanna Historical Society, Montrose, PA.

150. *Modified Register for Nathaniel Lewis*, 1.

151. Blackman, *History of Susquehanna County*, 95; Porter, *Origins of the Church*, 47; Staker, "Isaac and Elizabeth Hale," 38.

152. Staker and Jensen, "New Details," 7, fn. 38.

153. Chafee, *History of the Wyoming Conference*, 721.

154. Peck, *Early Methodism*, 331.

155. Chafee, *History of the Wyoming Conference*, 49; Susquehanna Branch History, March 2006, containing the *Lanesboro Methodist-Episcopal Church, Centennial Celebration*, March 3–5, 1912, 11–13; Porter, *Origins of the Church*, 47.

156. Peck, *Early Methodism*, 332; Chafee, *History of the Wyoming Conference*, 49.

157. Chafee, 485.

158. Blackman, *History of Susquehanna County,* 469.

159. Blackman, 581.

160. Staker, "Joseph and Emma Smith's Susquehanna Home," 80–81. Historian Mark Staker has concluded that the most logical location where some of the "money diggers" may have stayed is the Hales' log home. Staker, "Isaac and Elizabeth Hale," 49, 51–53.

161. Statement of Isaac Hale, in *The Susquehanna Register*; "Statement of Isaac Hale," in E. D. Howe, *Mormonism Unvailed* (Painesville, OH: s.n., 1834), 263; Stocker, *Centennial History of Susquehanna County,* 555.

162. Statement of Isaac Hale, in *The Susquehanna Register*; "Testimony of Isaac Hale," in *Mormonism Unvailed,* 263.

163. Historian Mark Staker has noted that Isaac Hale was raised in a culture of searching for gold. Staker, "Isaac and Elizabeth Hale," 11.

164. William Hale originally spoke with Oliver Harper to finance the digging. Oliver Harper was later allegedly murdered by Jason Treadwell, and Isaac Hale testified at Treadwell's trial. Staker and Smith, *The Trial of Jason Treadwell.*

165. Smith, *Biographical Sketches,* 92; Smith, *Lucy's Book,* 360–61 (Pratt version); Larry C. Porter, "Joseph Smith's Susquehanna Years," *Ensign,* Feb. 2001, 43.

166. Smith, *Biographical Sketches,* 92; Smith, *Lucy's Book,* 360–61 (Pratt version); Staker and Jensen, "New Details," 4

167. "Emma Hale Smith," *Encyclopedia of Mormonism,* ed. Daniel H. Ludlow (New York: Macmillan, 1992), 3:1321.

168. Kennedy, *Recollections of the Pioneers of Lee County,* 96.

169. Stocker, *Centennial History of Susquehanna County,* 554.

170. Frederic G. Mather, "The Early Mormons," *Binghamton Daily Republican,* July 29, 1880; Staker, "Joseph and Emma Smith's Susquehanna Home," 118.

171. Myers, *Long Crooked River,* 338–40.

172. Donna Hill, *Joseph Smith: The First Mormon* (Garden City, NY: Double Day & Company, Inc., 1977), 68; Black, "Isaac Hale: Antagonist of Joseph Smith," 6.

173. Carl Carmer, *The Susquehanna,* 338. Much of the folklore about Joseph was invented by people hostile to Joseph's message. Carmer, 339. Joseph admitted at one point that he was a money digger but never admitted to many of the exotic rituals attributed to him. For a discussion of these exotic legends and folklore, see Hollist, "Walking-on-Water Stories," 35–52; Stanley James Thayne, "In Harmony? Perceptions of Mormonism in Susquehanna, Pennsylvania," *Journal of Mormon History* (Fall 2007): 114–151.

According to local legend, Joseph at one point attempted to walk on water, across the Susquehanna River, as Peter did in the Bible. The site most commonly referenced for this event is at the border between Broome and Chenango Counties in New York, not far from the Stowell farm. Hollist, "Walking-on-Water Stories," 38.

A New York State historic iron marker was placed along the Susquehanna River at the Broome-Chenango County line in about 1933. The sign said, "Joseph Smith, Founder of Mormonism, Endeavored in 1827 to Walk on Water Nearby, The Venture Was Not a Success." The marker is no longer there today. It is believed to have been taken down two years later, in 1935, because it lacked historical foundation. Hollist, "Walking-on-Water Stories," 39.

Local folklore also spoke of Joseph Smith digging for treasure up Cornell Creek near Afton, New York. A marker was placed there to commemorate the location, stating, "JOSEPH SMITH IN 1827 DUG FOR AND CLAIMED TO FIND SOME OF THE PLATES FOR THE MORMON BIBLE ½ MILE UP THIS CREEK." The sign was later determined to be incorrect and was removed. Hollist, "Walking-on-Water Stories," 50, fn. 14.

174. Larry C. Porter, "The Joseph Knight Family," *Ensign*, Oct. 1978, 39.

175. Larry C. Porter, "The Colesville Branch and the Coming Forth of the Book of Mormon," *BYU Studies* 10, no. 3 (1970): 2; Mark Ashurst-McGee, "The Josiah Stowell Jr.—John S. Fullmer Correspondence," *BYU Studies* 38, no. 3 (1999): 109.

176. Porter, *Origins of the Church*, 71.

177. Isaac Hale et al., Agreement, Harmony, PA, Nov. 1, 1825, in "An Interesting Document," *Salt Lake Daily Tribune*, Apr. 23, 1880, 4, citing the *Susquehanna Journal*, Mar. 21, 1880.

178. Gordon A. Madsen, "Being Acquitted of a 'Disorderly Person' Charge in 1826," in Gordon A. Madsen, Jeffrey N. Walker, and John W. Welch, eds., *Sustaining the Law: Joseph Smith's Legal Encounters* (Provo, UT: BYU Studies, 2014), 71; Ashurst-McGee, "Josiah Stowell Jr.—John S. Fullmer," 110. Three principal accounts of the trial exist: (1) an article written five years later in 1831 by A. W. Benton; (2) a draft by William W. Purple in 1871 based on his supposed memory and notes, claiming he acted as scribe at the trial; and (3) accounts by Charles Marshall and Daniel S. Tuttle, which were purportedly based on the presiding judge's docket book written by his niece Emily Pearsall. Madsen, "Being Acquitted," 71–72.

179. Madsen, 72–75. The caption for the misdemeanor read "People vs. Joseph Smith The Glass Looker March 20, 1826." Albert Neely Jr. made $2.68 for examination of Joseph's case. Madsen, 72.

180. Madsen, 73.

181. Madsen, 85.

182. C[harles] M[arshall], "The Original Prophet," *Fraser's Magazine* 7 (Feb. 1873): 229–30.

183. Francis W. Kirkham, *A New Witness for Christ in America: The Book of Mormon* (Independence, MO: Zion's Printing and Publishing Co., 1959), 2:360.

184. Madsen, "Being Acquitted," 89–90. Because Mr. Stowell's testimony could not be impeached and there is no record of a sentence of fine being imposed, the only reasonable conclusion is that Joseph Smith was acquitted of the charges. Madsen, 89; Ashurst-McGee, "Josiah Stowell Jr.—John S. Fullmer," 110; Goodell and Topolewski, *Notes and Sketches*, 41. The following is an excerpt from William D. Purple's account:

"Justice Neely soberly looked at Deacon Isaiah Stowell, Josiah Stowell's son, and in a solemn, dignified voice, said, 'Deacon Stowell, do I understand you as swearing before God, under the solemn oath you have taken, that you believe the prisoner can see by the aid of the stone fifty feet below the surface of the earth, as plainly as you can see what is on my table?' 'Do I believe it?' says Deacon Stowell, 'Do I believe it? No, it is not a matter of belief. I positively know it to be true.'" Kirkham, *A New Witness*, 2:360; Madsen, "Being Acquitted," 88.

Oliver Cowdery concurred, stating that "there being no cause of action he was honorably acquitted." "Oliver Cowdery Letter VIII," 201.

The Pearsall account, however, in its last sentence notes that "the defendant [Joseph] was found guilty." This last sentence has been dismissed by legal experts as lacking credibility because of the lack of evidence of guilt being imposed. The fact that the Pearsall account consistently refers to Joseph Smith as the "prisoner" and not the "defendant" demonstrates a prejudice against Joseph. It is possible that the sentence was added later. Madsen, 89–90.

185. Goodell and Topolewski, *Notes and Sketches*, 41. On September 22, 1826, Joseph made the journey to Manchester, New York, and visited the Hill Cumorah as Moroni had directed. Porter, *Origins of the Church*, 73.

186. "Joseph Knight Sr., Reminiscences," no date, Church History Library, Salt Lake City; Joseph Knight Sr., "Joseph Knight's Recollection of Early Mormon History," ed. Dean Jessee, *BYU Studies* 17, no. 1 (1976): 29–32 (containing a transcription of Joseph Knight Sr.'s ten-page manuscript); Hartley, *Stand by My Servant Joseph*, 9. Joseph likely worked for a total of ten months on the Stowell's farm. Hartley, 8.

187. Porter, "The Colesville Branch," 3; "Joseph Knight Sr., Reminiscences"; Knight, "Joseph Knight's Recollection," 29.

188. Joseph Knight Jr., "Joseph Knight's Incidents of History from 1827 to 1844," compiled by Thomas Bullock from loose sheets in Joseph Knight Jr.'s possession, 1862, Church History Library, Salt Lake City; Porter, "The Joseph Knight Family," 39–40. The Knight family, at great sacrifice, followed

Joseph from New York to Ohio, Missouri, and Illinois and later followed Brigham Young to Utah. Allen and Leonard, *Story of the Latter-day Saints*, 42.

189. "Smith made his appearance in Afton and attended school in District No. 9." *Gazetteer and Business Directory of Chenango County, NY*, Hamilton Child Syracuse, 1869, 82. Josiah Stowell Jr. and Joseph were schoolmates and friends from 1825 to 1827. Ashurst-McGee, "Josiah Stowell Jr.—John S. Fullmer," 109. Although Joseph did not receive a full education, he nonetheless taught the importance of school and education later in his life. John A. Widtsoe, *Joseph Smith As Scientist* (Salt Lake City, UT: Eborn Books, 1908), 142–44. Taylor Hollist, personal interview with persons now living at the schoolhouse (on file with author).

190. Joseph Knight Jr., "Joseph Knight's Incidents," 1, fn. 1; Hartley, *Stand by My Servant Joseph*, 11; Porter, "The Joseph Knight Family," 39.

191. Newel Knight's Journal Manuscript, 47–48, Church History Library, Salt Lake City; "Newel Knight's Journal," *Classic Experiences and Adventures* (Salt Lake City, UT: Bookcraft, 1969), 46–104; "Joseph Smith's Youthful Life," *The Latter-Day Saints' Millennial Star* 44 (Oct. 30, 1882): 695; Hartley, *Stand by My Servant Joseph*, 12. Joseph Knight Sr., Joseph Knight Jr., and Newel Knight were the first three in the family to believe in Joseph Smith's visitations from heavenly beings. Hartley, 12.

CHAPTER 3

Inspired Texts

——— ◅◦◦▻ ———

William Penn is imprisoned in the Tower of London and writes
No Cross, No Crown, *a treatise dedicated to Jesus Christ that
becomes a guide on Quaker behavior. Joseph Smith flees New York
for Harmony and starts the translation of the Book of Mormon,
which becomes the keystone of The Church of Jesus Christ of Latter-
day Saints.*

William Is Imprisoned in the Tower of London

In 1668, only a year after converting to Quakerism, William
Penn published a pamphlet entitled *The Sandy Foundation Shaken*
in defense of the Quaker faith. William advocated that each person
could know God personally and that the traditions of English society
were contrary to God's laws.[1] Following publication and circulation of
the pamphlet, William was arrested and imprisoned for nearly eight
months in the Tower of London at Tower Hill, from December 1668
to July 1669.[2] While incarcerated, William authored one of his most
important statements on Christ and religion, *No Cross, No Crown*,
which became the guide on Quaker behavior.[3]

No Cross, No Crown is a discourse showing the nature and discipline required to obtain the holy cross of Jesus Christ. The treatise
is 365 pages and 22 chapters. William adds a personal touch to his
book and writes the preface in the form of a letter: "Reader, The great
business of man's life, is to answer the end for which he lives; and

that is to glorify God and save his own soul." William advises the "Reader" to search carefully and thoroughly in "thy life" because "thy soul is at stake." He further counsels the reader to deny the lusts of the world and receive Christ, which is the way to "Christ's Crown." He writes that he was "lead out of the pleasures, vanities, and hopes of the world" during his youth and then dedicated his life to Christ. By receiving the spirit of Christ, his soul was delivered, and he has been able to experience the "fruits of love, peace, joy, temperance, and patience." William closes the preface to *No Cross, No Crown* with the words "Thy fervent Christian Friend, William Penn."[4]

The South View of the Tower of London Engraving, 1737. Courtesy of the British Museum.

Essentially, William's message was that sacrifice for Christ brings eternal life:

> Let us lay aside every weight and burden, and the sin and vanities that do so easily beset us, and with a constant holy patience run our race, having our eye fixed upon Jesus, the Author and Finisher of our faith, not minding what is behind; (Heb. Xii. 1; Rom. V. 1–4;) so shall we be delivered from every snare. No temptations shall gain us, no frowns shall scare us from Christ's cross, and our blessed self-denial. (Phil. ii. 13; Rom. ii. 7.) And honour, glory, immortality, and a crown of eternal life shall recompense all our sufferings in the end.[5]

After being released from prison, William traveled back to Ireland to preach and share his Quaker faith. He met with authorities from towns and regions in his ongoing quest to mitigate the persecution of

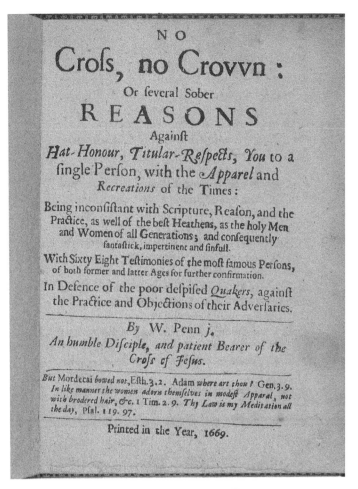

Title page of *No Cross, No Crown*, by William Penn, 1669.

the Quakers.[6] William made sure to visit Cork prison to comfort the prisoners detained there.[7] During his travels in Ireland, he published the first edition of *The Great Case of Liberty of Conscience*, a defense of the freedom of worship and the freedom to follow the laws of God.[8]

JOSEPH'S COURTSHIP AND MARRIAGE TO EMMA HALE OF HARMONY

Joseph Smith ultimately found something in Harmony of much more value than Spanish treasure. While employed with Mr. Stowell and Mr. Knight, Joseph made frequent visits to Emma in Harmony, and Emma visited Joseph in New York.[9] Emma was described as "being in her pride of beauty, fully-matured, charmingly figured, her face framed by jet-black locks and set off by dark, sparkling eyes."[10] Joseph would borrow a horse and cutter from Mr. Knight to make the twenty-mile journey to Emma's home.[11] Emma and Joseph enjoyed riding horses and could often be seen riding around the country.[12] During this time, Joseph also attended schools in the area.[13] In the 1820s books described the standards and customs of courtship, which included the exchange of romantic letters that the father of the daughter would read. Joseph's attendance at school may have been an effort to learn to write in order to comply with the custom and not disappoint Mr. Hale.[14]

Joseph eventually decided that he wanted to marry Emma, and he wrote his parents asking for permission: "If you have no objections to my uniting myself in marriage with Miss Emma Hale, she would be my choice in preference to any other woman I have ever seen."[15] Joseph's parents were pleased with his choice and requested that he bring her home with him.

Joseph mustered the courage and asked Mr. Hale for permission to marry his daughter.[16] Mr. Hale flatly refused: "Young Smith made several visits at my house, and at length asked my consent to his marrying my daughter Emma. This I refused, and gave him my reasons for so doing; some of which were, that he was a stranger, and followed a business that I could not approve; he then left the place."[17] Mr. Hale may not have wanted to give his daughter to Joseph, who was perceived by many as visionary, lacking a career path, and involved in money digging.[18] Indeed, it was customary at the time for young men to show means of making a living and a career before marrying.[19] Mr. Hale believed that a young man needed a house and property before marrying.[20] Joseph was anything but a traditional suitor, but he had a greater purpose that Mr. Hale did not understand.

In the fall, Joseph returned to Manchester with Josiah Stowell and Joseph Knight to recover the wheat crop for that year, arriving just in time to attend the wedding of Hyrum, Joseph's brother, on November 2, 1826. For Joseph, watching Hyrum get married likely conjured up thoughts of Emma and his desire to take her to wife. Following the wedding, he made the trip back to Mr. Stowell's, and while Mr. Hale was absent from his home, Emma left Harmony to visit Joseph in

New York, where Joseph asked her for her hand in marriage.[21] Emma later related the experience to her son:

> I was visiting at Mr. Stowell's who lived in Bainbridge, and saw your father there. I had no intention of marrying when I left home; but, during my visit at Mr. Stowell's your father visited me there. My folks were bitterly opposed to him; and being importuned by your father, aided by Mr. Stowell, who urged me to marry him, preferring to marry him to any other man I knew, I consented.[22]

On January 18, 1827, Joseph Smith Jr. took Emma Hale to be his wife.[23] Emma was twenty-three years old and Joseph twenty-one.[24] They eloped to the house of Esquire Zachariah Tarble, a justice of the peace in South Bainbridge, now Afton, New York, who lived about four miles from the Stowells.[25] Mr. Stowell and other guests attended the wedding on very short notice. Absent from the wedding party was Emma's family.[26] Following the ceremony, Joseph and Emma traveled to the Smiths' home in Manchester to stay with Joseph's parents.[27] Joseph recalled, "Owing to my continuing to assert that I had seen a vision, persecution still followed me, and my wife's father's family were very much opposed to our being married. I was, therefore, under the necessity of taking her elsewhere."[28] Lucy Smith, after hearing that Joseph and Emma would be visiting, made preparations to receive the newlyweds: "I set myself to work to put my house in order for the reception of my son's bride, and I felt all that pride and ambition in doing so that is common to mothers upon such occasions."[29]

Emma corresponded with her family while she and Joseph resided with the Smiths and requested her clothing, furniture, cows, and other belongings that she had left behind.[30] Her father obliged, and in August 1827 Joseph hired his neighbor Peter Ingersoll to travel to Harmony with him and Emma to retrieve the belongings.[31]

When they arrived, Mr. Hale saw Joseph for the first time since he had eloped with Emma. Peter Ingersoll described the face-to-face meeting:

> When we arrived at Mr. Hale's in Harmony, Pa. from which place he had taken his wife, a scene presented itself, truly affecting. His father-in-law (Mr. Hale) addressed Joseph in a flood of tears: "You have stolen my daughter and married her. I had much rather have

followed her to her grave. You spend your time digging for money—pretend to see in a stone, and thus try to deceive people." Joseph told Mr. Hale that "he had given up what he called *glass-looking*, and that he expected and was willing to work hard for a living."[32]

Mr. Hale accepted Joseph's explanation and offered to assist Joseph in pursuing a career if he would move to Pennsylvania and work for a living. Joseph apparently agreed to eventually return to Harmony, and after a short stay, he and Emma returned to Manchester with Emma's belongings.[33] Joseph may have felt pressure from Mr. Hale to pursue gainful employment to provide for Emma.[34] He was probably not sure what the Lord had planned for him, or the amount of time it would take him to accomplish the Lord's purpose. Joseph may have believed that he could obtain full-time work while at the same time accomplishing God's work.

On the return trip to Manchester, Joseph told Peter that renouncing money digging was difficult because the company of money diggers desperately wanted Joseph to assist them and aggressively recruited him: "They urged him [Joseph], day after day, to resume his old practice of looking in the stone."[35]

Soon after arriving in New York, Joseph departed on a business errand for his father, planning to return home by 6 p.m. that evening.[36] But 6 p.m. came and passed and Joseph had not returned, causing his parents and Emma to worry. It was not until late into the night that Joseph finally arrived. He entered the cabin and immediately threw himself into a chair in exhaustion. According to his mother, Joseph exclaimed, "I have taken the severest chastisement that I have ever had in my life . . . [a]s I passed by the hill of Cumorah, where the plates are, the angel met me and said that I had not been engaged enough in the work of the Lord; that the time had come for the record to be brought forth; and that I must be up and doing and set myself about the things which God had commanded me to do."[37] Joseph probably knew he had to overcome his weakness of treasure hunting and seek the gold plates solely for their spiritual value.

This historical marker identifies the site where Emma Hale and Joseph
Smith were married on January 18, 1827 in South Bainbridge, now
Afton, New York. Photograph by Kenneth Mays.
© By Intellectual Reserve, Inc.

THE GOLD PLATES ARE ENTRUSTED TO JOSEPH

Seven long years after his visit from God the Father and Jesus
Christ, on September 22, 1827, Joseph unearthed the plates from the
Hill Cumorah.[38] Emma accompanied him as they drove to the Hill
Cumorah before daylight in Joseph Knight Sr.'s carriage.[39] She awaited his return at the foot of the hill as Joseph climbed to the location
where the plates had laid hidden for 1,400 years.[40] Joseph found the
plates at the northwestern point near the top of the hill in a stone

box buried in the earth, where Moroni delivered the plates to him.[41] Joseph later described the plates in great detail:

> These records were engraven on plates which had the appearance of gold, each plate was six inches wide and eight inches long, and not quite so thick as common tin. They were filled with engravings, in Egyptian characters, bound together in a volume, as the leaves of a book with three rings running through the whole. The volume was something near six inches in thickness, a part of which was sealed. The characters on the unsealed part were small, and beautifully engraved. The whole book exhibited many marks of antiquity in its construction and much skill in the art of engraving.[42]

It is estimated that the plates weighed between forty and sixty pounds.[43]

The Angel Moroni Gives the Plates to Joseph Smith, by Kenneth Riley.
© By Intellectual Reserve, Inc.

Buried with the plates was the Urim and Thummim, which Moroni had referred to during his first meeting with Joseph.[44] The Urim and Thummim consisted of two white, polished, round stones that were about five-eighths of an inch thick and about two inches in diameter. They were joined by a four-inch silver bar and accompanied by a large breast plate.[45] The two stones were convex on both sides and appeared more like stones wrapped in a wire frame rather than actual glasses.[46] The spectacles could be connected by a single metal rod to the breastplate, which was intended to be strapped to a person's chest. The person then could freely move or use his or her hands while looking through the spectacles.[47]

The Interpreters. By Anthony Sweat. Used with permission.

The angel Moroni admonished Joseph to safeguard the plates and warned that evil persons would try to steal them.[48] Joseph was given a charge by the angel Moroni, as recorded in his own words, "that I should be responsible for them [the plates]; that if I should let them go carelessly, or through any neglect of mine, I should be cut off; but that if I would use all my endeavors to preserve them, until he, the messenger, should call for them, they should be protected."[49] Joseph hid the plates underneath his coat for a brief moment and then spotted an old decayed birch log nearby. Cutting a hole in the bark and peeling it back, he placed the plates in the cavity of the log and then replaced the bark and laid some dirt and brush over it.[50] Still in possession of the Urim and Thummim, Joseph returned to Emma where he had left her.[51]

Meanwhile, while Joseph and Emma were at the Hill Cumorah, Joseph Knight Sr., who had traveled from Colesville to Manchester along with Josiah Stowell to buy wheat, and who was staying at the Smiths, awoke and noticed that his horse and carriage were gone.[52] He did not know that Joseph had borrowed the carriage to travel to the Hill Cumorah to retrieve the plates. Quite disturbed, he stated, "Why Ms. Smith, my horse is gone and I can't find him on the premises."[53] Lucy Smith told him that the horse was in the stable and not to worry, but soon Mr. Knight noticed that his wagon was also gone. Mr. Knight concluded that both his horse and carriage were stolen.[54]

Joseph and Emma returned home early in the morning and related to Joseph's family what had occurred, cautioning them not to spread the news because people would want to kill them in order to obtain the gold.[55] After breakfast Joseph called Joseph Knight Sr. to his room and described the Urim and Thummin as "ten times better" than he expected—he could "see anything."[56]

OPPOSITION AND PERSECUTION MOUNT IN MANCHESTER, NEW YORK

As soon as Joseph took possession of the plates, persecution and opposition intensified against him. Joseph recorded, "False reports, misrepresentations and slander flew, as on the wings of the wind, in every direction; the house was frequently beset by mobs and evil designing persons. Several times I was shot at, and very narrowly escaped, and every device was made use of to get the plates away from me but the power and blessing of God attended me, and several began to believe my testimony."[57]

Only days after Joseph actually obtained possession of the gold plates, Joseph Smith Sr. learned that ten or twelve men were conspiring to steal them. Joseph Smith Sr. notified Emma, who rode at once to the nearby city of Macedon where Joseph was working to earn money to buy a wooden chest to hold the plates. Hearing the news, Joseph immediately left for Palmyra to make preparations to retrieve the plates from the hollowed log at the Hill Cumorah.[58] The next day, Joseph walked the three miles from his home to the Hill Cumorah. The plates were safe and undetected in the birch log where he had left them; he then removed them from the log and wrapped them in a linen frock. As he proceeded home, he was attacked several times, as later recounted by Joseph's mother:

> After proceeding a short distance, he thought it would be more safe to leave the road and go through the woods. Travelling some distance after he left the road, he came to a large windfall, and as he was jumping over the log, a man sprang up from behind it, and gave him a heavy blow with a gun. Joseph turned around and knocked him down, then ran at the top of his speed. About half a mile further he was attacked again in the same manner as before; he knocked this man down in the like manner as the former, and ran on again; and before he reached home he was assaulted the third time. In striking the last one, he dislocated his thumb, which, however, he did not notice until he came within sight of the house, when he threw himself down in the corner of the fence in order to recover his breath. As soon as he was able, he arose and came to the house. He was still altogether speechless from fright and fatigue of running.[59]

Joseph Smith's sister Katharine was at home when Joseph entered the house. "She took the plates from him and laid them on the table temporarily, and helped revive him until he got breathing properly and also examined his hand, and treated it for the bruises on his knuckles, where he had struck the villain and thus defended himself and the plates."[60] Learning of Joseph's assailants, Joseph Knight and Josiah Stowell immediately left the Smiths' home in pursuit of the three men but had no success.[61] Joseph had overcome and outran his three opponents over the course of three miles while carrying the heavy plates.

Although Joseph did not permit his family to see with their eyes the sacred items he had retrieved from the Hill Cumorah, he allowed them to feel the items. His mother handled the breastplate while it was wrapped in a thin muslin handkerchief.[62] She described it as follows:

> It was concave on one side and convex on the other, and extended from the neck downwards, as far as the center of the stomach of a man of extraordinary size. It had four straps of the same material, for the purpose of fastening it to the breast, two of which ran back to go over the shoulders, and the other two were designed to fasten to the hips. They were just the width of two of my fingers

(for I measured them), and they had holes in the end of them, to be convenient in fastening.[63]

Joseph allowed his brothers William, Hyrum, and Samuel, as well as other family members, to handle the plates while wrapped in a tow frock.[64] Most of Joseph's family members later spoke of touching, lifting, or seeing the plates.[65]

The local company of money diggers adamantly believed they had as much right to the plates as Joseph, and they refused to accept his renunciation of money digging.[66] According to them, Joseph was part of the company and had appropriated to himself that which rightfully belonged to them.[67] Joseph apparently rebuffed the company of money diggers and resisted their advances, demonstrating that he had overcome his weakness of treasure digging and was more focused on his divine mission. He was committed and focused on God's work.

Joseph stood on constant watch for mobs and persons seeking to steal the gold plates. He kept the Urim and Thummim (likely one or both of the stones) or his seer stone on his person at all times so he could determine whether the plates were in any danger.[68] He once told his mother that he had a "key"—the Urim and Thummim—which could track the location of the plates.[69]

The Urim and Thummim provided warning on several occasions. For instance, one time Joseph received inspiration that a mob was designing to ransack his house in search of the plates.[70] Sally Chase, the sister of local Methodist class leader Willard Chase, probably led the group.[71] Joseph immediately hid the plates in the cooper's shop across the road from his house. He removed the plates from the box and placed them in the loft while burying the empty box under the floorboards of the shop. That night, the mob plundered and destroyed the shop. The next morning, Joseph found the floor of the cooper's shop torn up and the hidden box shattered in pieces. The gold plates, however, laid untouched in the loft.[72]

Another time, "a great rodsman came to the Smith home and tried to bargain with Joseph Smith for a share of the plates. When Joseph refused, the rodsman took out his rods and held them up. When they pointed down to the hearth—where the plates were hidden—the rodsman identified them as being under the hearth."[73] To the rodsman's dissatisfaction, Joseph would not confirm the location of the plates or negotiate for their purchase.

Conjurors, diviners with peep stones, and other means were likewise employed to steal the plates. Some people offered Joseph cash and property in order to catch a glimpse of the plates, while others simply teased Joseph for his claims. Mobs gathered and searched the premises of the Smith home, even breaking into the house and ransacking it. One evening, Joseph was warned that a mob intended to steal the plates that night. He quickly left the field where he was working and placed the plates in a box below the hearth in the west room. Moments later, an armed mob rushed up to the house, only to be met by Joseph, who yelled as he opened the door as if he had a legion of men at his command. His father, his eleven-year-old brother Don Carlos, and others rushed outside. Confused by all the commotion and yelling, the mob disbanded and fled into the woods.[74]

In a matter of weeks, persecution increased and excitement surrounding the gold plates spread like wildfire through the village of Palmyra. Mobs threatened Joseph with tar and feathers, and several times he was shot at and narrowly escaped.[75] Referring to the persecutions he endured, Joseph recorded, "If I were to relate a thousandth part of them, it would fill up volumes."[76] It was only after these experiences that he understood why Moroni had given him such strict charges concerning the plates and why he had to return them to Moroni as soon as he finished his work.[77] Joseph likely realized that he could no longer protect the plates if he remained in Manchester.

REFUGE IN HARMONY, PENNSYLVANIA

In November or December 1827, because of the intense persecution and overwhelming opposition in Manchester, Joseph and Emma sought refuge in Susquehanna County, Pennsylvania, at the home of Emma's parents.[78] Joseph had only had the gold plates in his physical possession for about one or two months. Joseph and Emma, however, lacked money to pay for the 128-mile, four-day wagon ride.[79] Fortunately, a man by the name of Martin Harris, a reliable businessman from Palmyra, gave them fifty dollars.[80] Martin said, "Here are fifty dollars. I give this to you to do the Lord's work with; no, I give it to the Lord for his own work."[81] Joseph offered to sign a note to repay

Martin, but Martin insisted that Joseph accept the money as a gift.[82] Joseph may have realized at this point that he had to rely on others to accomplish the Lord's commandment. He could not do it alone, and others would share the burden.

Portrait of Martin Harris, by Lewis A. Ramsey.
© By Intellectual Reserve, Inc.

Martin Harris, forty-six years of age, was a landowner and long-time well-respected resident and businessman of Palmyra. He was industrious, hardworking, and shrewd in his business calculations.[83] Joseph worked on Martin's farm from time to time, which was a mile and a half north of the village of Palmyra.[84] At certain times, Martin associated with the Methodist Church and the Universalists.[85] When he first heard rumors of the gold plates, he questioned members of the Smith family separately to see if their stories matched, and he found that they did. He then approached Joseph and asked him about the plates. Joseph responded that "an angel had appeared to him, and told him it was God's work" and that "the plates must be translated, printed and sent before the world."[86] Martin remained skeptical: "If it is the devil's work, I will have nothing to do with it; but if it is the

Lord's, you can have all the money necessary to bring it before the world."[87] Later that same day, Martin implored God to know whether Joseph told him the truth and received his own witness. He wrote, "[God] showed me that it was his work, and that it was designed to bring in the fullness of his gospel to the gentiles to fulfill his word. . . . He showed this to me by the still small voice spoken in the soul. Then I was satisfied that it was the Lord's work."[88]

With the persecution in Palmyra intensifying, Martin told Joseph that "it was unsafe for him to remain in Palmyra."[89] The Hales sent Alva Hale, Emma's older brother, with a horse and wagon to transport Emma and Joseph to Harmony.[90] Word of Joseph and Emma's plans to leave Palmyra quickly spread. The mob in Palmyra and Manchester, made up of fifty men, endeavored to take possession of the plates and stop the Smiths from departing. A member of the mob approached Dr. McIntyre, the Smiths' family doctor, for assistance in stealing the gold plates.[91] Dr. McIntyre refused. Joseph wisely spread word that he and Emma would leave for Harmony on a Monday but left two days earlier in order to avoid detection by the mob. He enclosed the gold plates and breastplate in a box and buried them in a barrel filled with beans.[92]

All of Joseph and Emma's precautions, however, did not spare them hardship. Not long after leaving Manchester, an officer armed with a search warrant searched their wagon in order to obtain the plates. Later, yet another officer stopped them with the same intentions, "ransacking their wagon carefully." Neither attempt was successful. It appears that the officers were from the state of New York because after the two stops occurred, Joseph is said to have "pursued his journey until he came into the northern part of Pennsylvania." It is also unlikely that these searches occurred in Pennsylvania because Alva Hale was serving as the constable in Harmony Township, Pennsylvania, and he provided protection to Joseph and Emma on their trip once they crossed the border into Pennsylvania.[93]

With Martin's donation and the help of Emma's brother Alva, Joseph and Emma made the four-day wagon journey to the Hales' home, likely arriving in Harmony in the first week of December.[94] The weather that year was particularly rainy and wet, making traveling difficult for not only Emma and Joseph but their two cows as well.[95] At this time, Emma was in her first trimester of pregnancy and likely slept with Joseph at taverns along the route.[96]

Anxious to begin his work, upon arriving in Harmony, Joseph immediately started the arduous task of figuring out how to translate the gold plates.[97] He hid the plates in a pit on the hill above the Hales' home or under his bed.[98] Joseph initially believed that he needed to find a translator, or someone trained in linguistics, to translate the plates.[99] With the help of Emma and Emma's brother Reuben, he copied certain characters off the plates by means of the Urim and Thummim.[100] Joseph and Emma either occupied the log work kitchen attached to the Hales' frame home or their log home.[101] It is likely that Joseph made several copies of characters on the gold plates.

Isaac Hale Home. © By Intellectual Reserve, Inc.
Joseph and Emma likely stayed in Isaac Hales' home when they arrived in Harmony.

Joseph found odd jobs in Harmony in order to purchase goods and earn a little money when he was not occupied with translating the plates. For example, in January 1828, in order to pay for the leather covering of a pair of mittens, Joseph drew hay and worked for a neighbor.[102] He also bought a team of oxen and a horse and purchased hay to feed their two cows.[103]

Soon after Joseph arrived in Harmony with the gold plates, Nathaniel Lewis insisted on seeing the plates. According to Mr. Lewis, Joseph said he would show him the plates in eighteen months, around May or June 1829.[104] Joshua McKune, a son-in-law of Nathaniel Lewis, also claimed that he "and others should see [the plates] at a specified time."[105] Joseph allowed Mr. Hale to hold the plates while they were concealed in their box, but he would not allow Mr. Hale to see the plates. Mr. Hale stated, "I was allowed to feel the weight of the box—into which, however, I was not allowed to look. . . . After this I became dissatisfied, and informed him that if there was anything in my house of that description, which I could not be allowed to see, he must take it away; if he did not, I was determined to see it. After that the gold plates were said to be hid in the woods."[106]

Needless to say, Joseph and his father-in-law struggled to develop a meaningful relationship.[107] And Joseph's elopement with Emma may have remained a source of contention. Nonetheless, Mr. Hale maintained a certain respect for Joseph and never resorted to any type of legal challenge to Joseph eloping out of state with his daughter without his permission or knowledge.[108] Shortly after Mr. Hale's query, Joseph and Emma moved out of Mr. Hale's home and into the farm house of Emma's brother Jesse, which was approximately 150 yards southeast of the Hale home.[109] Joseph lacked the financial means to pay for the farm at the time and was generally without much money. His lack of full-time employment would continue to cause a rift between him and Mr. Hale, but he knew his divine mission and feared God more than the judgments of men.

Joseph and Emma Smith Home.
© By Intellectual Reserve, Inc.

Emma Serves as Scribe

During the winter of 1828, Joseph commenced translating the plates in the book of Lehi with Emma and her brother Reuben Hale as scribe.[110] Joseph was learning that he needed assistance from others to further the Lord's work—he could not carry the burden alone. Emma became Joseph's first primary scribe.[111] Later in her life, she recalled that she wrote for Joseph "day after day, often sitting at the table close to him, he sitting with his face buried in his hat, with the stone in it, and dictating hour after hour with nothing between [them]." When asked whether Joseph had a book or manuscript from which to read, she responded, "He had neither manuscript nor book to read from." Emma and Joseph spent hours translating, and following a meal or interruption, Emma remembered that Joseph "would once begin where he had left off, without either seeing the manuscript or having any portion of it read to him."[112]

When Emma assisted Joseph with the translation, she observed him dictate word for word without books or notes.[113] He spelled out proper names and corrected Emma's scribal errors even though he could not see what she had written.[114] Joseph, however, had little formal education and repeatedly stated that he was only able to translate the Book of Mormon by the gift and power of God.[115] Emma recalled, "If I made any mistake in spelling, he would stop me and correct my spelling, although it was impossible for him to see how I was writing them down at the time. Even the word *Sarah* he could not pronounce at first, but had to spell it, and I would pronounce it for him."[116] One time while translating, where the text spoke of the walls of Jerusalem, Joseph stopped and said, "Emma, did Jerusalem have walls surrounding it?" When Emma informed him that Jerusalem indeed had walls, he replied, "O, I thought I was deceived."[117]

Emma never saw the plates and never felt a need to do so. She related:

> The plates often lay on the table without any attempt at conceal-
> ment, wrapped in a small linen tablecloth, which I had given
> [Joseph] to fold them in. I once felt of the plates, as they thus lay on
> the table, tracing their outline and shape. They seemed to be pliable
> like thick paper, and would rustle with a metallic sound when the

edges were moved by the thumb, as one does sometimes thumb the edges of a book. . . . I did not attempt to handle the plates, other than [through the linen cloth]. . . . I was satisfied that it was the work of God, and therefore did not feel it to be necessary to do so. . . . I knew that [Joseph] had them, and was not specially curious about them. I moved them from place to place on the table, as it was necessary in doing my work.[118]

Joseph Smith translating the gold plates. By Anthony Sweat. Used with permission.

No one was more astonished by the quality of the translation than Emma. Commenting on her husband's writing ability, she stated:

Joseph Smith . . . could neither write nor dictate a coherent and well-worded letter; let alone dictating a book like the Book of Mormon. And, though I was an active participant in the scenes that transpired, and was present during the translation of the plates, and had cognizance of things as they transpired, it is marvelous to me, "a marvel and a wonder," as much so as to anyone else. . . . I am satisfied that no man could have dictated the writing of the manuscripts unless he was inspired; . . . It would have been improbable that a learned man could do this; and, for one so ignorant and unlearned as he was, it was simply impossible.[119]

Joseph's brother, William, said the entire Smith family was astonished by the translation: "Knowing that he was very young, that he had not enjoyed the advantages of a common education; and knowing too, his whole character and disposition, [Joseph's family was] convinced that he was totally incapable of arising before his aged parents, his brothers and sisters, and so solemnly giving utterance to anything but the truth. All of us, therefore, believed him, and anxiously awaited the results of his visit to the Hill Cumorah."[120]

With Emma's relatives living close by, Joseph frequently shared with them his experiences and mandate to translate the plates. On one such occasion, Mr. Lewis listened to Joseph and, when Joseph finished, asked with a tone of speculation, "Joseph, can anybody else translate strange languages by the help of them spectacles?" "O yes!" Joseph responded. "Well now," said Mr. Lewis, "I've got Clarke's Commentary, and it contains a great many strange languages; now, if you will let me try the spectacles, and if by looking through them I can translate these strange tongues into English, then I'll be one of your disciples." No response by Joseph is recorded.[121]

MARTIN HARRIS TRAVELS TO NEW YORK CITY WITH A COPY OF THE CHARACTERS

The Lord appeared to Martin in a vision and showed him the marvelous work he was about to perform and told Martin that he must go to New York City with characters copied from the plates.[122] Martin immediately left for Harmony, Pennsylvania, arriving two months after the Smiths in February 1828.[123] According to Joseph's mother, Martin and Joseph had previously arranged for Martin to travel to Harmony to obtain a copy of the characters on the plates and then exhibit them to scholars in ancient languages. Before Martin left for Harmony, his wife confronted him, insisting on going along and assisting in the translation. But Martin concluded it would be better to go alone and left without his wife's knowledge.[124]

When Martin arrived in Harmony, Joseph presented to him a copy of the ancient characters he had copied off the plates, and they proceeded to make other copies of the characters.[125] Neither Joseph nor Martin could recognize the characters on the plates or decipher them.[126] Martin was intrigued by the characters, and soon thereafter, he and Joseph showed the characters to Mr. Hale, who responded: "I told them, then, that I considered the whole of it a delusion, and advised them to abandon it."[127] Joseph and Martin took no heed.[128]

Characters on the gold plates.

On February 15, 1828, Martin left Harmony to embark on his trip to New York City with the characters in hand to show them to distinguished persons and scholars, including Luther Bradish, Professor Charles Anthon, and Dr. Samuel Latham Mitchill.[129] After returning home to Palmyra for a brief visit, Martin journeyed to Albany, New York, to visit Luther Bradish, a newly elected member of the New York State Assembly who was conversant in Middle East and Egyptian archaeological excavations.[130] Bradish had experience with languages and classical studies, and he may have been able to read the characters and point Martin in the right direction.[131] Next, Martin may have traveled to Philadelphia in search of a scholar in Native American studies who could translate the plates.[132]

Martin eventually made his way to New York City and present-ed the characters to Dr. Samuel Latham Mitchill, vice president of Rutgers Medical School and a well-known expert in the translation of ancient and modern languages.[133] Dr. Mitchill examined the char-acters and compared them to other ancient hieroglyphics but could not determine the linguistic origins of the characters.[134] Dr. Mitchill sent Martin to Professor Charles Anthon with a note requesting that Professor Anthon decipher the characters.[135] According to Martin, Dr. Mitchill confirmed that the writings were authentic.[136]

Martin visited Professor Anthon, an accomplished scholar in the area of ancient languages (Egyptology in particular) and professor at Columbia College.[137] According to Martin, after a careful examination of the characters, Professor Anthon affirmed that "they were Egyptian Chaldaic, Asseyric, and Arabic; and said they were true characters."[138] Professor Anthon handed Martin a certificate that confirmed the au-thenticity of the characters. As Martin was leaving, Professor Anthon asked where he found the gold plates, and Martin replied that "an an-gel of God had revealed it unto" a young man.[139] Troubled by Martin's response, Professor Anthon took back the certificate, tore it to pieces, and directed Martin to bring him the gold plates so he could trans-late them.[140] Martin informed Professor Anthon that the plates were sealed and that he was forbidden to bring them to him. The professor reacted by saying, "I cannot read a sealed book."[141]

Joseph concluded that Martin's experience with Professor Anthon was the fulfillment of Old Testament prophecy.[142] Isaiah prophesied, "And the vision of all is become unto you as the words of a book that is sealed, which men deliver to one that is learned, saying, Read this, I pray thee: and he saith, I cannot: for it is sealed" (Isaiah 29:11–14). Joseph believed the Book of Mormon was the "book that is sealed" that Isaiah spoke of, and that Dr. Anthon was the "one that is learned" who could not read it.[143] Following this experience, Joseph likely real-ized that because scholars could not translate the characters, he would have to translate the plates himself with the assistance of the Urim and Thummim.[144]

Seeing and examining the characters greatly increased Martin's faith, and from that point forward he was convinced of the divine nature of Joseph's mission.[145] The fact that Joseph was an illiterate man moved him to believe that Joseph was acting under divine inspiration. Martin reflected, "God had chosen the foolish things of the world to confound the wise, and the weak things to confound the mighty."[146] From this experience, Martin developed a willingness to sustain Joseph in carrying on the work of the Lord and determined that the translation of the plates should be published, even if it consumed all his worldly substance.[147] Martin returned to his home in Palmyra and apparently showed the characters to numerous people, including his wife, Lucy Harris.[148] Lucy was unhappy that she was not able to travel with Martin to New York City and insisted that she go with Martin to Harmony to see the plates.[149]

Martin Returns to Harmony with His Wife, Lucy

Martin agreed to take his wife to Harmony, and they made the trip sometime between February and April of that year.[150] When they arrived, Lucy immediately informed the Smiths that she had come to Harmony to see the plates. Without delay, she then proceeded to scour every square inch of the Smiths' home—chests, trunks, cupboards, and so on. Before she could locate the plates and breastplate, however, Joseph succeeded in removing them from the house and burying them on the northern side of the property. Lucy was unsuccessful in her efforts to find the plates that night in the house. The next morning, undaunted and with more determination, she canvassed the woods until 2:00 in the afternoon. As Lucy closely canvassed the ground for any indication of the plates, she apparently stumbled across a large black snake that hissed as it raised its head in front of her. Discouraged and startled by her encounter with the snake, she took up lodging at the house of a neighbor.[151]

While with the neighbors, Lucy spoke of Joseph as a grand imposter who had seduced her husband to obtain his property. She told others that she had found the location of the buried plates, but before she could obtain them, a large black snake frightened her so badly that she ended her search and ran back to the house.[152] She did all within her power to injure Joseph in the estimation of his neighbors, and much of the folklore and superstition surrounding Joseph likely emanated from Lucy's stories.[153] Two weeks later, Lucy gave up on Martin and Joseph and returned in anger to New York.[154] Martin returned to Manchester shortly after his wife departed.

Martin's participation in the translation of the plates likely caused tension with Lucy. She likely was worried that Martin would deplete their marital assets in assisting Joseph with the coming forth of the Book of Mormon. Indeed, possibly at Lucy's instance, that spring Martin and Lucy executed an agreement that provided Lucy her rights to one-third of Martin Harris's property.[155]

The Translation of the Book of Lehi with Martin as Scribe

Martin returned to Harmony on April 12, 1828, to serve as Joseph's scribe.[156] Joseph and Martin picked up the translation where Joseph and Emma had left off in the Book of Lehi, which was an abridgment of a larger section of the plates called the "large plates of Nephi."[157] Emma likely had written the majority of the Book of Lehi before Martin arrived.[158] Since acquiring the plates in September 1827, Joseph apparently had been attempting to translate the plates with limited success.[159] It was not until he arrived in Harmony that he succeeded in translating some of the characters and began to understand how to use the spectacles.[160] He may have realized that his gift for treasure seeking was in fact to be used for translating the plates. His gift had a divine purpose, and his weakness had now become a divine strength.

From about April 12 to June 14 or 15, roughly a two-month period, Martin and Joseph labored in dictation and writing, completing the 116 pages from the Book of Lehi.[161] Mr. Hale recorded, "About this time, Martin Harris made his appearance upon the stage; and Smith began to interpret the characters or hieroglyphics which he said were engraven upon the plates, while Harris wrote down the interpretation. It was said that Harris wrote down one hundred sixteen pages."[162]

A thick curtain or blanket may have been suspended in the middle of the room to separate Martin from Joseph, or Joseph may have covered the plates with a linen cloth and placed them on the table in front of him.[163] Martin described the process as follows: "[With] aid of the seer stone, sentences would appear and were read by the Prophet and written by [Martin], and when finished he would say, 'Written,' and if correctly written, the sentence would disappear and another appear in its place, but if not written correctly it remained until corrected."[164]

Book of Mormon Plates and Records

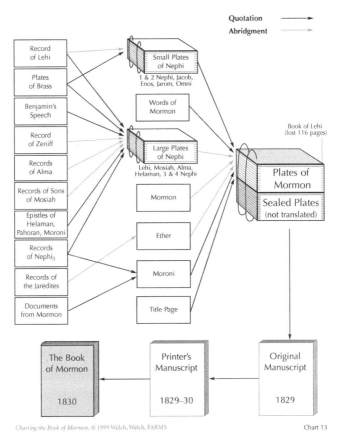

Book of Mormon Plates and Records. Charting the Book of Mormon.
© 1999 Welch, FARMS

Joseph looked through spectacles, or transparent stones, and repeated his interpretation of the hieroglyphics in English as he apparently saw the translated text on the spectacles. The transparent stones were placed in the bottom of a large-brimmed hat, and Joseph would look into the hat to see the text and block out extraneous light.[165] The darkness may have allowed Joseph to more clearly view the seer stones and text.[166] Once repeated aloud, Martin wrote down the words on foolscap paper.[167] The two men worked together in the lower chamber of the home day after day.

Joseph employed two different instruments to assist him in translating the plates—the Urim and Thummim and a seer stone. The two instruments were interchangeable and worked in the same manner, so that many of those who spoke of the translation process referred to both instruments as "interpreters" or the Urim and Thummim.[168] For convenience, Joseph often translated with the single seer stone rather than the two stones connected by wire.[169] The large and cumbersome seer stones connected by wire probably made the translation more difficult than a single stone.[170] Likewise, Joseph probably did not use the breastplate for translation since it was "large" and awkward, and persons familiar with the translation process said Joseph set it aside early on.[171] As Joseph continued to translate day after day, he gained familiarity with the plates and the use of the Urim and Thummim. His consistent, diligent study would prepare him to translate the majority of the plates in a short period of time.[172]

Since translating consumed each day for the entire day, Joseph and Martin were unable to gainfully work, leaving them in need of supplies. Fortunately, Joseph Knight Sr. graciously came to their rescue. Joseph Knight Sr. and Joseph Knight Jr. often visited Joseph and provided him with supplies.[173] Joseph Knight Sr. witnessed Joseph perform the translation and described the translation process as follows: "Now the way he translated was he put the Urim and Thummim into his hat and Darkened his Eyes than he would take a sentence and it would appear in Brite Roman Letters. Then he would tell the writer and he would write it. Then that would go away the next sentence would Come and so on. But if it was not Spelt rite it would not go away till it was rite, so we see it was marvelous."[174]

Notes

1. William Penn, *The Sandy Foundation Shaken* (London: Hackney C. Cradock, 1668), Google Books.

2. Andrew R. Murphy, *William Penn: A Life* (New York: Oxford University Press, 2019), 59; John A. Moretta, *William Penn and the Quaker Legacy* (New York: Pearson, 2007), 47–49.

3. Moretta, *William Penn*, 49–51. Penn made an initial draft and then substantially updated the draft in 1662 when he was establishing the colony in Pennsylvania.

4. William Penn, *No Cross, No Crown*, 2nd ed. (London: s.n., 1682).

5. Penn, *No Cross, No Crown*, conclusion.

6. "Irish Journal," in *The Papers of William Penn*, ed. Richard S. and Mary Maples Dunn (Philadelphia: University of Pennsylvania Press, 1981–1987), 1:107–9.

7. "Irish Journal," 1:110–117; Murphy, *William Penn: A Life*, 69.

8. William Penn, *The Great Case of Liberty of Conscience Once More Briefly Debated and Defended* [. . .] (London: s.n., 1670), 4 (original punctuation and spelling modernized); Murphy, *William Penn: A Life*, 83.

9. "Joseph Knight Sr., Reminiscences," no date, Church History Library, Salt Lake City; Joseph Knight Sr., "Joseph Knight's Recollection of Early Mormon History," ed. Dean Jessee, *BYU Studies* 17, no. 1 (1976): 32; History, circa June 1839–circa 1841 [Draft 2], 8, josephsmithpapers.org; B. H. Roberts, *A Comprehensive History of the Church of Jesus Christ of Latter-day Saints* (Salt Lake City, UT: Deseret News, 1948–57), 1:17; John Goodell and John L. Topolewski, eds., *Notes and Sketches from Along the Susquehanna* (Rutland, VA: Academy Books, 1984), 41.

10. Grant E. Carter, "Along the Susquehanna," *Improvement Era*, May 1960, 3.

11. "Joseph Knight Sr., Reminiscences"; Knight, "Joseph Knight's Recollection," 32; Larry C. Porter, "Joseph Smith's Susquehanna Years," *Ensign*, Feb. 2001, 43; Larry C. Porter, "The Joseph Knight Family," *Ensign*, Oct. 1978, 40.

12. Carter, "Along the Susquehanna," 5.

13. Mark Ashurst-McGee, "The Josiah Stowell Jr.—John S. Fullmer Correspondence," *BYU Studies* 38, no. 3 (1999): 109; Mark L. Staker, "A Comfort unto My Servant, Joseph," in *Women of Faith in the Latter Days: Volume 1, 1775–1820*, ed. Richard E. Turley Jr. and Brittany A. Chapman (Salt Lake City, UT: Deseret Book, 2011), 343–362.

14. Mark Lyman Staker, "Joseph and Emma Smith's Susquehanna Home: Expanding Mormonism's First Headquarters," *Mormon Historical Studies* 16, no. 2 (Fall 2015): 84.

15. Lucy Mack Smith, *Biographical Sketches of Joseph Smith the Prophet and His Progenitors for Many Generations* (Liverpool: S. W. Richards, 1853), 93; Lucy Mack Smith, *Lucy's Book: A Critical Edition of Lucy Mack Smith's Family Memoir*, ed. Lavina Fielding Anderson (Salt Lake City, UT: Signature Books, 2001), 362–3 (Pratt version).

16. Statement of Isaac Hale, Mar. 20, 1834, published in *The Susquehanna Register* (Montrose, PA), May 1, 1834; Larry C. Porter, *A Study of the Origins of the Church of Jesus Christ of Latter-day Saints in the States of New York and Pennsylvania, 1816–1831* (Provo, UT: BYU Studies, 2000), 73.

17. Statement of Isaac Hale, in *The Susquehanna Register*; "Isaac Hale, Affidavit, 20 Mar. 1834," in E. D. Howe, *Mormonism Unvailed* (Painesville, OH: s.n., 1834), 263; Rhamanthus M. Stocker, *Centennial History of Susquehanna County, Pennsylvania*, 2nd ed. (Baltimore, MD: Regional Publishing Company, 1974), 263. Some believe that Mrs. Hale approved of Emma and Joseph's relationship and thought they made a good match. Richmond E. Myers, *The Long Crooked River: The Susquehanna* (Boston: The Christopher Publishing House, 1949), 339.

18. Carter, "Along the Susquehanna," 5.

19. Mark Lyman Staker and Robin Scott Jensen, "New Details about Joseph and Emma Smith, the Hale Family, and the Book of Mormon," *BYU Studies Quarterly* 53, no. 3 (2014): 7 (expanded web version).

20. Staker and Jensen, "New Details," 11.

21. Statement of Isaac Hale, in *The Susquehanna Register*; Porter, *Origins of the Church*, 73.

22. Joseph Smith III, "Last Testimony of Sister Emma," *The Saints' Herald* (Oct. 1, 1879), 289; Porter, *Origins of the Church*, 75.

23. History, circa Summer 1832, 5, josephsmithpapers.org; History, 1834–1836, josephsmithpapers.org; History, circa June 1839–circa 1841 [Draft 2], 8, josephsmithpapers.org; Roberts, *History of the Church*, 1:17; Susan Easton Black, Milton V. Backman Jr., Richard O. Cowan, and Larry C. Porter, "The Times and Seasons of the Doctrine and Covenants," *Ensign*, Jan. 1993. Joseph and Emma were married for seventeen years. Joseph was murdered on June 27, 1844, leaving behind Emma with three sons, their adopted daughter Julia, and an unborn son. Linda King Newell and Valeen Tippetts Avery, "The Elect Lady: Emma Hale Smith," *Ensign*, Sept. 1979, 70. Out of their nine children, four died at a young age. Avery, "The Elect Lady," 70.

24. Roberts, *History of the Church*, 1:17.

25. History, circa June 1839–circa 1841 [Draft 2], 8, josephsmithpapers.org; Roberts, *History of the Church*, 1:17; Porter, *Origins of the Church*, 75. Today South Bainbridge is known as Afton, New York. Craig J. Ostler, "Early Church History Sites Along the Susquehanna River: A Photographic Essay," *Regional Studies in Latter-day Saint Church History, New York and Pennsylvania* (Provo, UT: BYU Department of Church History and Doctrine, 2002), 34.

26. It was customary in the Susquehanna Valley to marry in the parlor of the home of the bride. Mark Lyman Staker, "Isaac and Elizabeth Hale in Their Endless Mountain Home," *Mormon Historical Studies* 15, no. 2 (2014): 4.

27. Lucy Mack Smith, History, 1844–1845, book 5, 4, josephsmithpapers.org; Smith, *Lucy's Book*, 373 (manuscript version); Porter, *Origins of the Church*, 50.

28. History, circa June 1839–circa 1841 [Draft 2], 8, josephsmithpapers.org; Roberts, *History of the Church*, 1:17; Staker, "A Comfort unto My Servant," 343–362.

29. Carter, "Along the Susquehanna," 6.

30. Statement of Isaac Hale, in *The Susquehanna Register*; Porter, *Origins of the Church*, 50.

31. Statement of Peter Ingersoll, March 20, 1834, published in *The Susquehanna Register* (Montrose, PA), May 1, 1834. Peter stated, "In the month of August 1827 . . . I was hired by Joseph Smith, Junior, to go to Pennsylvania to move his wife's household furniture to Manchester." "Affidavit of Peter Ingersoll," in *Mormonism Unvailed*, 234; Staker and Jensen, "New Details," 16.

32. "Affidavit of Peter Ingersoll," in *Mormonism Unvailed*, 234–35.

33. "Affidavit of Peter Ingersoll," in *Mormonism Unvailed*, 234–35; Statement of Isaac Hale, in *The Susquehanna Register*; Porter, *Origins of the Church*, 50.

34. Alva Hale stated that Joseph "intended to quit the [money-digging] business, and labor for his livelihood." "Statement of Alva Hale," in *Mormonism Unvailed*, 268; Staker, "Joseph and Emma Smith's Susquehanna Home," 88.

35. "Affidavit of Peter Ingersoll," in *Mormonism Unvailed*, 235.

36. Lucy Mack Smith, History, 1844–1845, book 5, 4, josephsmithpapers.org; Smith, *Lucy's Book*, 373 (manuscript version).

37. Smith, *Biographical Sketches*, 99; Smith, *Lucy's Book*, 375 (Pratt version).

38. History, circa June 1839–circa 1841 [Draft 2], 8, josephsmithpapers.org; Roberts, *History of the Church*, 18. Joseph also discovered spectacles, a rod, and a breastplate. Knight, "Joseph Knight's Recollection," 33.

39. Lucy Mack Smith, History, 1844–1845, book 5, 4, josephsmithpapers.org; Smith, *Lucy's Book*, 376 (manuscript version); Porter, "The Joseph Knight Family," 41. A seer named Samuel Lawrence, who lived in the neighborhood, knew about the plates at the hill and was trying to obtain them. Near nightfall on the September 21, Joseph sent his father to the Lawrences' house to see if there were any signs that Samuel was going away that night. Joseph was worried that Samuel would leave that night and find him at the Hill Cumorah. Fortunately, Samuel stayed home, and Joseph's father left having seen no preparations by Samuel to search out the plates at the Hill Cumorah. Andrew H. Hedges, "'All My Endeavors to Preserve Them': Protecting the Plates in Palmyra, 22 September—December 1827," *Journal of Book of Mormon Studies* 8, no. 2 (1999), 18–20.

40. Stocker, *Centennial History of Susquehanna County*, 554; Porter, "Joseph Smith's Susquehanna Years," 44; Terryl L. Givens, *By the Hand of Mormon:*

The American Scripture that Launched a New World Religion (New York: Oxford University Press, 2002), 12.

Joseph obtained the plates on Rosh Hashanah, the Jewish New Year beginning at sundown on September 21, 1827. At Rosh Hashanah, the faithful were commanded to set a day aside as "a Sabbath, a memorial of blowing of trumpets, an holy convocation" (Leviticus 23:24). Larry E. Morris, "'I Should Have an Eye Single to the Glory of God': Joseph Smith's Account of the Angel and the Plates," *FARMS Review* 17, 1 (2005): 34.

In her account of Joseph's visits to the Hill Cumorah, Katharine Smith Salisbury, Joseph's younger sister, recorded that Joseph was to bring Alvin with him to recover the plates, but when Alvin died, he was told to bring Emma. Kyle R. Walker, "Katharine Smith Salisbury's Recollections of Joseph's Meetings with Moroni," *BYU Studies Quarterly* 41, no. 3 (2002): 14. Emma was the "right person" to accompany Joseph, perhaps as a safeguard to protect the record and preserve it for its intended purposes. Jennifer Reeder, *First: The Life and Faith of Emma Smith* (Salt Lake City, UT: Deseret Book, 2021), 79.

41. "Mormonism—II," *Tiffany's Monthly* 5 (Aug. 1859), 163. David Whitmer said he saw the stone box where Joseph found the plates and knew several money diggers who had seen the same. "Mormonism," *Kansas City Daily Journal*, June 5, 1881, 1; Michael Hubbard MacKay and Gerrit J. Dirkmaat, *From Darkness unto Light: Joseph Smith's Translation and Publication of the Book of Mormon* (Provo, UT: BYU Religious Studies Center, 2015), 8–9. Martin Harris said he found the stone box and broke off one corner of the box. Ole A. Jens, "Testimony of Martin Harris," Church History Library, Salt Lake City; MacKay and Dirkmaat, *From Darkness unto Light*, 22.

42. "Wentworth Letter," *Times and Seasons* (Nauvoo, IL), Mar. 1, 1842, vol. 3, no. 9, 707; *History of the Church* 4:537. "The letters had been cut or engraved in the thin leaves of a metal which would not corrode or alter its appearance with the passing of time." "Mormonism—II," 163. The thin leaves of gold were bound together by massive rings passing through the back edges, which served as a great convenience for carrying them. The leaves were stained with a black, hard stain, so as to make the letters more legible and easier to read. The characters were cut into the plates with some sharp instrument. Kirk B. Henrichsen, "How Witnesses Describe the 'Gold Plates,'" *Journal of Book of Mormon Studies* 10, no. 1 (2001).

43. "Mormonism—II," 163.

44. History, circa June 1839–circa 1841 [Draft 2], 8, josephsmithpapers.org; "Wentworth Letter," 707. The Book of Mormon often refers to the Urim and Thummim as the "interpreters." Gospel Topics Essays, "Book of Mormon Translation," Gospel Library.

45. "Mormonism—II," 165–66. Prophets of the Bible used other similar means to determine the will of God. For example, Aaron had a rod and Joseph of Egypt had a divining cup.

CHAPTER 3

46. "Mormonism—II," 165–66; MacKay and Dirkmaat, *From Darkness unto Light,* 63.

47. History, circa June 1839–circa 1841 [Draft 2], 5, josephsmithpapers.org; MacKay and Dirkmaat, *From Darkness unto Light,* 63. Urim and Thummim means "lights and perfections" in Hebrew and is mentioned several times in the Bible and Book of Mormon. In Exodus 28:30, the Lord commanded Moses, "Thou shalt put in the breastplate of judgment the Urim and Thummim." In Numbers 27:21, it is mentioned in connection with Joshua's elevation to the leadership of Israel: "The priest . . . shall ask counsel for him after the judgment of Urim before the Lord." In 1 Samuel 28:6, Saul's famous encounter with the witch of Endor is the result of his failure to obtain revelation by "dreams, prophets, or Urim." In the Book of Mormon, in Ether 3:23 and Ether 4:5, the Lord gave the brother of Jared "two stones" or "interpreters." And in Mosiah 28:13, King Mosiah translated plates of brass "by the means of those two stones which were fastened into the two rims of a bow." Givens, *By the Hand of Mormon,* 22–23.

48. Lucy Mack Smith, History, 1844–1845, book 6, 1, josephsmithpapers.org; Smith, *Lucy's Book,* 388 (Pratt version).

49. History, circa June 1839–circa 1841 [Draft 2], 8, josephsmithpapers.org; Roberts, *History of the Church,* 1:18.

50. Lucy Mack Smith, History, 1844–1845, book 5, 11, josephsmithpapers.org; Smith, *Lucy's Book,* 385 (Pratt version); Hedges, "All My Endeavors," 17. Martin Harris apparently said that Joseph hid the plates "in an old black oak treetop which was hollow." "Mormonism," 165.

51. Stocker, *Centennial History of Susquehanna County,* 554; Andrew H. Hedges, "'Take Heed Continually': Protecting the Gold Plates," *Ensign,* Jan. 2001, 38.

52. "Joseph Knight Sr., Reminiscences"; Knight, "Joseph Knight's Recollection," 33.

53. Smith, *Biographical Sketches,* 100; Smith, *Lucy's Book,* 377 (Pratt version).

54. Smith, *Biographical Sketches,* 101; Smith, *Lucy's Book,* 378 (Pratt version).

55. Smith, *Biographical Sketches,* 101; Smith, *Lucy's Book,* 378 (Pratt version); Hedges, "All My Endeavors," 1.

56. "Joseph Knight Sr., Reminiscences"; Knight, "Joseph Knight's Recollection," 33.

57. "Wentworth Letter," 708; History, circa June 1839–circa 1841 [Draft 2], 8, josephsmithpapers.org. Some people desired to tar and feather Joseph. Hedges, "All My Endeavors," 20.

58. Lucy Mack Smith, History, 1844–1845, book 5, 10, josephsmithpapers.org; Smith, *Lucy's Book,* 383–84 (Pratt version); Hedges, "All My Endeavors," 19.

59. Smith, *Biographical Sketches,* 105; Smith, *Lucy's Book,* 386 (Pratt version).

60. "The Prophet's Sister Testifies She Lifted the Book of Mormon Plates," Interview, Aug. 31, 1954, by Isaac B. Ball, 2, Church History Library, Salt Lake City; MacKay and Dirkmaat, *From Darkness unto Light,* 12.

61. William G. Hartley, *Stand by My Servant Joseph: The Story of the Joseph Knight Family and the Restoration* (Salt Lake City, UT: Deseret Book, 2003), 41.

62. Smith, *Biographical Sketches,* 107; Smith, *Lucy's Book,* 390 (Pratt version); Hedges, "All My Endeavors," 19.

63. Smith, *Biographical Sketches,* 107; Smith, *Lucy's Book,* 390 (Pratt version); Givens, *By the Hand of Mormon,* 25.

64. *Deseret Evening News* (Salt Lake City, UT), Jan. 20, 1894, 11. Joseph Smith Sr. asked to see the gold plates but Joseph declined, heeding the instructions of Moroni.

65. MacKay and Dirkmaat, *From Darkness unto Light,* 15.

66. "Affidavit of Peter Ingersoll," in *Mormonism Unvailed,* 235.

67. "Mormonism—No. II," 166–67. David Whitmer said that Oliver Cowdery told him, "I had conversation with several young men who said that Joseph Smith [Jr.] certainly had golden plates, and that before he had attained them he had promised to share with them, but had not done so and they were very much incensed with them." "Mormonism," 1; Lyndon W. Cook, ed., *David Whitmer Interviews: A Restoration Witness* (Orem, Utah: Grandin Book, 1993), 113–14. For a discussion of Willard Chase's and Samuel T. Lawrence's supposed involvement and claim that they rightfully had an interest in the plates, see MacKay and Dirkmaat, *From Darkness unto Light,* 8–9.

68. Lucy Mack Smith, History, 1844–1845, book 5, 12, book 6, 1, josephsmith-papers.org; Smith, *Lucy's Book,* 384, 389 (manuscript version).

69. Lucy Mack Smith, History, 1844–1845, book 5, 12, book 6, 1, josephsmith-papers.org; Smith, *Lucy's Book,* 384, 389 (manuscript version); MacKay and Dirkmaat, *From Darkness unto Light,* 69.

70. Lucy Mack Smith, History, 1844–1845, book 6, 2, josephsmithpapers.org; Smith, *Lucy's Book,* 392 (manuscript version).

71. James B. Allen and Glen M. Leonard, *Story of the Latter-day Saints,* 2nd ed. (Salt Lake City, UT: Deseret Book, 1992), 46.

72. Lucy Mack Smith, History, 1844–1845, book 6, 2, josephsmithpapers.org; Smith, *Lucy's Book,* 392 (manuscript version). It was only afterward that Joseph learned how the mob knew to search the cooper's shop. One of Sally Chase's discoveries was where Joseph kept the gold plates. The mob obeyed her directions but, as explained above, only found the box in which the plates were held and not the plates themselves. Smith, *Lucy's Book,* 392 (manuscript version).

73. "Joseph Knight Sr., Reminiscences"; Knight, "Joseph Knight's Recollection," 33–34; Morris, "I Should Have an Eye Single," 27; Hartley, *Stand by My Servant Joseph,* 34.

74. Lucy Mack Smith, History, 1844–1845, book 6, 2, josephsmithpapers.org; Smith, *Lucy's Book*, 391–92 (manuscript version); Hedges, "All My Endeavors," 19–20; Pearson H. Corbett, *Hyrum Smith, Patriarch* (Salt Lake City, UT: Deseret Book, 1963), 41.

75. Appendix: Orson Pratt, *A[n] Interesting Account of Several Remarkable Visions*, 1840, 13, josephsmithpapers.org.

76. History, circa June 1839–circa 1841 [Draft 2], 8, josephsmithpapers.org; Roberts, *History of the Church*, 1:19; Ivan J. Barrett, *Joseph Smith and the Restoration* (Provo, UT: Brigham Young University Press, 1970), 52.

77. History, circa June 1839–circa 1841 [Draft 2], 8, josephsmithpapers.org; Roberts, *History of the Church*, 1:18.

78. History, circa Summer 1832, 5, josephsmithpapers.org; "Historical Introduction," Agreement with Isaac Hale, 6 April 1829, josephsmithpapers. org. Historian Mark Staker observed that Joseph and Emma likely had planned to move to Harmony, Pennsylvania, in the early spring of 1828 when the home occupied by Emma's brother would become available. The intense persecution in Palmyra likely prompted Joseph and Emma to move to Harmony earlier than anticipated, thus causing them to take up residence with Emma's parents until their home was available. Staker and Jensen, "New Details," 17.

79. Staker and Jensen, "New Details," 16–25; Susan Easton Black, "Isaac Hale: Antagonist of Joseph Smith," in *Regional Studies in Latter-day Saint Church History: New York* (Provo, UT: BYU Department of Church History and Doctrine, 1992), 7.

80. History, circa Summer 1832, 5, josephsmithpapers.org. For a detailed and comprehensive in-depth biography of the life of Martin Harris, see Susan Easton Black and Larry C. Porter, *Martin Harris: Uncompromising Witness of the Book of Mormon* (Provo, UT: Brigham Young University, 2018).

81. Smith, *Biographical Sketches*, 113; Smith, *Lucy's Book*, 400–401 (Pratt version).

82. On another occasion, Martin bought Joseph a black suit and clothes at a local store. Martin believed the clothes were necessary for a man of God. "Mormonism—No. II," 166–68; Susan Easton Black and Larry C. Porter, "For the Sum of Three Thousand Dollars," *Journal of Book of Mormon Studies* 14, no. 2 (2005): 7.

83. "Mormonism—No. II," 164, 166–68; Black and Porter, "For the Sum," 5–7.

84. "Mormonism—No. II," 164, 166–68; Richard Lyman Bushman, *Joseph Smith: Rough Stone Rolling* (New York: Alfred A. Knopf, 2005), 62.

85. "Mormonism—No. II," 164, 166–68.

86. "Mormonism—No. II," 167–69. Martin Harris's wife, Lucy Harris, and his daughter visited Joseph at his Manchester home. Joseph apparently allowed Martin's wife and daughter to hold the wooden box containing the plates. "Mormonism—No. II," 168.

87. "Mormonism—No. II," 168–70; Bushman, *Joseph Smith: Rough Stone Rolling*, 62. When asked about the plates before he had met Joseph, Martin replied, "The Scripture says, He that answereth a matter before he heareth it, it is foolishness unto him." "Mormonism—No. II," 167.

88. Orson Pratt, *Remarkable Visions: By Orson Pratt, One of the Twelve Apostles of the Church of Jesus Christ of Latter-day Saints* (Liverpool: R. James, 1848), 15; "Mormonism—No. II," 167–69.

89. "Mormonism—No. II," 170; Staker and Jensen, "New Details," 17.

90. Statement of Isaac Hale, in *The Susquehanna Register*; Smith, *Biographical Sketches*, 120; Smith, *Lucy's Book*, 417 (Pratt version); Carter, "Along the Susquehanna," 6.

91. Smith, *Biographical Sketches*, 113; Smith, *Lucy's Book*, 401 (Pratt version).

92. Pratt, *Remarkable Visions*, 14; "Mormonism—No. II," 170; Hedges, "All My Endeavors," 21; Stocker, *Centennial History of Susquehanna County*, 554–55; Goodell and Topolewski, *Notes and Sketches*, 43. Apparently Martin Harris advised Joseph to "start a day or two in advance." "Mormonism—No. II," 170.

93. Orson Pratt, *Remarkable Visions*, 14; Staker and Jensen, "New Details," 21. In May 1828 Alva Hale was replaced as constable of Harmony. "Returned to the Court as Elected Township and Burough [sic] Officers for the Ensuing Year." Staker and Jensen, "New Details," 20, fn. 61.

94. History, circa Summer 1832, 5, josephsmithpapers.org; History, circa June 1839–circa 1841 [Draft 2], 8, josephsmithpapers.org; Roberts, *History of the Church*, 1:19; Lucy Mack Smith, History, 1844–1845, book 6, 6–7, josephsmithpapers.org; Smith, *Lucy's Book*, 400–401 (manuscript version); Black and Porter, "For the Sum," 7; Staker and Jensen, "New Details," 21, 25. Alva Hale, in his role as constable in Harmony Township, Pennsylvania, apparently provided protection to Joseph and Emma on their trip, especially when they crossed the border into Pennsylvania. Staker and Jensen, "New Details," 21.

95. "Testimony of Isaac Hale," in *Mormonism Unvailed*, 264; Staker and Jensen, "New Details," 23.

96. Staker and Jensen, "New Details," 20.

97. Joseph Knight Sr. stated, "[Joseph] began to be anxious to get them translated." "Joseph Knight Sr., Reminiscences"; Knight, "Joseph Knight's Recollection," 3; Hartley, *Stand by My Servant Joseph*, 37; MacKay and Dirkmaat, *From Darkness unto Light*, 34.

98. Stocker, *Centennial History of Susquehanna County*, 555; Mark Lyman Staker, "Where Was the Aaronic Priesthood Restored?: Identifying the Location of John the Baptist's Appearance, May 15, 1829," *Mormon Historical Studies* 12, no. 2 (2011): 50–51; Staker, "A Comfort unto My Servant," 343–362.

99. Hartley, *Stand by My Servant Joseph*, 42–43.

100. History, circa June 1839–circa 1841 [Draft 2], 9, josephsmithpapers.org. From December 1827 to February 1828, copying the characters and examining the plates occupied Joseph's time. Today there exist three documents that purportedly show the characters copied by Joseph Smith from the gold plates. Scholars have concluded that these documents likely are representative of characters Joseph Smith copied from the plates. See Appendix 2, Document 1. Characters Copied by John Whitmer, circa 1829–1831, josephsmithpapers.org.

101. Staker, "Joseph and Emma Smith's Susquehanna Home," 89.

102. Staker and Jensen, "New Details," 26 (analyzing David Hale's store ledger and providing a transcription).

103. Tax Records, Harmony Township, Susquehanna County, Pennsylvania, 1828, 1829, 1830, cited in Staker, "Where Was the Aaronic Priesthood Restored?," 158; Staker and Jensen, "New Details," 26.

104. Nathanial Lewis said, "Smith frequently said to me that I should see the plates at the time appointed." "Affidavit of Nathanial Lewis," in *Mormonism Unvailed*, 266; Staker, "Joseph and Emma Smith's Susquehanna Home," 95.

105. "Affidavit of Joshua M'Kune," in *Mormonism Unvailed*, 267.

106. Statement of Isaac Hale, in *The Susquehanna Register*; Porter, *Origins of the Church*, 51.

107. Mr. Hale claimed that Joseph had promised to show him the plates. He said, "At one time . . . [Joseph Smith] came to my house, and asked my advice, whether he should proceed to translate the Book of Plates or not. He said that God had commanded him to translate it, but he was afraid of the people: he remarked, that he was to exhibit the plates to the world, at a certain time, which was then about eighteen months distant. I told him I was not qualified to give advice in such cases. Smith frequently said to me that I should see the plates at the time appointed. After the time stipulated, had passed away, Smith being at my house was asked why he did not fulfill his promise to show the Golden Plates and prove himself an honest man? He replied that he, himself was deceived, but that I should see them if I were where they were, I reminded him then, what I stated at the time he made the promise, I was fearful 'the enchantment would be so powerful' as to remove the plates when the time came in which they were to be revealed." Statement of Isaac Hale, in *The Susquehanna Register*.

108. Historian Mark Staker notes that during this time period, a mother had her son-in-law arrested after he eloped with her daughter without permission, on charges of stealing parts of her daughter's wedding outfit. "Stealing a Wife," *AntiMasonic Telegraph*, Sept. 26, 1829, cited in Staker, "Joseph and Emma Smith's Susquehanna Home," 90.

109. Jesse Hale had recently built a new home across the river and moved his family into it so that Joseph and Emma could occupy the small farm home close the Hales' home. But David Hale and his wife, Rhoda Jane Hale, were

living in the home when Joseph and Emma arrived in Harmony. Staker and Jensen, "New Details," 28. It is believed that Emma and Joseph likely moved into the small farm home in February (probably the time when David and Rhoda Hale moved out of the home), which means Joseph and Emma lived with Emma's parents for around three months. "Historical Introduction," Agreement with Isaac Hale, 6 April 1829, fn. 2, josephsmithpapers.org. For a thorough discussion of the Jesse and Mary Hale home and its history with accompanying photographs, see Staker, "Joseph and Emma Smith's Susquehanna Home," 70–78.

110. "Joseph Knight Sr., Reminiscences"; Knight, "Joseph Knight's Recollection," 35; Gospel Topics Essays, "Book of Mormon Translation," Gospel Library.

111. MacKay and Dirkmaat, *From Darkness unto Light*, 85.

112. Smith, "Last Testimony of Sister Emma," 289–90.

113. Smith, "Last Testimony of Sister Emma," 289–90; John W. Welch, "The Miraculous Translation of the Book of Mormon," in John W. Welch, ed., *Opening the Heavens: Accounts of Divine Manifestations, 1820–1844* (Provo, UT: Brigham Young University Press, 2005), 88–89. In an interview, when asked whether Joseph used books or notes, Emma stated, "If he had anything of the kind he could not have concealed it from me." Smith, "Last Testimony of Sister Emma," 290; "Book of Mormon Translation By Joseph Smith," *Encyclopedia of Mormonism*, ed. Daniel H. Ludlow (New York: Macmillan, 1992), 1:210.

114. E. C. Briggs, "Brother Joseph Smith" *Saints' Herald* 31, no. 25 (21 June 1884): 397; Welch, "The Miraculous Translation," 129.

115. Gospel Topics Essays, "Book for Mormon Translation," Gospel Library.

116. Briggs, "Brother Joseph Smith," 454.

117. Briggs, "Brother Joseph Smith," 397; Mark L. McConkie, *Remembering Joseph: Personal Recollections of Those Who Knew the Prophet Joseph Smith* (Salt Lake City, UT: Deseret Book, 2003), 1305. E. C. Briggs reported that Emma made this statement in 1884. Welch, "The Miraculous Translation," 129.

118. Smith, "Last Testimony," 289–90; McConkie, *Remembering Joseph*, 1303–4; Richard L. Bushman, "The Recovery of the Book of Mormon," in Noel B. Reynolds, ed., *Book of Mormon Authorship Revisited: The Evidence for Ancient Origins* (Provo, UT: F.A.R.M.S., 1997), 22.

119. Smith III, "Last Testimony of Sister Emma," 289–90.

120. William B. Smith, *William B. Smith on Mormonism* (Lamoni, IA: Herald Steam, 1883), 9–10; Morris, "I Should Have an Eye Single," 62; "Joseph Smith Jr.," *Encyclopedia of Mormonism*, 3:1331–48.

121. George Peck, *Early Methodism* (New York: Carlton & Porter, 1860), 332–33.

122. History, circa Summer 1832, 5, josephsmithpapers.org. The Lord appeared to Martin because of Martin's faith and the assistance he rendered to Joseph.

123. Porter, *Origins of the Church*, 53; Roberts, *History of the Church*, 1:19. Martin Harris arrived in Harmony about the time that Joseph and Emma moved into their own home 150 yards southeast of Isaac Hale's frame home. Staker and Jensen, "New Details," 29. Emma and Joseph likely moved into their home in January or early February. Staker, "Joseph and Emma Smith's Susquehanna Home," 93.

124. Lucy Mack Smith, History, 1844–1845, book 6, 7, josephsmithpapers.org; Smith, *Lucy's Book*, 402 (manuscript version). From the beginning, Lucy Harris had insisted on assisting in the work and seeing the plates. To appease Lucy, and at her insistence, Joseph apparently accepted twenty-eight dollars from her to assist in the work. Lucy Mack Smith, History, 1844–1845, book 6, 4–5, josephsmithpapers.org; Smith, *Lucy's Book*, 398–99 (manuscript version). Joseph's acceptance of the money resulted in Lucy Harris being the first donor to the translation of the plates. Black and Porter, *Martin Harris: Uncompromising Witness*, 83.

125. History, circa Summer 1832, 5, josephsmithpapers.org; Bushman, *Joseph Smith: Rough Stone Rolling*, 63.

126. MacKay and Dirkmaat, *From Darkness unto Light*, 42.

127. Statement of Isaac Hale, in *The Susquehanna Register*.

128. Statement of Isaac Hale, in *The Susquehanna Register*; Black, "Isaac Hale: Antagonist," 8.

129. History, circa June 1839–circa 1841 [Draft 2], 9, josephsmithpapers.org; Roberts, *History of the Church*, 1:19–20; Bushman, "The Recovery of the Book of Mormon," 22. When Martin returned, Joseph knew that he must translate the plates. Hartley, *Stand by My Servant Joseph*, 45.

   Years later, in 1832, while staying at the Pearl Street House in New York City, Joseph recorded his thoughts of New York City in a letter to his wife Emma: "This day I have been walking through the most splendid part of the City of New York. The buildings are truly great and wonderful to the astonishing of every beholder." Joseph was disappointed, however, with the iniquity of some of the people in New York City. Joseph Smith, Letter, New York City, NY, to Emma Smith, Kirtland Township, OH, Oct. 13, 1832, Community of Christ Library Archives, Independence, Missouri.

   For a detailed study of the qualifications of the aforementioned experts and professors, please see Richard E. Bennett, "'Read This I Pray Thee': Martin Harris and the Three Wise Men of the East," *Journal of Mormon History* 36 (Winter 2010): 178–216.

130. Bennett, "Read This," 180; Stanley B. Kimball, "The Anthon Transcript: People, Primary Sources, and Problems," *BYU Studies* 10:3 (Spring 1970): 335; Porter, *Origins of the Church*, 53.

131. MacKay and Dirkmaat, *From Darkness unto Light*, 41. For an analysis of Joseph's and Martin's lack of knowledge as to language of the characters, see MacKay and Dirkmaat, 41–44.

132. "Joseph Knight Sr., Reminiscences"; Knight, "Joseph Knight's Recollection," 34; Richard E. Bennett. "Read This," 178–216; MacKay and Dirkmaat, *From Darkness unto Light,* 45. At this time, Martin may have believed that the characters were in a Native American language, and several scholars in Native American languages resided in Philadelphia. MacKay and Dirkmaat, 45.

133. MacKay and Dirkmaat, *From Darkness unto Light,* 48; Roberts, *History of the Church,* 1:20; Bushman, *Joseph Smith: Rough Stone Rolling,* 64. Dr. Mitchill was a member of dozens of scientific and scholarly societies and wrote a number of books, pamphlets, and articles. He was known as a "living encyclopedia" of knowledge. Hartley, *Stand by My Servant Joseph,* 40.

134. A. W. B., "Mormonites," *Evangelical Magazine and Gospel Advocate* 2, no. 25 (Apr. 9, 1831); Howe, *Mormonism Unvailed,* 270; MacKay and Dirkmaat, *From Darkness unto Light,* 49.

135. Howe, *Mormonism Unvailed,* 270. Author William Berrett believes that "Professor Anthon knew nothing as to the correctness of the translation or the genuineness of the characters" because no single American was skilled in reading Egyptian hieroglyphics or languages formed therefrom. William E. Berrett, *The Restored Church* (Salt Lake City, UT: Deseret Book, 1969), 33.

136. History, circa June 1839–circa 1841 [Draft 2], 9, josephsmithpapers.org; Roberts, *History of the Church,* 1:20; Porter, *Origins of the Church,* 54.

137. Professor Anthon was the best-known scholar in the science of Egyptology at that time. Kimball, "The Anthon Transcript," 330–31; Porter, *Origins of the Church,* 54.

138. History, circa June 1839–circa 1841 [Draft 2], 9, josephsmithpapers.org; Roberts, *History of the Church,* 1:20. Historian Stanley Kimball remarked that the two professors' areas of expertise, while extremely educationally advanced for their day, would only have allowed them to recognize that the characters were Egyptian, not to translate them into English. Kimball, "The Anthon Transcript," 335–37.

139. History, circa June 1839–circa 1841 [Draft 2], 9, josephsmithpapers.org; Roberts, *History of the Church,* 1:20.

140. History, circa Summer 1832, 5, josephsmithpapers.org.

141. History, circa June 1839–circa 1841 [Draft 2], 9, josephsmithpapers.org; Roberts, *History of the Church,* 1:20. Professor Anthon tells a dramatically different version of his encounter with Martin and adamantly disagrees with Martin's characterizations. He described his visit with Martin in a letter to Eber D. Howe written on February 17, 1834, and claims he never verified the authenticity of the writing. Charles Anthon, New York, to Eber D. Howe, Painesville, OH, Feb. 17, 1834, in Howe, *Mormonism Unvailed,* 270–72. Some historians believe that Professor Anthon later denied affirming the authenticity of the writing because his intellectual reputation would have

been harmed if he were connected to the gold plates. Givens, *By the Hand of Mormon*, 31; MacKay and Dirkmaat, *From Darkness unto Light*, 51.

142. It is unclear when Joseph ascertained that Martin's experience with Professor Anthon was a fulfillment of Old Testament prophecy. It may have occurred in the spring of 1829 when Joseph was translating a similar passage in the Book of Mormon (2 Nephi 27:15, 17–18).

143. History, circa Summer 1832, 5, josephsmithpapers.org. For an in-depth discussion on Martin's trip to New York City, see MacKay and Dirkmaat, *From Darkness unto Light*, 39–53.

144. MacKay and Dirkmaat, *From Darkness unto Light*, 62.

145. Affidavit of William Pilkington, Testimony sworn before Joseph W. Peterson, Apr. 3, 1934, Church History Library, Salt Lake City.

146. John A. Clark, *Gleanings by the Way* (Philadelphia: W. J. and J. K. Simon 1842), 230, quoting Clark's interview with Martin Harris.

147. Clark, *Gleanings by the Way*, 230.

148. History, circa June 1839–circa 1841 [Draft 2], 9, josephsmithpapers.org; Roberts, *History of the Church*, 1:20; MacKay and Dirkmaat, *From Darkness unto Light*, 80.

149. Lucy Mack Smith, History, 1844–1845, book 6, 9, josephsmithpapers.org; Smith, *Lucy's Book*, 405 (manuscript version).

150. Lucy Mack Smith, History, 1844–1845, book 6, 8, josephsmithpapers.org; Smith, *Lucy's Book*, 404–405 (manuscript version). According to Lucy Mack Smith, who is believed by many historians to have a prejudice against Lucy Harris (MacKay and Dirkmaat, *From Darkness unto Light*, 25–26), Lucy Harris devised a scheme to obtain a copy of the transcript with the Egyptian characters. As Martin exhibited the characters to friends and acquaintances along the way to Harmony, Lucy would take "out of her pocket an exact copy of the same; and she told those present that 'Joe Smith' was not the only one who was in possession of this great curiosity, that she had the same characters, and, they were quite as genuine as those shown by Mr. Harris." Lucy Mack Smith, History, 1844–1845, book 6, 8–9, josephsmithpapers.org; Smith, *Lucy's Book*, 404–5 (manuscript version).

151. Lucy Mack Smith, History, 1844–1845, book 6, 9, josephsmithpapers.org; Smith, *Lucy's Book*, 405–6 (manuscript version).

152. Lucy Mack Smith, History, 1844–1845, book 6, 9–10, josephsmithpapers. org; Smith, *Lucy's Book*, 406 (manuscript version).

153. MacKay and Dirkmaat, *From Darkness unto Light*, 83. The snake was likely a black rat snake or timber rattlesnake (black phase), both native and common in the area. Staker, "Where Was the Aaronic Priesthood Restored?," 151.

154. Lucy Mack Smith, History, 1844–1845, book 6, 10, josephsmithpapers.org; Smith, *Lucy's Book*, 407 (manuscript version). "Historical Introduction," Revelation, July 1828 [D&C 3], josephsmithpapers.org.

155. Wayne Co., NY, Deed Records, 1823–1904, vol. 5, 530–532, Nov. 29, 1825, microfilm 478, 782, US and Canada Record Collection, Family History Library, Salt Lake City; "Historical Introduction" Revelation, July 1828 [D&C 3], josephsmithpapers.org. This agreement was called a "jointure agreement," which under New York state law at the time allowed a wife to elect to take land as part of her marital property instead of money. David S. Garland and Lucius P. McGehee, eds, *The American and English Encyclopedia of Law*, 2nd ed. (Long Island, NY: Edward Thompson Company, 1899), 209.

156. History, circa June 1839–circa 1841 [Draft 2], 9, josephsmithpapers.org; Roberts, *History of the Church*, 1:20; Porter, *Origins of the Church*, 55.

157. *Church History in the Fullness of Times Student Manual* (2000), 59; MacKay and Dirkmaat, *From Darkness unto Light*, 90–91.

158. MacKay and Dirkmaat, *From Darkness unto Light*, 90

159. MacKay and Dirkmaat, *From Darkness unto Light*, 71; David E. Sloan, "The Anthon Transcripts and the Translation of the Book of Mormon: Studying It Out in the Mind of Joseph Smith," *Journal of Book of Mormon Studies* 5, no. 2 (1996): 57–81. Joseph also had years of experience using a seer stone to rely on as he translated the plates.

160. History, circa June 1839–circa 1841 [Draft 2], 9, josephsmithpapers.org; MacKay and Dirkmaat, *From Darkness unto Light*, 66.

161. History, circa June 1839–circa 1841 [Draft 2], 9, josephsmithpapers.org; Roberts, *History of the Church*, 1:20–21; "Historical Introduction," Revelation, July 1828 [D&C 3], josephsmithpapers.org.

162. Statement of Isaac Hale, in *The Susquehanna Register*.

163. Clark, *Gleanings by the Way*, 230; MacKay, *From Darkness unto Light*, 90–91.

164. "One of the Three Witnesses," *Deseret Evening News*, Dec. 13, 1881.

165. Gospel Topics Essays, "Book of Mormon Translation," Gospel Library.

166. MacKay and Dirkmaat, *From Darkness unto Light*, 89.

167. Clark, *Gleanings by the Way*, 230; MacKay and Dirkmaat, *From Darkness unto Light*, 69.

168. Gospel Topics Essays, "Book of Mormon Translation," Gospel Library. Joseph Smith and others understood the term "Urim and Thummin" to refer to the broad category of instruments used for translations, not one specific instrument.

169. "One of the Three Witnesses," 4; Gospel Topics Essays, "Book of Mormon Translation," Gospel Library.

170. MacKay and Dirkmaat, *From Darkness unto Light*, 92.

171. "One of the Three Witnesses," 4; MacKay and Dirkmaat, *From Darkness unto Light*, 89.

172. Joseph Fielding Smith, *Doctrines of Salvation*, comp. Bruce R. McConkie (1955), 3:5. Many people believe that Joseph obtained his knowledge of the Book of Mormon and skill in translating by studying and practicing. See Joseph Fielding Smith, *Doctrines of Salvation*, 1:582.

173. "Joseph Knight Sr., Reminiscences"; Larry C. Porter, "The Colesville Branch and the Coming Forth of the Book of Mormon," *BYU Studies* 10, no. 3 (1970): 4.

174. "Joseph Knight Sr., Reminiscences"; Knight, "Joseph Knight's Recollection," 35.

CHAPTER 4

WILLIAM PENN'S IMPRISONMENT IN NEWGATE PRISON

——— ⟨∾⊚⌒⟩ ———

Chapters 4 and 5 recount some of the trials experienced by William Penn and Joseph Smith. Both William and Joseph showed incredible zeal and courage during these trials. They rose to the challenge and relied on God to fulfill their divine purposes.

AFTER RETURNING FROM HIS MISSIONARY WORK IN IRELAND, William Penn continued to publicly advocate for his Quaker faith in London. On August 14, 1670, William was on the street outside a Quaker meetinghouse on London's Gracechurch Street preaching to a crowd of several hundred people. He was accompanied by a recent Quaker convert, William Mead.[1] They preached in the street because the government had closed the Quaker meetinghouse, as William Penn recalled: "We were by force of arms kept out of our lawful house and met as near it in the street, as the soldiers would give us leave." The two Friends were arrested and sent to Newgate Prison, under charges that they "unlawfully and tumultuously did assemble and congregate themselves together, to the disturbance of the Peace."[2]

William Penn's and William Mead's case was highly publicized and set for trial. Sir Samuel Starling, the Sheriff of London who harbored a particular animus against William Penn's father and expressed his disdain openly in court, presided over the trial. After an initial hearing, William Penn and William Mead were detained at the nearby Black Dog Inn and were held in custody during trial. At the beginning of the trial, Sheriff Starling asked William Penn and William Mead to enter into a plea agreement. William Penn requested a copy of the indictment, the document charging him with a crime, but Sheriff Starling refused to show it to him: "You must first plead [guilty] to the indictment, before you can have a copy of it," he retorted. Both William Penn and William Mead entered a plea of not guilty and were not shown the indictment.[3]

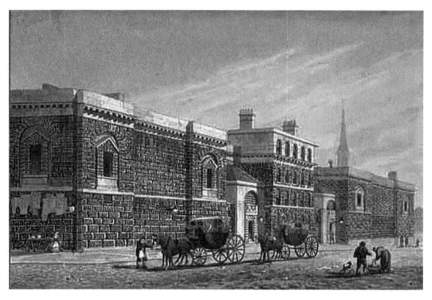

West view of Newgate Prison, by George Shepherd, 1810.

The trial was adjourned and then resumed a few days later. Sheriff Starling called witnesses to testify of William Penn's purported disturbance of the peace. As the witnesses testified, it became clear that there was insufficient evidence to convict the two Friends. Many witnesses had heard William Penn preaching, but they could not hear, nor recall, the words he preached. After the government's witnesses testified, William Penn insisted that the charges against him, founded on "common law," were not sufficiently specific: "For if it be common, it should not be so hard to produce . . . [and] unless you shew me, and the people, the law you ground your indictment upon, I shall take it for granted, your proceedings are merely arbitrary."[4] He continued: "I have asked but one question [what law have I broken] and you have not answered me; though the rights and privileges of every

Englishmen be concerned in it." He then concluded: "The Question is not whether I am guilty of this indictment, but whether this indictment be legal."[5] William Penn at this point was relying on his legal education and making technical legal arguments in his own defense.

Sheriff Starling responded by removing William Penn and William Mead from the courtroom and placing them in the bail-dock—a cage where those accused of crimes awaited their cases to be called. From the bail-dock, William Penn continued to argue that he had "at least ten or twelve material points to offer, in order to invalidate their indictment."[6]

The trial concluded, and the jury completed its deliberation. Then the jury reported its verdict: eight on one side and four on the other side—a hung jury, which under modern law would mean the prosecution had failed to prove its case and the indictment would be dismissed. But legal protections for juries common today—such as deference to jury verdicts, no tampering with the jury, and no influencing the jury—did not exist in England at the time. Sheriff Starling pressured the jury and sent them back to deliberation. Upon further deliberation, the jury then returned a verdict against William Penn and William Mead of "guilty of speaking in Gracechurch street," which was not a crime and not the charge against them. Once again Sheriff Starling sent the jurors back for deliberation, but they returned the same verdict again: "We the jurors, hereafter named, do not find William Penn to be guilty of speaking or preaching to an assembly, met together in Gracious [Gracechurch]. Street, the 14th of August last, 1670, and that William Mead is not guilty of the indictment."[7]

Sheriff Starling became irate, ordering the jury, "You shall not be dismiss'd, till we have a verdict that the court will accept; and you shall be lock'd up, without meat, drink, fire, and tobacco: You shall not think thus to abuse the court; we will have a verdict by the help of God, or you shall starve for it." William Penn responded to Sheriff Starling, insisting that the independence and integrity of the jury's verdict was a fundamental aspect of English law.[8]

Sheriff Starling then ordered that the jury be confined overnight without food or drink. The next morning the jury reported the verdict of not guilty. They were then instructed to reconsider their verdict and came back yet again with a verdict of not guilty. In a desperate attempt, Sheriff Starling fined the jury and defendants and sent William Penn and William Mead to prison based on contempt of court for an earlier incident during the trial when William Penn and William Mead would not remove their hats as a sign of submission to the court.[9] While confined in prison, William Penn wrote three letters to his father requesting that no one pay the unjust fines, but someone did pay the fines and William Penn and William Mead were released from prison.[10]

Prison did not deter William Penn in his missionary zeal, but after his release, he quickly returned home to his father's bedside. His father, Sir William Penn, had become deathly ill and died on September 16, 1670. Those last moments with his father were precious. Years later, William recounted a tearful reconciliation between father and son. In one of their last conversations, Sir William Penn had encouraged his son to be true to his Quaker faith: "Son William, if you and your friends will keep to your plain way of preaching, and keep to your plain way of living, you will make an end of the priests to the end of the world."[11]

William followed the last words of his father and continued to profess Quakerism in London. In February 1671 he preached at a Quaker meeting at the Wheeler Street Meetinghouse in Spitalfields. According to William, English soldiers observed the meeting and allowed him to speak. But then "the sergeant came and pulled him down, and led him through the throng of the Meeting into the street, where the constable and his watchmen joined the soldiers, and . . . brought him to the Tower [of London]."[12] William was charged with a violation of the Five Mile Act, an English law that prohibited "dissenters"—people who did not belong to the Church of England—from coming within five miles of any incorporated English town. Persons accused of violating the Five Mile Act were not guaranteed a jury trial. Sir John Robinson, lieutenant of the Tower of London, presided over the trial. William advocated his innocence but was ultimately incarcerated for six months.[13]

While in prison, William expanded and refined his epistle *The Great Case of Liberty of Conscience*. He defined "Liberty of Conscience" as "the free and uninterrupted exercise of our consciences, in that way of worship, we are most clearly persuaded, God requires us to serve

Him in (without endangering our undoubted Birthright of English Freedoms) which being Matter of faith; we Sin if we omit, and they can't do less, that shall endeavor it."[14]

According to William, Liberty of Conscience was an "English Birthright" and a "divine right." William signed the epistle "From a Prisoner for Conscience-Sake."[15] Liberty of Conscience was more than freedom to believe—it was freedom to worship without restraint:

> First, By Liberty of Conscience, we understand not only a mere Liberty of the Mind, in believing or disbelieving this or that Principle or Doctrine, but the Exercise of ourselves in a visible Way of Worship, upon our believing it to be indispensably required at our Hands, that if we neglect it for Fear or Favor of any Mortal Man, we Sin, and incur Divine Wrath. . . . Secondly, By Imposition, Restraint, and Persecution, we don't only mean, the strict Requiring of us to believe this to be true, or that to be false; and upon Refusal, to incur the Penalties enacted in such Cases; but by those Terms we mean thus much, any coercive Lett or Hindrance to us, from meeting together to perform those Religious Exercises which are according to our Faith and Persuasion.[16]

In 1669 William began courting Gulielma Springett, who came from a similar social background.[17] After three years of courting, they were married on April 4, 1672.[18] The marriage ceremony took place at King John's Farm in Chorleywood, where they "solemnly and express-ly [took] each other in marriage, mutually promising to be loving, true and faithful to each other in that relation, so long as it shall please the Lord to continue their natural lives."[19] Gulielma had a daughter in January 1673 and twins in January 1674, but the daughter and twins died within a few months of birth.[20] Gulielma and William were later blessed with three children, Springett, Laetitia, and William Jr. ("Bille"), who would survive infancy.[21]

NOTES

1. Andrew R. Murphy, *William Penn: A Life* (New York: Oxford University Press, 2019), 76.

2. William Penn, *The Peoples Ancient and Just Liberties Asserted* (London: s.n., 1670), 18 (Penn-Mead trial transcript).

3. Penn, *The Peoples*, 6; "To Sir William Penn, 15 August 1670," in *The Papers of William Penn*, ed. Richard S. and Mary Maples Dunn (Philadelphia: University of Pennsylvania Press, 1981–1987), 1:173.

4. Penn, *The Peoples*, 10.

5. Penn, *The Peoples*, 11.

6. Penn, *The Peoples*, 14.

7. Penn, *The Peoples*, 17.

8. Penn, T*he Peoples*, 17.

9. "To Sir William Penn, 5 September 1670," in *Papers of William Penn*, 1:177; Murphy, *William Penn: A Life*, 79.

10. "To Sir William Penn, 5 September 1670," "To Sir William Penn, 6 September 1670," "To Sir William Penn, 7 September 1670," in *Papers of William Penn*, 1:177–180; Murphy, *William Penn: A Life*, 80.

11. William Penn, *No Cross, No Crown*, 2nd ed. (London: s.n., 1682), 571–72.

12. "Injustice Detected, February 1671," in *Papers of William Penn*, 1:200–201.

13. "Injustice Detected," 1:200–201; Murphy, *William Penn: A Life*, 82.

14. William Penn, *The Great Case of Liberty of Conscience Once More Briefly Debated and Defended* [. . . .] (London: s.n., 1670), 4 (original punctuation and spelling modernized).

15. Penn, *Great Case of Liberty of Conscience*, 15. The epistle contained six substantive chapters examining the foundations of Liberty of Conscience and vigorously defended the freedom of worship. Murphy, *William Penn: A Life*, 71.

16. Penn, *Great Case of Liberty of Conscience*, 11–12 (original punctuation and spelling modernized).

17. Murphy, *William Penn: A Life*, 150–151.

18. *Papers of William Penn*, 1:231.

19. "Marriage Certificate, 4 April 1672," in *Papers of William Penn*, 1:238.

20. *Papers of William Penn*, 1:249.

21. "To Springett Penn, Letitia Penn, and William Penn Jr., 29 August 1682," in *Papers of William Penn* 2:280–81.

JOSEPH SMITH'S TRIALS OF 1828

LIKE WILLIAM PENN, JOSEPH SMITH ALSO EXPERIENCED MANY TRI-als. As the translation of the Book of Mormon progressed, Martin grew desperate to see the plates and to show the manuscript to his family so that he "might convince them of the truth" of his work.[1] Martin may have hoped that displaying the manuscript would re-vive his strained relationship with his wife and rectify his reputation. Martin pled with Joseph to inquire of the Lord through the Urim and Thummim on his behalf.[2] Joseph valued Martin's friendship, for Martin had been there for him when he needed support and assis-tance.[3] Joseph inquired, and the Lord said Martin should not be per-mitted to take the manuscript.[4] Unsatisfied with the response, Martin again requested that Joseph inquire of the Lord. Joseph did so a sec-ond time, only to receive the same answer.[5]

Martin may not have requested the manuscript a third time but for the instance of his wife, Lucy. According to a neighbor in New York, when Martin told Lucy that his second request had been de-nied, Lucy "was awfully worked up, and threatened to kick him out of the house if he didn't bring the manuscript." Martin recalled, "I loved my wife and wanted to please her. So I told her I would ask the prophet a third time." He importuned Joseph a third time and Joseph reluctantly agreed, receiving permission from the Lord to de-liver the manuscript to Martin with certain conditions.[6] Martin was to show the manuscript only to five people—his wife, Lucy Harris;

his brother, Preserved Harris; his father, Nathan Harris; his mother, Rhoda Lapham Harris; and his wife's sister, Polly Harris Cobb.[7] In addition to these conditions, Joseph obligated Martin to bind himself in a covenant, in a most solemn manner, that he would not show the manuscript to any others.[8] Around June 14, Martin left Harmony for New York with the manuscript.[9] Joseph in this circumstance uncharacteristically gave into the pressure of Martin, likely because Martin had provided the means for Joseph to travel to Harmony, had searched for a translator for the gold plates, and had served as his scribe. Joseph also may have thought this could renew the tense relationship between Martin and his wife. In this instance, Joseph feared man more than God.

THE DEATH OF THE SMITHS' FIRST CHILD AND EMMA'S ILLNESS

On June 15, 1828, Emma gave birth to the Smiths' firstborn son.[10] The baby was either stillborn or died shortly after birth and was buried in the cemetery situated just east of the Smiths' home.[11] The inscription on his headstone reads, "In Memory of An Infant Son of Joseph And Emma Smith Jun 15th 1828." The tragic event left Emma in poor health and spirits; she soon became deathly ill. Joseph's mother recalled that Emma felt "more like sinking with her infant into the mansion of the dead than remaining with her husband among the living."[12] Joseph and Emma were not alone in mourning the death of a beloved child, as months earlier, on January 29, 1828, Jesse and Mary Hale lost their two-and-a-half-year-old daughter, Nancy Hale. An epidemic may have passed through the Susquehanna Valley during this time, leaving tragedy and sorrow in Harmony.[13]

Chagrin and concern enveloped Joseph as he cared for his wife day after day. Sleeping proved to be a painful burden as thoughts of his wife's grave condition preoccupied him. Two distressing weeks passed and Emma's condition began to improve. Seeing his wife regain her health boosted Joseph's spirits, and his thoughts reluctantly turned to Martin and the 116-page manuscript.[14] Three weeks had passed since Martin had left with the manuscript, and Joseph had not received word from him.[15] Joseph did not dwell on the matter, for it sorely troubled him, and he would not think of leaving his wife in her poor condition. More days passed, and noticing Joseph's concern, Emma raised the subject of the manuscript and encouraged Joseph to seek out Martin. She said, "Go and enquire into the reason of his not writing or sending any word back since he left us."[16] Joseph adamantly objected. But after seeing Emma so cheerful and knowing that her mother would care for her, and after even more persuasion from Emma, Joseph consented to go after Martin. Joseph boarded the next stagecoach to Manchester.[17]

The gravestone of the Smiths' first son. The original gravestone was encased in grey ceramic cement to preserve it. Photograph by the author.

The Stagecoach to Manchester

Only one passenger traveled on the stagecoach with Joseph that day. Traveling by stagecoach was rather uncomfortable and strenuous. Although stagecoaches were equipped with strong leather springs for the comfort of passengers, jolts still rattled the carriage at each bump and turn.[18] An English woman described her trip on a stagecoach through Pennsylvania in 1830 as follows: "We were tossed about like a few potatoes in a wheelbarrow. Our knees, elbows, and heads required too much care for their protection to allow us leeway to look out of the windows."[19] Stages or "stations" were situated every fifteen miles on the route that passed in front of the Hales' home, allowing the horses to be changed often.[20] By 1830 the standard speed for a stagecoach was only ten miles an hour and the average fare was six cents a mile, to be paid in advance with cash.[21]

As Joseph sat in the stagecoach, he could not stop thinking about Martin and the 116-page manuscript. He deeply regretted permitting Martin to take the manuscript and feared its loss.[22] The loss troubled his spirit and soul. And although he was fatigued and hungry, sleep fled from his eyes and his desire for food abated, for he felt he had acted gravely improper.[23] After observing Joseph for a considerable time, the passenger in the coach perceived that Joseph was indeed troubled and mired in sadness and affliction.[24] The man offered his assistance, but Joseph declined and thanked him kindly. Joseph briefly mentioned the death of his first and only child and that he had left his wife in a sick condition and feared she would not be alive when he returned.[25] He did not eat or sleep during the entire ride.[26]

When Joseph was preparing to leave the stage at 10 p.m. that night, he told the passenger that he had another twenty miles to go on foot to reach his parents' home.[27] The stranger would not allow Joseph to go alone and said, "I feel to sympathize with you, and I fear that your constitution, which is evidently not strong, will be inadequate to support you. You will be in danger of falling asleep in the forest, and of meeting with some awful disaster."[28] At Joseph's stop, the stranger descended the stagecoach to accompany him for the twenty-mile trek. They proceeded at a gentle pace toward Manchester to accommodate Joseph's weakened condition. As they approached sixteen miles, Joseph's strength completely failed and exhaustion overcame him. The stranger grasped Joseph by the waist and supported him for the last four miles. Joseph stumbled along in a state of slumber and fatigue.[29] When they reached Joseph's parents' home, it was nearly daylight. Joseph likely would not have made the journey without the stranger's assistance.

The Manuscript Lost

Joseph and the stranger ate breakfast, after which the stranger quickly left on his way. Not a moment passed before Joseph requested to see Martin. The Smith family then waited, the table set, to receive Martin for breakfast at 8 a.m. They continued to wait until 9:00, but Martin still had not come—10:00, 11:00, and still no sign of him. Finally, at 12:30 p.m., Martin came within sight of the Smiths' home, walking slowly with his eyes fixed on the ground. At the gate in the yard, he stopped and, instead of passing through, climbed on the fence and sat there for some time with his hat over his eyes. Martin eventually entered the home and sat down at the table but could not eat. Hyrum Smith asked, "Martin, why do you not eat; are you sick?" Martin pressed his hands upon his temples and cried out in a tone of deep anguish, "Oh, I have lost my soul! I have lost my soul!"[30]

Joseph sprang from the table, exclaiming, "Martin, have you lost the manuscript?" "Yes, it is gone," replied Martin, "and I know not where." Clenching his hands, Joseph responded, "All is lost! all is lost! What shall I do? I have sinned—it is I who tempted the wrath of God. I should have been satisfied with the first answer which I received from the Lord; for he told me that it was not safe to let the writing go out of my possession." Joseph cried and groaned, continually pacing back and forth across the floor until that evening when he finally agreed to eat some food. Joseph determined that he would go and search for the manuscript himself. "And how shall I appear before the Lord? Of what rebuke am I not worthy from the angel of the Most High," he clamored. Martin, however, dissuaded Joseph from searching further: "I have ripped open beds and pillows; and I know it is not there."[31]

The following morning, Joseph departed Manchester under a cloud of sadness and disappointment. He thought to himself, "Must I return to my wife with such a tale as this? I dare not do it, lest I should kill her at once." His mother wrote, "We parted with heavy hearts, for it now appeared that all which we had so fondly antici-pated, and which had been the source of so much secret gratification, had in a moment fled, and fled forever." When Joseph delivered the news to Emma, she was undoubtedly disappointed because she had also sacrificed to translate the manuscript and was fully engaged in God's work.[32]

Although it remains unclear what actually happened to the manuscript, Martin later explained his view of the events surrounding the disappearance of the manuscript. Soon after arriving in Palmyra with the manuscript, Martin showed it to his wife and family.[33] His wife, Lucy, was so pleased with the manuscript that she permitted Martin to lock it up in her own set of drawers, which was a special favor to him. Soon thereafter, a close friend of Martin's visited. They discussed the manuscript at length, and the friend earnestly desired to see it. Notwithstanding Joseph's cautions and his own covenant with Joseph, Martin deeply desired to show the manuscript to his friend. He hurriedly ran to his wife's cabinet to remove the manuscript from the drawer, but the key was missing. He tried for some time to locate the key but was unsuccessful. Anxious to gratify his friend's curiosity, Martin carelessly forced his way into the drawer, severely damaging it in the process. To his relief, the manuscript was still intact, and he showed it to his friend. Upon her return home, Lucy Harris saw the damaged dresser. As recorded by Joseph's mother, "When Mrs. Harris . . . discovered the marred state of her bureau, her irascible temper was excited to the utmost pitch, and an intolerable storm ensued, which descended with the greatest violence upon the devoted head of her husband."[34]

Having shown the manuscript to his friend and broken his promise, Martin was no longer bothered in exposing the manuscript. He showed the manuscript to any good friend who happened to call on him.[35] As time passed, Martin became careless with the manuscript and paid little attention to its security. When Joseph sent for him that day, Martin went immediately to the drawer where he kept it, but it was gone.[36] He never saw the manuscript again.

Martin and several others suspect that Mrs. Harris took the manuscript from the drawer with the purpose of obtaining another translation that differed from the original.[37] Mrs. Eliza Winters Squires, an intimate friend of Emma Smith's, said that "Mrs. Harris destroyed about one hundred pages of her husband's manuscript, and that Joseph dare not attempt another translation of it for fear that it would not conform with the first translation."[38] Joseph's mother said, "There is no doubt but Mrs. Harris took it from the drawer, with the view of retaining it until another translation should be given, then to alter the original translation, for the purpose of showing a discrepancy between them and thus make the whole appear to be a deception."[39]

Martin's carelessness with the manuscript rendered him unfit to serve as Joseph's scribe, but no bitter feelings came between Joseph and Martin because of it. Joseph and his family valued their relationship with Martin and were grateful for his contributions to the work.[40] Martin is recognized as being the first man of any stature in Palmyra to give credit to the story of Joseph.[41]

HUMBLE AND PENITENT JOSEPH

As a consequence of Joseph's wearying the Lord in asking permission for Martin to take the manuscript, upon returning to Harmony in late July 1828, the Lord divested him of the Urim and Thummim and the plates.[42] Joseph straightaway humbled himself in mighty prayer, pouring out his soul to God for mercy and forgiveness. His repentance was deep and sincere. An angel soon appeared to him and gave him back the Urim and Thummim.[43] The angel told Joseph that he had transgressed the commandants and laws of God and "should not have feared men more than God," while reminding Joseph that God was merciful and that he was still "called to the work." The angel stated that the plates had been preserved so that the Lord's people might know His promises and believe the gospel of Jesus Christ in order to obtain salvation.[44] This is considered to be the first revelation recorded by Joseph.[45] While in the crucible of affliction, and in his humblest state, Joseph received inspiration from God. He was gaining his prophetic voice. From this point forward, he would more regularly receive official revelations for the Church.

After Joseph received this message from the angel, the Urim and Thummim and plates were again taken from him.[46] According to Joseph, his probationary period without these sacred objects lasted only "a few days," for when Joseph inquired of the Lord concerning the 116 pages of the lost manuscript, the Lord permanently returned to him the plates and Urim and Thummim.[47] Later in his life, Joseph formulated for himself the rule "When the Lord commands, do it."[48]

Following these tribulations, Joseph stopped translating and fo-cused on earning money to pay for his farm.[49] He was also visited and strengthened by family and close friends. Joseph was learning that he could not accomplish God's work alone—he had to rely on God and others. Working on the farm gave him time to reflect on his mission and Moroni's charge to translate the plates. Losing the translation of the Book of Lehi was a significant setback for him, and he probably wondered if God would allow him to continue.

During this time, Joseph bought a broad shovel, pocketbook, and pocketknife and slaughtered animals to stock up meat for the win-ter.[50] His purchases of the pocketbook and pocketknife suggest he was intent on writing and knew he had to find a way to translate the plates.[51] Joseph also used this time to dig a well, which required him to hire help to dig the hole and border it with stones.[52] This likely put him in debt, and over the next few months he performed odd jobs in order to the pay the debt. On October 18, 1828, he threshed buck-wheat for a neighbor for half a day; on October 24, he used his oxen to plow one of his neighbor's fields; and on November 5, he worked for two days husking corn for a neighbor.[53]

Joseph only managed to translate a few pages that winter.[54] Being without a steady scribe and without time to write inhibited his prog-ress.[55] Emma was willing to serve as Joseph's scribe, as she had done previously, but with the demands of work around the house, she had little time to help.[56] The Hales were opposed to helping with the trans-lation, except for Reuben, who could write only occasionally.[57] And Joseph's brother Samuel, who provided limited assistance as a scribe, was occupied with other matters.[58] A permanent scribe was needed.[59]

JOSEPH'S PARENTS VISIT, AND JOSEPH SMITH SR. IS CALLED TO THE WORK

Concerned after not hearing from their son for two months, Joseph's parents traveled to Harmony in September 1828.[60] While there, they became acquainted with the Hales. Joseph's mother wrote of the Hales, "They were an intelligent and highly respectable family. They were pleasantly situated, and lived in good style, in the town of Harmony, on the Susquehanna river, within a short distance of the place where Joseph resided."[61] Lucy was particularly impressed by the

Hales' frame home, describing it as a "mansion" with every "convenient appendage necessary."[62] Joseph's parents' visit in Harmony lasted at least three months, after which they returned to Palmyra.[63] Lucy remarked, "The time of our visit with them we passed very agreeably, and we returned home relieved of a burden which was almost insupportable, and our present joy far overbalanced all our former grief."[64]

During his stay in Harmony, Joseph Smith Sr. asked to know by revelation the will of the Lord concerning his role in the work. The Lord responded that the people were prepared to hear the gospel of Jesus Christ, and He called Joseph Smith Sr. to be a missionary. The Lord also revealed the qualities required to be a missionary, which include "faith, hope, charity and love, . . . temperance, patience, . . . humility, diligence" (Doctrine and Covenants 4:5–6).[65] When Joseph Smith Sr. returned to Palmyra, this revelation may have prompted him to freely share the details of Joseph's task to translate the plates with a local schoolteacher named Oliver Cowdery, who would later serve as the permanent scribe for the translation of the Book of Mormon.[66]

JOSEPH KNIGHT SR. PROVIDES ASSISTANCE

Through the winter of 1828–1829, Joseph Knight Sr. graciously supported and encouraged Joseph and Emma. Joseph and Emma had few provisions that winter and were in desperate need of assistance. Joseph had little means to work, and his father-in-law may not have been willing to provide any further assistance. Joseph and Emma decided to visit Joseph Knight Sr., who recalled, "Now he Could not translate But little Being poor and nobody to write for him But his wife and she Could not do much and take Care of her house and he Being poor and no means to live But work."[67] Joseph Knight Sr. provided some assistance that included "some little provisions and some few things of the store, [like] a pair of shoes and three dollars in money."[68] Joseph was at least able to earn three dollars in early December by working for a neighbor.[69]

In January 1829 Joseph Smith Sr. and Joseph's brother, Samuel, traveled to Harmony. On their way, they stopped to see Joseph Knight Sr., who took them by sleigh to see Joseph and Emma. Joseph Knight Sr. stayed the night in Harmony and in the morning gave Joseph some money to buy paper for translation and gave Joseph Smith Sr. a half-dollar.[70] Joseph could not have continued the Lord's work without Joseph Knight Sr.'s assistance. Joseph also chopped wood and performed other similar tasks to earn money. Samuel Smith did not return to Palmyra with his father but remained in Harmony with Joseph during the spring and helped him work on his property so Joseph could focus on completing the translation.[71]

In March, Joseph Knight Sr. and his wife traveled to Harmony and gave Joseph more money to buy paper to translate.[72] While Joseph Knight Sr. and his wife were in Harmony, Joseph spoke about the translation and some revelations he had received, which caused Joseph Knight Sr.'s wife to believe in Joseph's message. She remained faithful to the church her entire life.[73]

Meanwhile, back in Manchester, the Smiths with five of their younger children were forced to move back into their log house, which was already occupied by Hyrum and his wife.[74] False rumors of Joseph's work persisted in Palmyra and the persecution continued.

Martin Visits Harmony

Even though Martin Harris was undoubtedly disappointed in the disappearance of the Book of Lehi, he never lost interest in Joseph's work and again offered his support. In March 1829 the people in the Palmyra area began gathering testimony "against the Plates" in an effort to file a lawsuit against Joseph and put him and his father in jail.[75] Martin's wife, Lucy Harris, is believed to have been the source of the mounting opposition, as she traveled "from house to house making diligent enquiry at every house for miles where she had the least hope of gleaning" any information to undermine Joseph's credibility.[76]

Martin traveled to Harmony to see Joseph and Emma, for he "desired of the Lord to know whether Joseph, had, in his possession, the [plates]."[77] Martin may have wanted further assurance of the truthfulness of the plates as he faced constant opposition to the plates from his wife and others.[78] Martin said he was also concerned about the potential lawsuit that might be filed against Joseph in New York.[79] A man by the name of Thomas Rogers accompanied Martin for the journey. Rogers had heard of the plates and wanted to see if Joseph actually possessed them. Martin later learned that Rogers had pledged to give Lucy Harris one hundred dollars to verify the authenticity of the plates and had told Lucy Harris that he would cut off the covering of the plates with his knife.[80]

This may have been Martin's first contact with Joseph since the disappearance of the manuscript and may have been awkward.[81] While in Harmony, Martin again assisted as scribe in the translation of the plates.[82] As they translated hour after hour, day after day, they would become fatigued and go down to the river and exercise by skipping stones. While down at the river on one occasion, Martin found a stone like the ones used for translation. Before resuming translation, he replaced a seer stone with the stone he had found by the river. Martin recalled that Joseph remained silent, intently gazing into darkness, the usual sentences not appearing. Surprised, Joseph exclaimed, "Martin! What is the matter? All is as dark as Egypt!" Martin's expression on his face revealed the joke, and he admitted that he had replaced the seer stone with an ordinary stone to disprove those that disbelieved that Joseph was actually translating the record. When the ordinary stone was replaced with the seer stone, the translation resumed as usual.[83]

Since meeting Joseph and serving as scribe for the translation of the Book of Lehi, however, Martin had never seen the plates and thus desired to see them.[84] Showing the plates to another person would relieve Joseph of the heavy burden of being their sole witness. At the request of Martin, Joseph inquired of the Lord.[85]

The Lord responded that three persons would have the opportunity to witness the plates and testify of their authenticity to the world.[86] Martin was promised that he would be one of the Three Witnesses if he humbled himself and bowed down in mighty prayer and faith, requesting in sincerity of heart that the Lord allow him to see the plates.[87] Martin was further taught that *spiritual* manifestations convey the truth of Joseph's work, not the physical event of seeing the plates. Physically seeing the plates would not convince a person of the truth of Joseph's work if the person was not receptive to manifestations of the Spirit.[88] Although Martin was not permitted to view the plates during his visit to Harmony, he was overjoyed that he would eventually witness the gold plates.[89] Following his visit to Harmony, Martin departed for Palmyra by stagecoach with bright spirits and a burning testimony, freely sharing with the other passengers the story of the gold plates.[90]

Visits from his friends and close family provided Joseph much needed relief and comfort, but the gravity of his mission bore down upon him. Apparently Mr. Hale was disappointed when he learned from Joseph that only three persons would witness the plates.[91] Others may have been disappointed as well, including Nathaniel Lewis and Joshua McKune. This may have prompted Mr. Hale to withdraw his financial support of Joseph and Emma.[92] Joseph said, "We had become reduced in property and my wife's father was about to turn me out of doors and I had not where to go and I cried unto the Lord that he would provide for me to accomplish the work whereunto he had commanded me."[93] The Lord told Joseph to cease translating for the present time and wait until commanded to recommence the translation. The Lord promised that he would "provide means" whereby Joseph could "accomplish the thing" that the Lord commanded him to do.[94]

According to Joseph's mother, around this same time, in March 1829, Lucy Harris filed a civil lawsuit against Joseph in Lyons, New York.[95] Martin's agreement to pay for the Book of Mormon likely caused Lucy to bring the lawsuit. She believed that "the chief object which Joseph Smith had in view, was to defraud her husband out of all his property, and that she did not believe that Joseph Smith had ever been in possession of the gold plates which he talked so much about."[96] Deeply troubled by the lawsuit, Lucy Smith prayed on Joseph's behalf:

> Not being accustomed to lawsuits of this character, I trembled for the issue, for this was the first time a suit had ever been preferred before a court against any of my family. I retired to a secluded place, and poured out my whole soul in entreaties to God, for the safety of my son, and continued my supplication for some time; at length the spirit fell upon me so powerfully, that every foreboding of ill was entirely removed from my mind, and a voice spoke to me, saying, "not one hair of his head shall be harmed." I was satisfied. I arose, and repaired to the house. I had never before in my life experienced such happy moments.[97]

At the hearing, Lucy Harris submitted an affidavit alleging that Joseph had defrauded her husband out of his property. In addition to

Mrs. Harris' testimony, three other witnesses took the stand, claiming that Joseph sought to deceive people with his story of the gold plates.[98] In contradiction to his wife's testimony and the other witnesses, Martin boldly defended Joseph Smith's character and honesty, declaring:

> I can swear, that Joseph Smith never has got one dollar from me by persuasion since God made me. I did once, of my own free will and accord, put fifty dollars into his hands, in the presence of many witnesses, for the purpose of doing the work of the Lord. This, I can pointedly prove; and I can tell you, furthermore, that I have never seen in Joseph Smith, a disposition to take any man's money without giving him a reasonable compensation for the same in return. And as to the plates which he professes to have, gentlemen, if you do not believe it, but continue to resist the truth, it will one day be the means of damning your souls.[99]

The judge reportedly halted the hearing and asked that the written testimony be brought and placed in front of him. According to Joseph's mother, the judge tore the written testimony in pieces and "told them to go home about their business and trouble him no more with such ridiculous folly."[100] Notably, Lucy Harris chose to file this lawsuit in New York and not in Pennsylvania where Joseph was residing at the time.

NOTES

1. History, circa Summer 1832, 5, josephsmithpapers.org; Lucy Mack Smith, History, 1844–1845, book 7, 1, josephsmithpapers.org; Lucy Mack Smith, *Lucy's Book: A Critical Edition of Lucy Mack Smith's Family Memoir*, ed. Lavina Fielding Anderson (Salt Lake City, UT: Signature Books, 2001), 410 (manuscript version); Richard Lyman Bushman, *Joseph Smith: Rough Stone Rolling* (New York: Alfred A. Knopf, 2005), 66.

2. History, circa Summer 1832, 5, josephsmithpapers.org; History, circa June 1839–circa 1841 [Draft 2], 9, josephsmithpapers.org; B. H. Roberts, *A Comprehensive History of the Church of Jesus Christ of Latter-day Saints* (Salt Lake City, UT: Deseret News, 1948–57), 1:21.

3. Lucy Mack Smith, History, 1844–1845, book 7, 1, josephsmithpapers.org; Smith, *Lucy's Book*, 410 (manuscript version).

4. History, circa Summer 1832, 5, josephsmithpapers.org; History, circa June 1839–circa 1841 [Draft 2], 9, josephsmithpapers.org; Roberts, *History of the*

Church, 1:21; Lucy Mack Smith, History, 1844–1845, book 7, 1, josephsmith-papers.org; Smith, *Lucy's Book*, 410 (manuscript version).

5. History, circa Summer 1832, 6, josephsmithpapers.org; History, circa June 1839–circa 1841 [Draft 2], 9, josephsmithpapers.org; Roberts, *History of the Church*, 1:21; William Pilkington, *Autobiography and statements 1934–39*, MS 1041, fd. I, 16, Church History Library, Salt Lake City (spelling modernized); Black and Larry C. Porter, *Martin Harris: Uncompromising Witness of the Book of Mormon* (Provo, UT: Brigham Young University, 2018), 110.

6. History, circa Summer 1832, 6, josephsmithpapers.org; History, circa June 1839–circa 1841 [Draft 2], 9, josephsmithpapers.org; Roberts, *History of the Church*, 1:21; Lucy Mack Smith, History, 1844–1845, book 7, 1, josephsmith-papers.org; Smith, *Lucy's Book*, 410 (manuscript version).

7. History, 1838–1856, volume A-1 [23 December 1805–30 August 1834], 9, josephsmithpapers.org; Lucy Mack Smith, History, 1844–1845, book 7, 1, josephsmithpapers.org; Smith, *Lucy's Book*, 411 (manuscript version). It is noteworthy that Joseph's 1832 history indicates that Martin was only to show the manuscript to "four persons." History, circa Summer 1832, 6, josephsmithpapers.org.

8. History, circa Summer 1832, 6, josephsmithpapers.org; History, circa June 1839–circa 1841 [Draft 2], 9–10, josephsmithpapers.org; Roberts, *History of the Church*, 1:21; Lucy Mack Smith, History, 1844–1845, book 7, 1, josephsmithpapers.org; Smith, *Lucy's Book*, 411 (manuscript version).

9. Lucy Mack Smith, History, 1844–1845, book 7, 1, josephsmithpapers.org; Smith, *Lucy's Book*, 411 (manuscript version). Lucy states that Martin left with the 116 pages of manuscript in July, but Joseph recorded that the event took place in June. Most scholars agree with Joseph's recollection of the events. See Smith, *Lucy's Book*, 411, fn. 165; "Historical Introduction," Revelation, July 1828 [D&C 3], josephsmithpapers.org.

10. Lucy Mack Smith, History, 1844–1845, book 7, 1, josephsmithpapers.org; Smith, *Lucy's Book*, 412 (manuscript version). Historians have debated whether the Smiths' baby boy was given a name. Larry Porter has concluded that the Smiths' son was named Alvin based on credible evidence—the name "Alvin Smith" recorded next to the birth and death of this baby in the Smith family bible. LaMar C. Berrett and Larry C. Porter, *Sacred Places: A Comprehensive Guide to Early LDS Historical Sites: New York and Pennsylvania* (Salt Lake City, UT: Deseret Book, 2000), 2:264. But recently other historians have argued that the words "Alvin Smith" were recorded after the birth and death by someone other than Emma, and they concluded the boy did not receive a name. "Historical Introduction" to Revelation, July Revelation, July 1828 [D&C 3], fn. 6, josephsmithpapers.org.

11. Lucy Mack Smith, History, 1844–1845, book 7, 1, josephsmithpapers.org; Smith, *Lucy's Book*, 412 (manuscript version). Sophia Lewis, the Smiths' neigh-bor who stated she was present at the birth, said that the baby was "still born

and very much deformed," while Lucy Mack Smith, who was not present at the birth, seemed to suggest in her writings that the baby died shortly after birth. Compare Statement of Sophia Lewis, March 20, 1834, published in *The Susquehanna Register* (Montrose, PA), May 1, 1834; "Statement of Sophia Lewis," in E. D. Howe, *Mormonism Unvailed* (Painesville, OH: s.n., 1834), 263; Rhamanthus M. Stocker, *Centennial History of Susquehanna County, Pennsylvania*, 2nd ed. (Baltimore, MD: Regional Publishing Company, 1974), 269 with Lucy Mack Smith, History, 1844–1845, book 7, 1, josephsmithpapers.org; Smith, *Lucy's Book*, 412 (manuscript version).

12. Lucy Mack Smith, *Biographical Sketches of Joseph Smith the Prophet and His Progenitors for Many Generations* (Liverpool: S. W. Richards, 1853), 118; Smith, *Lucy's Book*, 412 (Pratt version); William G. Hartley, *Stand by My Servant Joseph: The Story of the Joseph Knight Family and the Restoration* (Salt Lake City, UT: Deseret Book, 2003), 47.

13. Mark Lyman Staker and Robin Scott Jensen, "New Details about Joseph and Emma Smith, the Hale Family, and the Book of Mormon," *BYU Studies Quarterly* 53, no. 3 (2014): 30 (expanded web version). In 1828, within a few months, several children were buried in the local Harmony cemetery, including Nancy Hale, Joseph and Emma's firstborn son, and the Smiths' neighbor's son. Mark L. Staker, "A Comfort unto My Servant, Joseph," in *Women of Faith in the Latter Days: Volume 1, 1775–1820*, ed. Richard E. Turley Jr. and Brittany A. Chapman (Salt Lake City, UT: Deseret Book, 2011), 343–362.

14. Lucy Mack Smith, History, 1844–1845, book 7, 2, josephsmithpapers.org; Smith, *Lucy's Book*, 412–13 (manuscript version).

15. Smith, *Biographical Sketches*, 118; Smith, *Lucy's Book*, 412–13 (Pratt version).

16. Lucy Mack Smith, History, 1844–1845, book 7, 2, josephsmithpapers.org; Smith, *Lucy's Book*, 413 (manuscript version).

17. Smith, *Biographical Sketches*, 118; Smith, *Lucy's Book*, 13 (Pratt version).

18. Larry E. Morris, "The Conversion of Oliver Cowdery," *Journal of Book of Mormon Studies* 16, no. 1. (Provo, UT: Maxwell Institute, 2007), 15.

19. Stevenson Whitcomb Fletcher, *Pennsylvania Agriculture and Country Life, 1640–1840*, 2nd ed. (Harrisburg, PA: Pennsylvania Historical and Museum Commission, 1971), 469.

20. Staker, "New Details," 21, quoting Rhamanthus M. Stocker, *Centennial History of Susquehanna County, Pennsylvania*, 2nd ed. (Baltimore, MD: Regional Publishing Company, 1974), 21.

21. Fletcher, *Pennsylvania Agriculture*, 468.

22. Smith, *Biographical Sketches*, 118–119; Smith, *Lucy's Book*, 413 (Pratt version). Joseph's experience on the stagecoach is told by his mother.

23. Smith, *Biographical Sketches*, 118–119; Smith, *Lucy's Book*, 413–14 (Pratt version).

24. Lucy Mack Smith, History, 1844–1845, book 7, 4, josephsmithpapers.org; Smith, *Lucy's Book*, 415 (manuscript version).

25. Smith, *Biographical Sketches*, 119; Smith, *Lucy's Book*, 415–16 (Pratt version).

26. Lucy Mack Smith, History, 1844–1845, book 7, 2, josephsmithpapers.org; Smith, *Lucy's Book*, 415 (manuscript version).

27. Smith, *Biographical Sketches*, 119; Smith, *Lucy's Book*, 415 (Pratt version).

28. Smith, *Biographical Sketches*, 119–20; Smith, *Lucy's Book*, 416 (Pratt version).

29. Lucy Mack Smith, History, 1844–1845, book 7, 5, josephsmithpapers.org; Smith, *Lucy's Book*, 416 (manuscript version).

30. Lucy Mack Smith, History, 1844–1845, book 7, 5, josephsmithpapers.org; Smith, *Biographical Sketches*, 120–21; Smith, *Lucy's Book*, 416–18 (manuscript and Pratt versions).

31. Lucy Mack Smith, History, 1844–1845, book 7, 6, josephsmithpapers.org; Smith, *Biographical Sketches*, 121; Smith, *Lucy's Book*, 418–19 (manuscript and Pratt versions).

32. Smith, *Biographical Sketches*, 122; Smith, *Lucy's Book*, 419–20 (Pratt version).

33. This portion of the story is told by Lucy Mack Smith, who may have had a slight prejudice against Lucy Harris.

34. Lucy Mack Smith, History, 1844–1845, book 7, 7–8, josephsmithpapers.org; Smith, *Biographical Sketches*, 123; Smith, *Lucy's Book*, 420–21 (manuscript and Pratt versions).

35. Smith, *Biographical Sketches*, 121; Smith, *Lucy's Book*, 421 (Pratt version).

36. Lucy Mack Smith, History, 1844–1845, book 7, 8, josephsmithpapers.org; Smith, *Lucy's Book*, 422 (manuscript version).

37. Lucy Mack Smith, History, 1844–1845, book 7, 8, josephsmithpapers.org; Smith, *Lucy's Book*, 422 (manuscript version); John A. Clark, *Gleanings by the Way* (Philadelphia: W. J. and J. K. Simon 1842), 247–48. Orsamus Turner noted, "With sacrilegious hands, she [Mrs. Harris] seized over an hundred of the manuscript pages of the new revelation, and burned or secreted them." *History of the Pioneer Settlement of Phelps and Gorham's Purchase, and Morris' Reserve* (Rochester, NY: William Alling, 1852), 215. Some scholars agree that Martin's wife played a central role in the disappearance of the manuscript. For example, see Susan Easton Black, *Who's Who in the Doctrine & Covenants* (Salt Lake City, UT: Deseret Book, 1997), 125.

38. Stocker, *Centennial History of Susquehanna County*, 556. Eliza Squires settled in Harmony, Pennsylvania, near the McKune Cemetery in 1825 and married in 1827. Stocker, 557. Emma apparently told Eliza about the gold plates.

39. Smith, *Biographical Sketches*, 123; Smith, *Lucy's Book*, 422 (Pratt version); Ivan J. Barrett, *Joseph Smith and the Restoration* (Provo, UT: Brigham Young University Press, 1970), 55. Joseph later explained in the Palmyra edition of

the Book of Mormon why he could not publish the lost manuscript, called the "Book of Lehi," if he were to translate it again:

"As many false reports have been circulated respecting the following work, and also many unlawful measures taken by evil designing persons to destroy me, and also the work, I would inform you that I translated, by the gift and power of God, and caused to be written, one hundred and sixteen pages, the which I took from the Book of Lehi, which was an account abridged from the plates of Lehi, by the hand of Mormon; which said account, some person or persons have stolen and kept from me, notwithstanding my utmost exertions to recover it again—and being commanded of the Lord that I should not translate the same over again, for Satan had put it into their hearts to tempt the Lord their God, by altering the words, that they did read contrary from that which I translated and caused to be written; and if I should bring forth the same words again, or, in other words, if I should translate the same over again, they would publish that which they had stolen, and Satan would stir up the hearts of this generation, that they might not receive this work." Preface to Book of Mormon, circa August 1829, 1, josephsmithpapers.org; Barrett, *Joseph Smith and the Restoration*, 57.

40. Lucy Mack Smith, History, 1844–1845, book 8, 10, josephsmithpapers.org; Smith, *Lucy's Book*, 451 (manuscript version).

41. James G. Bennett, "History of Mormonism" *Hillborough Gazette* (Ohio), Oct. 29, 1831.

42. "Historical Introduction," Revelation, July 1828 [D&C 3], josephsmithpapers.org; Doctrine and Covenants 3:3–8, 10; Smith, *Biographical Sketches*, 125; Smith, *Lucy's Book*, 424–25 (Pratt version).

43. History, circa June 1839–circa 1841 [Draft 2], 10, josephsmithpapers.org; Roberts, *History of the Church*, 1:21–22. It is unclear whether the angel also gave Joseph back the gold plates at this time or at another time. In any event, the plates were returned to him at some point because following this revelation, Joseph states that the gold plates were again taken from him. History, circa June 1839–circa 1841 [Draft 2], 11, josephsmithpapers.org.

44. Revelation, July 1828 [D&C 3], josephsmithpapers.org; Doctrine and Covenants 3:3–8, 10.

45. Bushman, *Joseph Smith: Rough Stone Rolling*, 68.

46. History, circa June 1839–circa 1841 [Draft 2], 11, josephsmithpapers.org; Roberts, *History of the Church*, 1:23.

47. History, circa June 1839–circa 1841 [Draft 2], 11, josephsmithpapers.org; Roberts, *History of the Church*, 1:23. According to Lucy Mack Smith, however, it was not until September 22, 1828, that an angel returned the plates to Joseph. Smith, *Biographical Sketches*, 126; Smith, *Lucy's Book*, 428 (Pratt version). Because of these conflicting accounts, the exact timing of the angel returning the plates and Urim and Thummim is uncertain. See Staker and Jensen, "New Details," 32, fn. 105.

48. Roberts, *History of the Church*, 2:170.

49. History, circa June 1839–circa 1841 [Draft 2], 11, josephsmithpapers.org; Roberts, *History of the Church*, 1:28.

50. Staker and Jensen, "New Details," 32–33, 35.

51. Staker and Jensen, 34.

52. Staker and Jensen, 34–35. Joseph hired someone to help him dig the well from September 8 to September 17, but they took a break from digging on Sunday, September 14. Staker and Jensen, 34.

53. Staker and Jensen, 36.

54. Revelation, Harmony, PA, Mar. 1829, Newel K. Whitney, Papers, Brigham Young University, Provo, UT, 2–3; Doctrine and Covenants 5:30; "Book of Mormon Translation By Joseph Smith," *Encyclopedia of Mormonism*, ed. Daniel H. Ludlow (New York: Macmillan, 1992), 1:210.

55. Wayne Culter Gunnell, "Martin Harris—Witness and Benefactor to the Book of Mormon" (master's thesis, Brigham Young University, 1955), 37–38; Larry C. Porter, *A Study of the Origins of the Church of Jesus Christ of Latter-day Saints in the States of New York and Pennsylvania, 1816–1831* (Provo, UT: BYU Studies, 2000), 57.

56. Lucy Mack Smith, History, 1844–1845, book 8, 4, josephsmithpapers.org; Smith, *Lucy's Book*, 438 (manuscript version). "An examination of the fragmentary original manuscript shows no evidence of Emma's handwriting, which indicates that very little translation work was actually accomplished during this time." John W. Welch and Tim Rathbone, "How Long Did It Take to Translate the Book of Mormon?," in *Reexploring the Book of Mormon* (Provo, UT: F.A.R.M.S., 1992), 46.

57. "Joseph Knight Sr., Reminiscences," no date, Church History Library, Salt Lake City; Joseph Knight Sr., "Joseph Knight's Recollection of Early Mormon History," ed. Dean Jessee, *BYU Studies* 17, no. 1 (1976): 32.

58. Emma noted that she and Samuel both served as scribe for Joseph. Joseph Smith III, "Last Testimony of Sister Emma," *Saints' Herald* 26 no. 19 (Oct. 1, 1879), 289–90.

59. Larry C. Porter, "Joseph Smith's Susquehanna Years," *Ensign*, Feb. 2001, 45. Reuben Hale, in commenting on the translation process, stated that Joseph Smith's hat "was a very large one, and what is commonly called a 'stove-pipe.' The hat was on the table by the window and the stone in the bottom or rather in the top of the hat. Smith would bend over the hat with his face buried in it so that no light could enter it, and thus dictate to the scribe what he should write." Stocker, *Centennial History of Susquehanna County*, 556.

60. History, circa June 1839–circa 1841 [Draft 2], 11, josephsmithpapers.org; Roberts, *History of the Church*, 1:28.

61. Smith, *Biographical Sketches*, 127; Smith, *Lucy's Book*, 430 (Pratt version); Porter, "Joseph Smith's Susquehanna Years," 45.

62. Smith, *Biographical Sketches*, 127; Smith, *Lucy's Book*, 430 (Pratt version); Mark Lyman Staker, "Isaac and Elizabeth Hale in Their Endless Mountain Home," *Mormon Historical Studies* 15, no. 2 (2014): 3.

63. Porter, "Joseph Smith's Susquehanna Years," 45. Upon returning to Palmyra, Joseph Smith Sr. and Lucy found their children Sophronia and Samuel to be ill. Morris, "The Conversion of Oliver Cowdery," 6.

64. Smith, *Biographical Sketches*, 127; Smith, *Lucy's Book*, 430 (Pratt version).

65. Revelation, Harmony, PA, to Joseph Smith Sr., [Feb.] 1829, Edward Partridge, Papers, Church History Library, Salt Lake City; Doctrine and Covenants 4:5–6. Joseph Fielding Smith stated, "This revelation is very short . . . but it contains sufficient counsel and instruction for a life-time of study. No one has yet mastered it. It was not intended as a personal revelation to Joseph Smith [Sr.], but to be of benefit to all who desire to embark in the service of God. . . . Perhaps there is no other revelation in all our scriptures that embodies great instruction pertaining to the manner of qualification of members of the Church for the service of God, and in such condensed form than this revelation. It is as broad, as high, and as deep as eternity. No elder of the Church is qualified to teach in the Church, or carry the message of Salvation to the world, until he has absorbed, in part at least, this heaven-sent instruction." Joseph Fielding Smith, *Church History and Modern Revelation* (Salt Lake City, UT: Deseret Book, 1946), 1:35.

66. "Historical Introduction," Revelation, February 1829 [D&C 4], josephsmith-papers.org.

67. "Joseph Knight Sr., Reminiscences"; Knight, "Joseph Knight's Recollection," 35; Staker and Jensen, "New Details," 36. On December 4, 1828, Joseph purchased a comb that may have been intended as a gift for his wife Emma on December 6, the day that many settlers at the time celebrated Christmas. Staker and Jensen, 37–39.

68. "Joseph Knight Sr., Reminiscences"; Knight, "Joseph Knight's Recollection," 36; Hartley, *Stand by My Servant Joseph*, 38.

69. Staker and Jensen, "New Details," 36.

70. "Joseph Knight Sr., Reminiscences"; Knight, "Joseph Knight's Recollection," 36; Hartley, *Stand by My Servant Joseph*, 38.

71. Staker and Jensen, "New Details," 39.

72. "Joseph Knight Sr., Reminiscences"; Knight, "Joseph Knight's Recollection," 36.

73. "Joseph Knight Sr., Reminiscences"; Knight, "Joseph Knight's Recollection," 36; Hartley, *Stand by My Servant Joseph*, 46. Joseph Knight Sr. may have visited Joseph in Harmony and provided assistance at other times between

January and May 1829. "Historical Introduction," Revelation, May 1829–B [D&C 12], josephsmithpapers.org.

74. In early 1829 the Smith family was forced to move back into the log cabin they had occupied previously. The cabin was barely able to hold one family, let alone eleven people. Occupants of the home at the time were Joseph and Lucy and their five children (Samuel, age 20; William, 17; Katharine, 15; Don Carlos, 12; and Lucy, 7); Hyrum and his wife, Jerusha, and their eighteen-month-old daughter, Lovina; and Oliver. Hyrum and Jerusha had lived in the cabin since their marriage in 1826. Morris, "The Conversion of Oliver Cowdery," 12; Lucy Mack Smith, History, 1844–1845, book 8, 3, josephsmithpapers.org; Smith, *Lucy's Book*, 437 (manuscript version); Bushman, *Joseph Smith: Rough Stone Rolling*, 47.

75. "Testimony of Martin Harris," Sept. 4, 1870, 4, Edward Stevenson Collection, Church History Library, Salt Lake City; "Historical Introduction," Revelation, March 1829 [D&C 5], josephsmithpapers.org.

76. Lucy Mack Smith, History, 1844–1845, book 8, 5, josephsmithpapers.org; Smith, *Lucy's Book*, 441 (manuscript version).

77. *A Book of Commandments, for the Government of the Church of Christ, Organized according to Law, on the 6th of April, 1830* (Zion [Independence], MO: W. W. Phelps & Co., 1833), 10, Church History Library, Salt Lake City; Gunnell, "Martin Harris," 29–30; Porter, *Origins of the Church*, 57.

78. Statement of Isaac Hale, Mar. 20, 1834, published in *The Susquehanna Register* (Montrose, PA), May 1, 1834; "Historical Introduction," Revelation, March 1829 [D&C 5], josephsmithpapers.org.

79. "Testimony of Martin Harris."

80. "Testimony of Martin Harris"; Morris, "The Conversion of Oliver Cowdery," 14; "Historical Introduction," Revelation, March 1829 [D&C 5], josephsmithpapers.org. The Joseph Smith Papers historians believe that "Rogers" is "Joseph Rogers" living in Phelpstown, New York, during the time period, who provided negative accounts of the Smiths and may have been the Rogers mentioned by Martin Harris. "Historical Introduction," Revelation, March 1829 [D&C 5], josephsmithpapers.org.

81. "Historical Introduction," Revelation, March 1829 [D&C 5], josephsmithpapers.org. A "temporary rift" may have formed between Joseph and Martin. Michael Hubbard MacKay and Gerrit J. Dirkmaat, *From Darkness unto Light: Joseph Smith's Translation and Publication of the Book of Mormon* (Provo, UT: BYU Religious Studies Center, 2015), 105.

82. Isaac Hale stated that Martin Harris wrote for Joseph around March 1829. Statement of Isaac Hale, in *The Susquehanna Register*; Edward Stevenson, Sandusky, OH, to Franklin D. Richards, Jan. 10, 1887, in Stevenson, Journal, Oct. 1886–Mar. 1887, 106–113; "Historical Introduction," Revelation, February 1829 [D&C 4], fn. 4, josephsmithpapers.org.

83. *Monday Evening News* (Salt Lake City, Utah Territory), Sept. 5, 1870; "The Three Witnesses to the Book of Mormon," *The Latter-Day Saints' Millennial Star* 48 (June 21, 1886): 390. Historians have noted that this experience may have occurred in the summer of 1828, but it is more likely that it occurred during Martin's visit in March 1829 because Joseph was using a seer stone at this time and not the spectacles, which Joseph was likely using in the summer of 1828. MacKay and Dirkmaat, *From Darkness unto Light*, 111, fn. 22.

84. Gunnell, "Martin Harris," 29–30; Porter, *Origins of the Church*, 57.

85. Revelation, March 1829 [D&C 5], 1, josephsmithpapers.org; Doctrine and Covenants 5:1.

86. Revelation, March 1829 [D&C 5], 1, josephsmithpapers.org; Doctrine and Covenants 5:11, 15.

87. Revelation, March 1829 [D&C 5], 2, josephsmithpapers.org; Doctrine and Covenants 5:24, 28; "Historical Introduction," Revelation, March 1829 [D&C 5], josephsmithpapers.org.

88. Revelation, March 1829 [D&C 5], 1, josephsmithpapers.org; Doctrine and Covenants 5:7, 15; "Historical Introduction," Revelation, March 1829 [D&C 5], josephsmithpapers.org.

89. History, circa June 1839–circa 1841 [Draft 2], 11–13, josephsmithpapers.org; Roberts, *History of the Church*, 1:28–31; Revelation, March 1829 [D&C 5], josephsmithpapers.org; Doctrine and Covenants 5.

90. William S. Sayre, Bainbridge, NY, to James T. Cobb, [Salt Lake City, Utah Territory], Aug. 31, 1878, in Theodore Albert Schroeder Papers, 1845–1901, microfilm ([Madison, WI]: State Historical Society of Wisconsin, Division of Archives and Manuscripts, [ca. 1987]), Church History Library, Salt Lake City; Morris, "The Conversion of Oliver Cowdery," 15.

91. "Isaac Hale, Affidavit," Mar. 20, 1834, in Howe, *Mormonism Unvailed*, 263; Mark Lyman Staker, "Joseph and Emma Smith's Susquehanna Home: Expanding Mormonism's First Headquarters," *Mormon Historical Studies* 16, no. 2 (Fall 2015): 69.

92. Staker, "Joseph and Emma Smith's Susquehanna Home," 96.

93. History, circa Summer 1832, 6, josephsmithpapers.org; Dean C. Jessee, comp. and ed., *The Personal Writings of Joseph Smith* (Salt Lake City, UT: Deseret Book, 2002), 8. Since Joseph did not own his home, he was dependent on Mr. Hale's generosity.

94. Revelation, March 1829 [D&C 5], 3, josephsmithpapers.org; Doctrine and Covenants 5:34. In March 1829 Joseph was able to pay off his last dollar of debt to David Hale and close his account at David's local store. Staker and Jensen, "New Details," 39.

95. Lucy Mack Smith, History, 1844–1845, book 8, 5, josephsmithpapers.org; Smith, *Lucy's Book*, 441 (manuscript version); Morris, "The Conversion of Oliver Cowdery," 13. No written account of the proceeding has been found.

"Historical Introduction," Revelation, March 1829 [D&C 5], josephsmith-papers.org. The account of the hearing related in this text is derived from the journal of Joseph's mother. Although Lucy Smith states that the trial took place in August 1829, it is believed that this hearing occurred in March 1829. As historian Larry Morris shows, March 1829 coincides with Samuel's return to Harmony in the spring of 1829, and this is the date provided by Martin in his testimony. Morris, "The Conversion of Oliver Cowdery," 82, fn. 50.

96. Smith, *Biographical Sketches*, 132; Smith, *Lucy's Book*, 441 (Pratt version).

97. Smith, *Biographical Sketches*, 133; Smith, *Lucy's Book*, 442–43 (Pratt version).

98. Lucy Mack Smith, History, 1844–1845, book 8, 6–7, josephsmithpapers.org; Smith, *Lucy's Book*, 443–44 (manuscript version). "The 1st Witness testified that Joseph Smith told him that the box which he had contained nothing but sand and he only said it was gold plates to deceive the people. 2nd Witness swore that Joseph Smith told upon a certain occasion that it was nothing but a box of lead and he was determined to use it as he saw fit. 3rd Witness declared under oath that he inquired of Joseph Smith what he had in that box and Joseph told him that there was nothing in the box saying I have made fools of the whole of you and all I want is to get Martin Harris's money away from. Witness also stated that Joseph had already got $200 or $300 from Martin by his persuasion." Lucy Mack Smith, History, 1844–1845, book 8, 6–7, josephsmithpapers.org; Smith, *Lucy's Book*, 443–44 (manuscript version); Morris, "The Conversion of Oliver Cowdery," 13.

99. Smith, *Biographical Sketches*, 134; Smith, *Lucy's Book*, 445 (Pratt version); Morris, "The Conversion of Oliver Cowdery," 13; Susan Easton Black and Larry C. Porter, "For the Sum of Three Thousand Dollars," *Journal of Book of Mormon Studies* 14, no. 2 (2005): 8. Apparently Lucy Smith was not aware of the lawsuit brought by Peter Bridgeman against Joseph for being a "disorderly person" in 1826.

100. Lucy Mack Smith, History, 1844–1845, book 8, 7, josephsmithpapers.org; Smith, *Lucy's Book*, 445 (manuscript version); Morris, "The Conversion of Oliver Cowdery," 13. In 1831 Martin and Lucy Harris separated.

CHAPTER 6

WILLIAM PENN'S "HOLY EXPERIMENT"

———— ❧ ————

Often miracles follow trials. Chapters 6 and 7 recount William Penn and Joseph Smith fulfilling their divine mandates. William establishes the colony of Pennsylvania, and Joseph translates the majority of the Book of Mormon and receives the priesthood of God.

IN EARLY 1675 WILLIAM PENN WAS ASKED TO MEDIATE A DISPUTE between two Quakers over the proprietorship of a piece of land in West New Jersey. The next year, in the summer of 1676, William and about 150 others signed the West New Jersey Concessions, which established the structure of government and the fundamental laws for the colony of West New Jersey in the Americas. The West New Jersey Concessions included protections of Liberty of Conscience but were never enacted into law.[1] Many of the concessions ended up being included in the United States Constitution's Bill of Rights. William's role in establishing the colony of West New Jersey likely ignited his interest in the colonization of Pennsylvania.[2]

WILLIAM PURSUES HIS OWN COLONY

William decided to pursue his own colony and make Liberty of Conscious the hallmark of its laws and policies. In May 1680 he filed a petition with King Charles I for a land grant in America.[3] This began an arduous ten-month process of filings, hearings, arguments, bargaining, and bureaucratic hurdles.

William appeared before the Committee of Trade, the government body that considered petitions for land, to discuss his proposed province and its boundaries. He insisted on a deep water port to allow ships access to his colony.[4] Many interested parties voiced opinions and concerns, including Lord Baltimore, the proprietor of the colony of Maryland; Sir John Werden, the Duke of York; and the Bishop of London.[5] In March 1681, after "many waitings, watchings, solicitings, and disputes in council," William received a Royal Charter granting him proprietorship, "powers[,] and privileges" of his American colony—"Pennsylvania".[6] William wrote that "my God . . . has given it me through many difficulties [and] will I believe bless and make it the seed of a nation."[7]

William had proposed "New Wales" as the name of the colony. But the secretary of state, Leoline Jenkins, had objected to the name, and William had suggested his second choice, "Sylvania." Jenkins and his undersecretaries then added "Penn" to "Sylvania," which William had objected to because it was vain and unnecessary. King Charles ultimately insisted that the name "Penn" stay.[8]

William said he was inspired by God to establish the colony of Pennsylvania: "God hath made it a matter or religious exercise to my soul in getting and settling this Land. And it is the Lords and to his service do I dedicate my days in the help of his people here, I am not Idle, I have not time for it, but good is the Lord to me in it all, my health and strength are continued and renewed."[9] The Royal Charter gave William complete authority over Pennsylvania and specifically references furthering the love of "Christian Religion."[10] William wrote "that it hath pleased the Lord to dispose the mind of the King . . . to grant a country to me, in America," and committed that he would "secure all in their civil and religious rights."[11] He knew he had a divine mission in securing Pennsylvania as a land of free worship and Liberty of Conscience. He saw his colonialization of Pennsylvania as a similar mission to that of Moses, Lycurgus, Theseus, and Romulus.[12]

William described his aspirations for the colony of Pennsylvania. "I desire . . . that an example may be set up to the nations. There may be room there, though not here, for such a holy experiment."[13] William wrote letters encouraging others to settle in Pennsylvania.[14] He promised fair treatment in any disputes and ended his letter stating, "I am your friend. William Penn."[15]

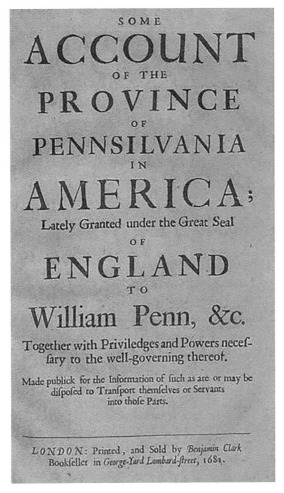

Title page of *Some Account of the Province of Pennsylvania,* by William Penn, 1681.

William's first promotional material of Pennsylvania was entitled *Some Account of the Province of Pennsylvania in America.* In it, he stated, "Since (by the good providence of God) a country in *America* is fallen to my lot, I thought it not less my duty than my honest interest to give some public notice of it to the world." William concluded his promotion by invoking the blessings of God: "I beseech Almighty God to direct us, that His blessing may attend our honest endeavor, and then the consequence of all our undertaking will turn to the glory of His great name, and the true happiness of us and our posterity. Amen."[16]

Pennsylvania's Founding Documents

After receiving his Royal Charter, William drafted the Fundamental Constitution of Pennsylvania, which he intended to be the law governing his colony. He never made the document public, and it was not passed into law, but it shows his initial thinking in creating his colony. The Fundamental Constitution of Pennsylvania emphatically declared the right to Liberty of Conscience:

> I do hereby declare . . . the First Fundamental of the government of my country, that every person that does or shall reside therein shall have and enjoy the free possession of his or her faith and exercise of worship towards God, in such way and manner as every person shall in conscience believe is most acceptable to God. . . . [Each person] shall be protected in the enjoyment of the aforesaid Christian liberty by the civil magistrate.[17]

William consulted with friends and colleagues as his thinking continued to evolve. In 1682 he published the first laws of Pennsylvania, which included documents called the 1682 Frame of Government of Pennsylvania and more than three dozen laws that were agreed on in England. The 1682 Frame of Government followed the Fundamental Constitution in guaranteeing Liberty of Conscience to those who publicly confessed a belief in God and behaved peacefully. It provided the following:

> That all persons living in this province, who confess and acknowledge the one Almighty and eternal God, to be the Creator, Upholder and Ruler of the world; and that hold themselves obliged in conscience to live peaceable and justly in civil society, shall, in no ways, be molested or prejudiced for their religious persuasion or practice, in matters of faith and worship, nor shall they be compelled, at any time, to frequent or maintain any religious worship, place or ministry whatever.[18]

The May 1682 Frame reflected William's firm commitment to suppressing vice in the colony to promote Liberty of Conscience.[19] Vices were considered "offences against God" and undermined Liberty of Conscience. These vices included:

> Swearing, cursing, lying, prophane talking, drunkenness, drinking, of healths, obscene words, incest, sodomy, rapes, whoredom, fornication, and other uncleanness . . . all treasons, misprisions, murders, duels, felony, seditions, maims, forcible entries, and other violences, to the persons and estates of the inhabitants within the province; all prizes, stage-plays, cards, dice, May-games, gamesters, masques, revels, bull-battings, cock-fightings, bear-battings, and the like, which excite the people to rudeness, cruelty, looseness, and irreligion, shall be respectively discouraged, and severely punished.[20]

The May 1682 Frame further provided that "if any person shall abuse or deride any other for his or her different persuasion and practice in matters of religion such shall be looked upon as a disturber of the peace and punished accordingly."[21]

William enthusiastically prepared to sail to Pennsylvania. For the first half of 1682, he arranged his affairs, which required all his energy and mental capacity. By August 1682 he was prepared to make the two-month voyage to the new world. In mid-August he wrote one final time to each of his three young children. To his eldest son, Springett, William wrote, "Be good, learn to fear God, avoid evil, love thy book, be kind to thy brother and sister and God will bless thee and I will exceedingly love thee. Farewell dear child." To his daughter, Letitia, he wrote, "I dearly love thee, and would have thee sober, learn thy book, and love thy brothers. I will send thee a pretty book to learn in. The Lord bless thee and make a god woman of thee. Farewell." And to his son Billy, who was only seventeen months old, he wrote, "I love thee much, therefore be sober and quiet, and learn his book, I will send one, so the Lord bless thee. Amen."[22]

The Landing of William Penn from the *Welcome* at Uppland,
Pennsylvania, by Arnold Anderson, 1931.

WILLIAM SAILS FOR PENNSYLVANIA

On August 30, 1682, William sailed for Pennsylvania on the ship
the *Welcome*. William's journey across the Atlantic Ocean lasted eight
weeks; about thirty passengers and crew died from smallpox during
the passage.[23] On October 28, 1682, the *Welcome* landed in New
Castle, Delaware. The following day or the day after, on October 28
or 29, 1682, William Penn first set foot in Pennsylvania in Uppland,
which he renamed Chester.[24] William inspected his proposed capital city of Philadelphia and visited the neighboring colonies. In early
December he convened the first Pennsylvania Assembly in Chester,
Pennsylvania. The Chester Assembly approved a version of the May
1682 Frame of Government and called it the "Great Law," which established a stable foundation for Pennsylvania's representative government and promoted freedom of worship.[25] The Great Law provided
in its preamble, "Whereas the Glory of Almighty God and the Good
of Mankind is the Reason and End of Government and therefore
Government in it selfe is a Venerable ordinance of God and for as
much as it is principally desired and intended by the Proprietary and
Governor and the Freemen of the Province of Pennsylvania."[26]

The first chapter of the Great Law addressed Liberty of Conscience:

Almighty God being only Lord of Conscience Father of Lights & Spirits and the Author as well as Object of all divine Knowledge Faith and Worship who only can Enlighten the Mind and perswade and Convince the Understanding of People. . . . No Person now or at Any time hereafter Liveing in this Province who Shall Confess and acknowledge one Almighty God to be the Creatour . . . shall he or she at any time be Compelled to frequent or Maintaine any Religious Worshipp place or Ministry whatever Contrary to his or her mind but shall freely and fully Enjoy his or her Christian Liberty without any Interuption or reflection and if any Person shall abuse or deride any Other for his or her Diferant Perswasion and Practice in Matters of Religion Such shall be Lookt upon as a disturber of the Peace and be punished accordingly.[27]

William fell in love with Pennsylvania and wrote of its wonders and beauties in letters to England. He said in one letter, "The air, heat and cold resemble the heart of France; the soil good, the springs many and delightful. The fruits, roots, corn and flesh, as good as I have commonly eaten in Europe, I may say of most of them better. Strawberry's ripe in the woods in April, and in the last month peas, beans, cherrys and mulberries. Much black walnut, chestnut, Cyprus, or white cedar and mulberry are here. The sorts of fish in these parts are excellent and numerous."[28] In another letter, William described in eloquent detail the soil, air, water, seasons, and produce of Pennsylvania. He wrote, "[The] air is sweet and clear, the heavens serene, like the south parts of France, rarely overcast" and the "woods are adorned with lovely flowers, for color, greatness, figure, and variety. I have seen the gardens of London best stored with that sort of beauty." William included a map of the developing city of Philadelphia, a grid with public squares similar to London.[29]

Little time passed before William became aware of rumors in England concerning him and his colony—for example, that he was a Jesuit, that he had died, or that Maryland and Pennsylvania were engaged in armed conflict.[30] William perceived this as an effort to discredit him and destroy his ability to sell land and attract more settlers to Pennsylvania.[31]

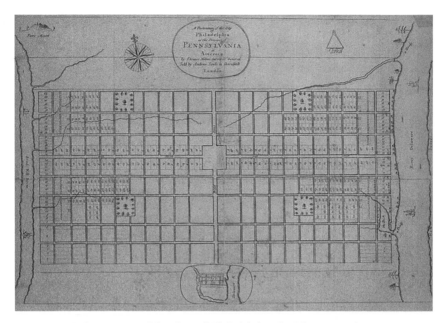

A Portraiture of the City of Philadelphia, by Thomas Holme,
1683. The Miriam and Ira D. Wallach Division of Art, Prints and
Photographs: Print Collection, The New York Public Library.

William managed the colony, which included mediating disputes between settlers, collecting taxes, running the government, and establishing relationships with neighboring colonies. A dispute quickly developed between William and Lord Baltimore over the southernmost counties of Pennsylvania. Lord Baltimore disputed William's authority over the lower counties, arguing that he had royal authority over the lands. Lord Baltimore also had frequent disputes with Virginia authorities over control of the Potomac River.[32]

William wanted to maintain control over the lower counties so that Pennsylvania could have direct access to the Atlantic Ocean. He and Lord Baltimore met in person in May 1683, and William told Lord Baltimore that he had "upon serious thoughts, determined with myself, to embark for England by the first convenience" if Lord Baltimore did not accept his proposals of compromise.[33] In June 1683 Lord Baltimore sent William a list of grievances and William responded.[34] Soon both sides were mailing letters directly to England, addressed to the Lord of Trade in England.[35] The dispute escalated in the fall of 1863 as Lord Baltimore undertook his own surveys, made claims to territories claimed by William, and harassed or threatened settlers who refused to acknowledge his authority.[36] By early 1684 several colonists from Delaware had rejected William's authority. Armed conflict between the colonies became a strong possibility, and William realized he had no alternative but to return to England and argue his position in person before the Lord of Trade in England.[37]

William Returns to England to Defend Pennsylvania

After living in Pennsylvania for almost two years, William agonized over leaving his new home of religious freedom. Before returning to England, he delivered what is recognized today as his "farewell" to Pennsylvania. He delivered the remarks from the ship *Endevour*:

> My love and my life is to you and with you, and no waters can quench it nor distance war it out or bring it to an end. I have been with you, cared over you, and served you with unfeigned love, and you are beloved of me and near to me beyond utterance. I bless you in the name and power of the Lord, and may God bless you with His righteousness, peace, and plenty all the land over. Oh, that you would eye Him in all, through all, and above all the works of your hands, and let it be your first care how you may glorify God in your undertakings. . . . But if any forget God and call not upon His name in Truth, He will pour out His plagues upon them and they shall know who it is that judges the children of men.[38]

William prayed for Philadelphia to "be kept from the evil that would overwhelm thee." His prayer continued: "My soul prays to God for thee that thou may stand in thy day of trial, that thy children may be blessed of the Lord and thy people saved by His power." He signed the speech "Your friend and lover in truth."[39]

On August 18, 1684, William departed for England, and when he arrived, he continued his dispute with Lord Baltimore. In early September 1685 William and Lord Baltimore appeared before the Lord of Trade. William presented his evidence that the lower counties rightfully belonged to him, and Baltimore protested. The Lord of Trade considered the evidence and ruled in favor of William, and on November 13, 1685, the decision was affirmed by the King of England.[40] But William's legal victory did not end the dispute, as Maryland officials continued to encourage residents of the lower counties to refute William's authority.[41]

William intended to return to his beloved Pennsylvania following his victory over Lord Baltimore, and in his letters he frequently expressed his desire to do so, but he knew that his presence in England was critical to keeping Pennsylvania's charter. His most important purpose was to preserve Liberty of Conscience, which he called "my old post and province."[42] But since William could not return to Pennsylvania, he continued to pursue better treatment for the Quakers in England.

In 1686, in an abrupt change, the English government began to recall colonial charters. William protested giving up Pennsylvania and willingly entered the chaos of English politics.[43] He wrote in the fall of 1686, "My being here has not only advanced the reputation of the province [of Pennsylvania], and again many great persons into our interest, but prevented a storm as to us, that is falling upon other colonies."[44]

William's relationship with those in power helped him serve the interest of Liberty of Conscience and preserve the Charter of Pennsylvania. In particular, William had a long history with King James, who was only ten years older than him and had served with his father in the Royal Navy against the Dutch. William also was well acquainted with Robert Spences from his days at Oxford and traveling Europe. Robert Spences was the secretary of state in England and president of the Privy Council. William's relationships also helped him secure rights for Quakers and protect them from unfair imprisonment and persecution. He recalled, "I have been an instrument to open the prison doors for our brethren all over the nation."[45]

William's life in England quickly presented several life-defining challenges as he continued his defense of Pennsylvania. In November 1688, William the Orange invaded England and ordered King James to leave London. On July 14, 1690, and February 5, 1691, proclamations were issued for William's arrest based on high treason for his contacts with King James.[46] He was imprisoned for one month following the first proclamation and was forced to go into hiding for much of the following three years.[47] William had intended to return to Pennsylvania and once again had to postpone his voyage: "I was going at the farthest, all things preparing . . . when this trouble broke out on me."[48] While in hiding, he continued to manage his colony, but in October 1691 rumors circulated that the government of Pennsylvania neglected its duties, and William was stripped of his Royal Charter.[49] He spent a long and difficult three years in hiding. Being a public outcast and losing his charter to Pennsylvania weighed upon his soul.

In November 1693 William was finally acquitted of any charges against him, and his name was cleared.[50] But in early 1694 his wife, Gulielma Springett Penn, became ill and suddenly passed away. William mourned her loss and with sadness wrote, "My extreme great affliction for the decease of my dear wife, makes me unfit to write much, whom the Great God took to himself, from the troubles of this exercising world." William suffered deep affliction, which he described as "incomparable loss."[51]

After grieving his wife's passing, William hesitantly turned back to petitioning the English government to return his colonial charter. Finally, in August 1694, after three years without his colony, Queen Mary restored William to his colony.[52] He then embarked on a two-year ministering tour around southwestern England, accompanied by his son, Springett.[53] As he was accustomed, in one city, William was apprehended while preaching and taken before the mayor of the city for questioning. According to William, he was ultimately "dismissed honorably."[54]

William Briefly Returns to Pennsylvania

In November 1694 William met Hannah Callowhill, a daughter of a prominent Quaker family from Bristol, and they began courting. A year and a half later, on March 15, 1696, William and Hannah were married in the Bristol. They promised "each to other to live together husband and wife in love and faithfulness according to gods holy ordinance until by death they shall be separated."[55] Hannah and William welcomed many children during their marriage, including four boys—John, Thomas, Richard, and Dennis—and two girls, Margaret and Hannah.[56] Shortly after his marriage to Hannah, William's oldest son Springett became fatally ill and died at Lewes Sussex on April 10, 1696. William deeply lamented the passing of his oldest son: "The Lord has taken from me my excellent child, to my deepest grief."[57]

In September 1699 William finally succeeded in arranging his affairs in England to permit him to return to Pennsylvania. William embarked on a voyage to Pennsylvania with his wife, Hannah, and his twenty-year-old daughter Letitia (from his previous marriage). The ocean crossing was "a long and sometimes rude passage" lasting thirteen weeks.[58] William quickly returned to directly managing the affairs of Pennsylvania. He resumed mediating quarrels and presiding over the governing body of Pennsylvania. One challenge was collecting taxes to run the government and pay for William's investment in Pennsylvania. Many early settlers did not have sufficient funds to pay, and collecting taxes proved challenging.

William maintained peaceful relations with local native Indian tribes and directly handled negotiations with them. Instead of treating them as inferior to him, he negotiated with them at arms length and treated them as equals—the Quaker way. In late April 1701 some forty natives—along with the chiefs of the Susquehannock, Shawnee, Piscataway, and Iroqois tribes—met with William in Philadelphia and signed a treaty of friendship and alliance.[59]

Treaty with the Indians. The Miriam and Ira D. Wallach Division of Art, Prints and Photographs: Print Collection, The New York Public Library.

During the year 1701 William became increasingly concerned about the Charter of Pennsylvania. Disparaging rumors circulated in England that he was neglecting his duties and that Pennsylvania was in dire condition. He wrote, "The necessity of my going [to England] makes it absolutely necessary that I have" supplies to return to England.[60] As one of his last official acts before departing from Pennsylvania, never to return again, William Penn approved a Charter of Privileges, listing privileges belonging to the people of Pennsylvania.

The Charter of Privileges remained in effect until the passing of Pennsylvania's Constitution of 1776. William prioritized the list of privileges in order of importance, listing the first privilege as "The Law Concerning Liberty of Conscience." The privilege explained that "no people can be truly happy though under the greatest enjoyment of civil liberties, if abridged of the freedom of their consciences as to their religious profession and worship."[61]

The first privilege protected Liberty of Conscience from molestations and prejudice and declared that those who acknowledged God would not "be compelled to frequent or maintain any religious worship, place or minister whatsoever, contrary to his or her mind, but shall freely and fully enjoy his or her Christian liberty in that respect, without any interruption or reflection." If any person persecuted another "for his or her different persuasion and practice in matter of religion, such person" was regarded "as a disturber of the peace and [would] be punished accordingly." The final sections of the charter separated the upper and lower counties if their deputies could not reach an agreement. A few years later, a formal separation was arranged, permanently separating Delaware (the lower counties) from Pennsylvania.[62]

After returning to England, William faced financial challenges and was encouraged to sell everything in his possession, including his Royal Charter. But William held tightly to his charter, hoping that maybe the discovery of silver mines in Pennsylvania would be the answer to his financial hardship.[63] Even when offered a generous settlement to settle his debts, William refused to sell Pennsylvania, stating, "For God was with me in seeking, getting, and settling of it, and there some that have not forsaken their first love to truth and me, whom I would live and die with."[64]

WILLIAM'S VISION OF RELIGIOUS FREEDOM IN PENNSYLVANIA

William's incessant efforts to secure political and religious liberty to those in Pennsylvania was a bright success and benefited thousands of religious minorities.[65] In Pennsylvania, mainstream religions such as the Quakers, Presbyterians, and Anglicans thrived, while smaller minority religions like the Reformed, Lutherans, Mennonites, Baptists, and others developed.[66] In Lancaster County in 1762, one Reverend observed faithful settlers of many faiths: "German Lutherans, Calvinists, Mennonites, Moravians, New Born, Dunkers, Presbyterians, Seceders, New Lights, Covenanters, Mountain Men, Brownists, Independents, Papists, Quakers, Jews and so forth!"[67] Although William was a Quaker and protected Quaker values, he also actively recruited other religious minorities to join the colony of Pennsylvania.[68] Each person was inherently equal in worth.[69]

William believed that religion unified the community against disorder and promoted common good.[70] Religion could inspire individuals to be virtuous, and it was in the government's interest to inspire individuals to virtuous living.[71] The state was neutral toward any denomination and was favorable to all churches because religious practice contributed to civil order and common good by fostering morality, obedience to the law, hard work, and other civic virtues.[72] William believed that church and state should support one another on common ground. He said, "The government should stand on its own legs, and the church upon hers. The legs of the civil government, is the civil interest of the government, which is that of all the people under it, so that the government is obliged to secure all, because all are for their own interested bound to secure it."[73]

William believed God should be a part of government because both civil and natural laws come from God.[74] But religious truth was entirely individual and personal and beyond the reach of the government.[75] According to William, God was "the only Lord of conscience, Father of lights and spirits, and the Author as well as object of all divine knowledge, faith and worship, who only doth enlighten the mind and persuade and convince the understandings of people."[76] Liberty of Conscience was inseparably connected to "Understanding, Reason, Judgment and Faith."[77]

William focused on common beliefs and morals and ignored less important issues such as sacraments, church government, and ritual upon which there could be no unity. For him, the essence of religion was reverence for scripture, faith in God and Christ, and virtuous or moral living.[78]

The main role of government was to protect property rights and Liberty of Conscience while suppressing vices.[79] According to William, Liberty of Conscience required virtuous living. He wrote, "For there can be no pretense of conscience to be drunk, to whore, to be voluptuous, to game, swear, curse, blaspheme, and profane" because these "impieties . . . lay the ax to the root of human society, and are the common enemies of mankind."[80] As mentioned previously, the behaviors that were considered offenses against God were "swearing, cursing, drunkenness, duels, stage-plays, card games, dice games, May-games, revels, bull-baitings, cock-fighting, bear-baitings," and other activities that "excite the people to rudeness, cruelty, looseness, and irreligion."[81]

A government that infringed on Liberty of Conscience "enslaves [its] fellow creatures, invades their right of liberty, and so perverts the whole order of nature."[82] Indeed, "a government that is run by corrupt men will produce a corrupt government, which inevitably will fail to protect the rights and liberties of its citizens."[83] William understood that government and laws depended upon good, honorable men. He wrote, "Governments, like clocks, go from the motion men give them; and as governments are made and moved by men, so by them they are ruined too; wherefore governments rather depend upon men, then men upon governments. Let men be good, and the government can't be bad; if it be ill, they will cure it. But if men be bad, let the government be never so good, and they will endeavor to warp and spoil it to their turn"[84]

NOTES

1. "The West New Jersey Concessions, August 1676," in *Papers of William Penn*, 1:388–408.

2. *The Papers of William Penn*, ed. Richard S. and Mary Maples Dunn (Philadelphia: University of Pennsylvania Press, 1981–1987), 1:38.

3. *Papers of William Penn*, 2:32–33.

4. *Papers of William Penn*, 2:256; "Sir John Werden to William Blathwayt, 20 November 1680," in *Papers of William Penn*, 2:48; Andrew R. Murphy, *William Penn: A Life* (New York: Oxford University Press, 2019), 138.

5. "Minute of the Committee of Trade, 22 January 1681," in *Papers of William Penn*, 2:57.

6. "To Robert Turner, 5 March 1681," in *Papers of William Penn*, 2:83 (spelling modernized); John A. Moretta, *William Penn and the Quaker Legacy* (New York: Pearson, 2007), 105.

7. "To Robert Turner," 2:83 (spelling modernized).

8. "To Robert Turner," 2:83 (spelling modernized); Murphy, *William Penn*, 138–39; Moretta, *William Penn*, 105.

9. "To John Alloway, 29 November 1683," in *Papers of William Penn*, 2:504.

10. Charter of the Province of Pennsylvania, Statutes of Large of Pennsylvania, 303, Appendix I.

11. "To Friends in the Countries, March 1681(?)," in *Papers of William Penn*, 3:139 (microfilm); Murphy, *William Penn: A Life*, 142.

12. *Some Account of the Province of Pennsylvania in America, Lately Granted under the Great Seal of England to William Penn* [. . .] (London: Benjamin Clark, 1681), Historical Society of Pennsylvania, Philadelphia; Jean R. Soderlund, *William Penn and the Founding of Pennsylvania, 1680–1684: A Document History* (Philadelphia: University of Pennsylvania Press, 1983), 59.

13. "To James Harrison, 26 August 1681," in *Papers of William Penn*, 2:108.

14. "To the Kings of the Indians," in *Papers of William Penn*, 2:128–129; "To the Emperor of Canada, 21 June 1682," in *Papers of William Penn*, 2:261.

15. "To the Kings of the Indians," 2:128–129.

16. *Some Account of the Province of Pennsylvania.*

17. The Fundamental Constitutions of Pennsylvania, William Penn [summer 1681?], Historical Society of Pennsylvania, Philadelphia.

18. "The Frame of the Government of the Province of Pennsylvania in America [. . .]" (1682), Historical Society of Pennsylvania.

19. "Frame of Government," XXXV; Murphy, *William Penn: A Life*, 150–151.

20. "Frame of Government," XXXVII.

21. "Frame of Government," XXXV; Murphy, *William Penn: A Life*, 156.

22. "To Springett Penn, Letitia Penn, and William Penn Jr., 19 August 1682," in *Papers of William Penn*, 2:280–81.

23. Marion Balderston, "The Real *Welcome* Passengers," *Huntington Library Quarterly* 26 (1962): 31.

24. *Papers of William Penn*, 2:299; "John Moll's account of the surrender of the Three Lower Counties to William Penn, 1682," in *Papers of William Penn*, 2:305–308.

25. "Frame of Government"; *Papers of William Penn*, 2:211–27; Murphy, *William Penn: A Life*, 156.

26. "The Great Law; Or, The Body of Laws of the Province of Pennsylvania And Territories Thereunto Belonging [. . .]," preamble.

27. "The Great Law," chapter 1. The second Frame of Government preserved most of the features of the first Frame of Government but reduced the size of the government. Jean R. Soderlund, *William Penn and the Founding of Pennsylvania*, 265.

28. "To John Aubrey, 13 June 1683," in *Papers of William Penn*, 2:395.

29. William Penn, *A Letter . . . to the Committee of the Free Society of Traders* (London: s.n., 1683).

30. "To the Governor and Council of West New Jersey, 11 June 1683," in *Papers of William Penn*, 2:391; *Papers of William Penn*, 2:390.

31. "To the Governer and Council," 2:391: *Papers of William Penn*, 2:390; "To Thomas Lloyd, 7 October 1684," in *Papers of William Penn*, 2:604.

32. Murphy, *William Penn: A Life*, 164.

33. "To Lord Baltimore, 30 May 1683," in *Papers of William Penn*, 2:388.

34. "From Lord Baltimore, 24 June 1683," in *Papers of William Penn*, 2:405–409.

35. "To the Committee of Trade, 14 August 1683," in *Papers of William Penn*, 2:431–437.

36. Two residents of the lower counties described the "oppressions and wrongs" of Lord Baltimore and his attempts to draw settlers away from William. "From James William and John White, 8 September 1683," in *Papers of William Penn*, 2:485–486.

37. Murphy, *William Penn: A Life*, 165.

38. "Farewell to Pennsylvania," in *Papers of William Penn*, 2:590–91.

39. "Farewell to Pennsylvania," 2:590–91.

40. "Order in Privy Council, 13 November 1685," in *Papers of William Penn*, 3:69.

41. Murphy, *William Penn: A Life*, 179.

42. "A History of My Life from 1684, c. 1691—1692," in *Papers of William Penn*, 3:342.

43. "To Thomas Lloyd, 21 September 1686," in *Papers of William Penn*, 3:117; Murphy, *William Penn: A Life*, 180–181.

44. "To Thomas Lloyd, 21 September 1686," 3:117.

45. "To Thomas Lloyd, 21 September 1686," 3:117; Murphy, *William Penn: A Life*, 176–77.

46. *Papers of William Penn*, 3:275.

47. "To the Earl of Nottingham, 31 July 1690," in *Papers of William Penn*, 3:283; *Papers of William Penn* 3:275.

48. "To a Weighty Friend in England," in *Papers of William Penn*, 3:351.

49. "Minute of Lords of Trade and Plantations," Feb. 2, 1694, *CSP Colonial*, 1693–1696, 860; Murphy, *William Penn: A Life*, 216.

50. "To Friends in Pennsylvania, 11 December 1693," in *Papers of William Penn*, 3:383.

51. "To Robert Turner, 27 February 1694," in *Papers of William Penn*, 3:388.

52. *Papers of William Penn*, 3:393; "Report of the Lord of Trade, 3 August 1694," in *Papers of William Penn*, 3:397.

53. *Papers of William Penn*, 3:393.

54. "To Aaron Atkinson, 22 November 1695," in *Papers of William Penn*, 3:420.

55. "Marriage Certificate, 15 March 1696," in *Papers of William Penn*, 3:435.

56. "To Samuel and Hannah Carpenter, 7 September 1708," in *Papers of William Penn*, 4:614–15. Their second daughter, Hannah, only survived for five months and died on January 24, 1709.

57. "To Robert Turner, 25 December 1696," in *Papers of William Penn*, 3:470.

58. "To Francis Nicholson, 12 December 1699," in *Papers of William Penn*, 3:578.

59. "Articles of Agreement with the Susquehanna Indians, 23 April 1701," in *Papers of William Penn*, 4:51.

60. "To James Logan, 8 September 1701," in *Papers of William Penn*, 4:87.

61. "The Charter of Privileges, 28 October 1701," in *Papers of William Penn*, 4:105; "Charter of Privileges, granted by William Penn, Esq.: to the Inhabitants and Pennsylvania and Territories, dated at Philadelphia, 28th October, 1701," 4, Historical Society of Pennsylvania, Philadelphia.

62. "Charter of Privileges," 4; Murphy, *William Penn: A Life*, 279.

63. "To John Evans, 7 September 1708," in *Papers of William Penn*, 13:530.

64. "To James Logan, 16 September 1704," in *Papers of William Penn*, 11:355, reprinted in *Pennsylvania Magazine of History and Biography* 7 (1883): 229.

65. Murphy, *William Penn: A Life*, 5.

66. Jim Wedeking, "Quaker State: Pennsylvania's Guide to Reducing the Friction for Religious Outsiders under the Establishment Clause," *NYU Journal of Law and Liberty* 2, no. 1 (2006): 35

67. Letter to the Society for the Propagation of the Gospel by the Reverend Thomas Barton (Nov. 8, 1762), in William Stevens Perry, ed., *Historical Collections Relating to the American Colonial Church* (Hartford, CT: s.n., 1871), 366.

68. Christie L. Maloyed, "A Liberal Civil Religion: William Penn's Holy Experiment," *Journal of Church and State* 55, no. 4 (June 22, 2012): 673.

69. Maloyed, "A Liberal Civil Religion," 674.

70. Wedeking, "Quaker State," 78.

71. Maloyed, "A Liberal Civil Religion," 675.

72. Wedeking, "Quaker State," 163.

73. William Penn, *A Second Letter from a Gentleman in the Country to His Friends in London upon the Subject of the Penal Laws and Test* (London: s.n., 1687) (spelling modernized); Murphy, *William Penn: A Life*, 194.

74. J. William Frost, *A Perfect Freedom: Religious Liberty in Pennsylvania* (University Park, PA: Pennsylvania State University Press, 1993), 4.

75. Sally Schwartz, "William Penn and Toleration: Foundations of Colonial Pennsylvania," *Pennsylvania History* 50, no. 4 (Oct. 1983): 285.

76. "Charter of Privileges."

77. William Penn, *The Great Case of Liberty of Conscience Once More Briefly Debated and Defended* [. . . .] (London: s.n., 1670), 12.

78. J. William Frost, "Religious Liberty in Early Pennsylvania," *The Pennsylvania Magazine of History and Biography*, vol. 105, no. 4 (Oct. 1981): 422.

79. Frost, *A Perfect Freedom*, 12, 16.

80. William Penn, *An Address to Protestants upon the Present Conjuncture in II Parts / By a Protestant, William Penn* (London: s.n., 1679); Murphy, *William Penn: A Life*, 133.

81. *Political Writings of William Penn*, 2:209.

82. Penn, *Great Case of Liberty of Conscience*, 19.

83. Maloyed, "A Liberal Civil Religion," 13.

84. "Frame of Government."

CHAPTER 7

TRANSLATION AND
RESTORATION IN HARMONY

—— ⁂ ——

THE GOVERNMENT THAT WILLIAM PENN ESTABLISHED, AND HIS PO-
litical thinking and policies, provided religious protection for Joseph
Smith to succeed in translating the Book for Mormon and restoring
the holy priesthood of God. But Joseph knew he could not translate
the Book of Mormon alone, and Oliver Cowdery was the answer to
his prayers.

Oliver Cowdery was slight of build, about five feet and five inches
tall, with dark eyes and dark, wavy hair. He was a schoolteacher in
Manchester who had been boarding with the Smiths for some time.[1]
Oliver taught spelling, arithmetic, reading, grammar, and geography, and he frequently asked his students to read from the New
Testament.[2] When he first arrived in Manchester, he heard stories of
Joseph Smith and the gold plates. He inquired of the Smiths concerning these things, and due to the controversial nature of the subject,
the Smiths were reluctant to share their experiences. But as the Smiths
gained confidence in Oliver, they related to him more information.
Eventually the Smiths fully recounted to Oliver the circumstances in
which Joseph received the gold plates, possibly prompted by Joseph
Smith Sr.'s revelatory experience in Harmony. At some point, Oliver
told Joseph Smith Sr. that he had been in deep study over Joseph's

work that entire day and that he believed it was God's will that he should go to Harmony to write for Joseph.[3]

At the close of the school year, Oliver made the 128-mile trip to Harmony with Samuel, Joseph's younger brother, to hear the story firsthand from Joseph.[4] The roads were in poor condition due to freezing rain. The two men stopped at the house of Oliver's friend, David Whitmer, in Fayette Township, New York.[5] Oliver spoke to David about the purpose of his journey to Harmony and promised to send him his impressions of Joseph.[6] Oliver and Samuel continued their journey, arriving in Harmony without major incident. The rough journey in freezing rain, however, left them exhausted with frostbitten toes.[7]

THE TRANSLATION OF THE BOOK OF MORMON COMMENCES

On April 5, 1829, when Oliver Cowdery arrived in Harmony, Joseph happily greeted him with an expression of assurance and relief.[8] Joseph knew that the prayer he had offered three days earlier—for help in translating the plates—was answered, and that he would be able to now start the translation with Oliver as scribe. That night, sleep seemed a burden to Joseph and Oliver as they conversed until early into the morning, contemplating Joseph's experiences and the work to be accomplished.[9] Joseph followed the "Ask Principle" in requesting a permanent scribe since he knew he could not accomplish the translation without assistance from others.

The next morning, Oliver assisted Joseph in arranging the purchase of the home occupied by Joseph and Emma, which stood on a parcel of land that was thirteen and a half acres and met the Susquehanna River on its southernmost side. Oliver wrote the agreement for Joseph to purchase the property for $200 from Mr. Hale and also witnessed the agreement.[10]

The agreement did not require full payment up front but allowed for an installment payment of $114 by May 1, 1829, and payment of the remaining balance by May 1, 1830. The agreement carried a heavy penalty of $400 if the installment payments were late. That day Joseph made a down payment of sixty-four dollars, which showed a good faith effort to pay for his residence and allowed him to devote his

Joseph Smith's Agreement with Isaac Hale,
6 April 1829 (2 pages). © By Intellectual Reserve, Inc.

full attention to translating the plates.[11] Because Joseph did not have a full-time job and he and Emma "had become reduced in property," Oliver may have contributed a portion of his teacher's salary of sixty-five dollars and fifty cents to the down payment.[12] This agreement symbolizes Joseph's focus on his divine mission and that he feared God more than man. Instead of engaging in full-time employment and paying for his farm, he borrowed money and agreed to pay his father-in-law in installments.

On April 7, 1829, Joseph commenced the translation of the Book of Mormon with Oliver Cowdery as his scribe, likely starting in the book of Mosiah.[13] The translation occurred in the main room on the bottom floor of the two-story Smith home.[14] Oliver said that by looking through "two transparent stones, resembling glass, set in silver bows," Joseph "was able to read in English, the reformed Egyptian characters, which were engraven on the plates."[15] Samuel Richards, a friend of Oliver's, said Oliver described the translation process as follows:

> He represented Joseph as sitting at a table with the plates before him, translating them by means of the Urim and Thummim, while he (Oliver) sat beside him writing every word as Joseph spoke them to him. This was done by holding the "translators" over the hieroglyphics, the translation appearing distinctly on the instrument, which had been touched by the finger of God and dedicated and consecrated for the express purpose of translating languages. Every word was distinctly visible even to every letter; and if Oliver omitted a word or failed to spell a word correctly, the translation remained on the interpreter until it was copied correctly.[16]

As translation progressed, doubt clouded Oliver's mind, and concern over his role in the translation process created a mental block. Joseph sought help from the Lord through the Urim and Thummin and received a revelation directed to Oliver. The Lord told Oliver:

> If you desire a further witness, cast your mind upon the night that you cried unto me in your heart, that you might know concerning the truth of these things; did I not speak peace to your mind concerning the matter?—What greater witness can you have than from God? . . .

Fear not to do good my sons, for whatsoever ye sow, that shall
ye also reap; therefore, if ye sow good, ye shall also reap good for
your reward. Therefore, fear not, little flock; do good, let earth and
hell combine against you, for if ye are built upon my Rock, they
cannot prevail.[17]

Hearing the words of the Lord illuminated Oliver's mind and
touched his heart; he knew the work was true. The revelation prompted Oliver to share with Joseph the experience he had in Palmyra while
staying with Joseph's family. He told him about the night when, after speaking to Joseph Smith Sr. concerning Joseph's work, he called
upon the Lord to know if the work was true.[18] Joseph later recorded that the "Lord appeared unto . . . Oliver Cowd[e]ry [that night]
and shewed unto him the plates in a vision and also the truth of the
work."[19] Since that time, Oliver had kept his spiritual experience a
secret, even from Joseph.[20] When he received the revelation in which
the Lord referenced that revelatory night, this affirmed his faith in the
work because no one knew of this experience but God and him.[21] The
Lord further confirmed to Oliver that, if he desired, he could have the
gift "to translate even as my servant Joseph."[22]

The Lord also taught Oliver the importance of inquiring and the
"Ask Principle": "For what thou has done, for thou has inquired of me,
and behold as often as thou hast inquired, thou hast received instructions of my Spirit. If it had not been so, thou wouldst not have come
to the place where thou art at this time."[23]

THE TRANSLATION OF THE BOOK OF LEHI

As translation continued, Joseph and Oliver Cowdery questioned
whether they should retranslate the Book of Lehi—the 116 pages of
the lost manuscript. The Lord responded that Joseph could not retranslate the pages because men had altered the words of the manuscript. If Joseph retranslated it, then the men would claim he had
contradicted himself and was consequently a liar and a pretender.[24]

Although devastating to the progress of the translation and
Joseph's morale, not all was lost with the disappearance of the Book
of Lehi. When Mormon assembled the plates, the Lord directed him
to attach the small plates of Nephi, which contained a record of the
people covering the same period of time as the Book of Lehi. This

account focused on religious teachings of the people and the gospel of Jesus Christ and was of more spiritual value than the Book of Lehi.[25] As a result, there existed two accounts of the history of the people of Lehi in the plates received by Joseph: the abridgment, entitled the Book of Lehi, and the religious enriched account, or small plates of Nephi. In His infinite foresight, the Lord prepared two accounts of the people of Lehi and preserved the religious enriched account for translation.[26] This knowledge undoubtedly comforted Joseph in his despair over losing the manuscript.

OLIVER IS TOLD HE HAS THE GIFT TO TRANSLATE THE PLATES

In the course of the translation, Oliver became anxious to translate himself and inquired of the Lord.[27] The Lord responded that if Oliver asked "with an honest heart" and faith, he would "receive, a knowledge concerning the engravings of old" and could translate the plates.[28] This knowledge would be received by manifestations of the Spirit, which the Lord conveys in the following manner: "I will tell you in your mind and in your heart by the Holy Ghost which shall come upon you and which shall dwell in your heart. . . . And therefore, whatsoever you shall ask me to tell you by that means that will [I] grant unto you that ye shall know."[29]

JOHN THE APOSTLE

As Joseph and Oliver continued to translate, day after day, a difference of opinion arose between them with respect to John the Beloved of the New Testament—whether he continued to live on the earth or had died.[30] They both inquired of the Lord through the Urim and Thummim.[31] Through revelation, they learned that John asked the Lord to stay on the earth and continue the Lord's work, and the Lord granted John's request, giving him power over death that he might live and bring souls unto God.[32]

OLIVER ATTEMPTS TO TRANSLATE

After receiving the revelation that he could obtain the gift of translation, Oliver attempted to translate the plates, but he struggled.

His inexperience and lack of preparation slowed the translation process. The Lord admonished Oliver to be patient and urged him to be content to write rather than attempt to translate. The Lord said:

> Behold you have not understood, you have supposed that I would give it unto you, when you took no thought, save it was to ask me; but behold I say unto you, that you must study it out in your mind; then you must ask me if it be right, and if it is right, I will cause that your bosom shall burn within you; therefore, you shall feel that it is right; but if it be not right, you shall have no such feelings, but you shall have a stupor of thought, that shall cause you to forget the thing which is wrong.[33]

Oliver learned an important lesson that day: he needed to do as Joseph did—study, prepare, and learn to be a translator. Oliver humbly pondered the admonishment from the Lord, learned from his mistake, and continued to write for Joseph. Oliver later recalled, "These were the days never to be forgotten—to sit under the sound of a voice dictated by the inspiration of heaven, awakened the utmost gratitude of this bosom! Day after day I continued, uninterrupted, to write from his mouth, as he translated, with the Urim and Thummim, or, as the Nephites would have said, 'Interpreters,' the history, or record, called 'The Book of Mormon.'"[34]

Later in his life, Oliver bore testimony of his role as Joseph's scribe:

> I wrote, with my own pen, the entire Book of Mormon (save a few pages) as it fell from the lips of the Prophet Joseph Smith, as he translated it by the gift and power of God by the means of the Urim and Thummim, or, as it is called by that book, "holy interpreters." I beheld with my eyes, and handled with my hands, the gold plates from which it was transcribed. I also saw with my eyes and handled with my hands the "holy interpreters." The book is true. . . . I wrote it myself as it fell from the lips of the Prophet.[35]

Near the end of April, Joseph made a fifty dollar payment on his home in order to meet the May 1 deadline for the installment payment of $114.[36] Joseph Knight Sr. may have contributed the fifty dollar payment. Joseph Knight Jr. recorded, "Joseph [Smith] had commenced to translate the plates, he told my Father he wanted fifty dollars; my Father could not raise it; he then came to me, the same day I sold my house lot and sent him a one horse wagon."[37] The wagon provided by Mr. Knight may have been accepted as the fifty dollar payment.[38]

The translation continued into the month of May as Oliver and Joseph worked in the book of Third Nephi, which recounts Jesus Christ's visit to the people on the American continents. The Book of Mormon records that Jesus Christ visited the Americas and taught the inhabitants His gospel, blessed their children, and healed their sick. He also taught the proper method of baptism in order to settle disagreements among the people. Baptism was to be performed by immersion by someone holding the proper authority. Jesus Christ gave Nephi, the prophet of the people at that time, and other disciples the power and authority to baptize (see 3 Nephi 11:21). In reflecting on these passages, Oliver realized that the authority to baptize had in fact been lost for centuries and that no church at that time had the authority from God to administer the ordinances of the gospel.[39]

THE RESTORATION OF THE AARONIC PRIESTHOOD

Joseph and Oliver desired to be baptized but knew that no one had authority to administer the sacred ordinance, and they were at a loss as to how the authority was to be restored. On May 15, 1829, they "retired in the woods" adjacent to Joseph's home "at the Susquehanna River" to inquire of the Lord concerning baptism for the remission of sins, again following the "Ask Principle."[40] They recounted, "[Our] souls were drawn out in mighty prayer—to know how we might obtain the blessings of baptism and the Holy Spirit, according to the order of God, and we diligently sought for the right of the fathers and the authority of the Holy Priesthood and to administer the same; for we desired to be followers of righteousness, and in the possession of greater knowledge, even the knowledge of the mysteries of the kingdom of God."[41]

The Susquehanna River had inspired many others before Joseph and Oliver. The four-thousand-year-old Susquehanna River had stood as the keystone of Pennsylvania's geography throughout the ages.[42] Since the Susquehanna's discovery, explorers, travelers, tourists, and others marveled at its waters and surrounding terrain, authoring countless books and studies on its behalf. The Susquehanna ignites the imagination, stirs the senses, and inspires dreams. It is a writer's wellspring—generous, beckoning, and majestic.[43] The peaceful hum of the Susquehanna's wistful waters beckons the passerby to its banks. Considered a missionary's river, a geologist's river, an Indian's river, and a politician's river, the Susquehanna's far-reaching tributaries and branches seem to touch every aspect of human life.[44] Captain John Smith, one of the first English settlers to set eyes on the Susquehanna, commented on its beauties: "Heaven and earth seemed never to have agreed better to frame a place for man's commodious and delightful living."[45]

The Youthful Prophet, Joseph Smith, Jr., and Oliver Cowdery, Receiving the Aaronic Priesthood under the hands of John the Baptist, May 15, 1829.

Joseph Smith Jr. and Oliver Cowdery receiving the Aaronic Priesthood under the hands of John the Baptist, May 15, 1829. By George W. Crocheron, 1898. US Library of Congress.

Joseph and Oliver knelt in fervent prayer in the sugar maple groves located on the north side of Joseph's property.[46] A messenger suddenly appeared and descended in a cloud of light. He said his name was John the Baptist from the New Testament and that he acted under the direction of Jesus's disciples of the New Testament, Peter, James, and John.[47]

Laying his hands upon the heads of Oliver and Joseph, John the Baptist conferred upon them the power to baptize, saying: "Upon you my fellow servants in the name of the Messiah I confer the priest-hood of Aaron, which holds the keys of the ministering of angels and of the Gospel of repentance, and of baptism by immersion for the remission of sins and this shall never be taken again from the earth, until the sons of Levi do offer again an offering unto the Lord in righteousness."[48] The Priesthood of Aaron, also known as the prepara-tory priesthood, was named after Moses's brother Aaron of the Old Testament.[49]

John the Baptist told Joseph and Oliver that the Aaronic Priesthood did not have the power of laying on of hands for the gift of the Holy Ghost but only the authority to baptize.[50] He com-manded Joseph and Oliver to "repair to the river each of them to be baptized."[51] Joseph was to baptize Oliver, and Oliver to baptize Joseph, in the Susquehanna River. John the Baptist added that the keys of the Melchizedek Priesthood—the keys of which were held by Peter, James, and John—would be conferred on them in due time.[52]

They then went to the Susquehanna River where Joseph baptized Oliver and Oliver baptized Joseph.[53] Immediately upon coming up out of the water, Joseph and Oliver experienced spiritual enlighten-ment, inspiration, and glorious blessings from heaven beyond com-prehension and description. Oliver stood up and prophesied of things that should occur in the future. Joseph prophesied of the rise of the Church and many other things connected with the Church and this generation of the children of men: "Our minds being now enlight-ened, we began to have the Scriptures laid open to our understand-ings, and the true meaning and intention of mysterious passages re-vealed unto us in a manner which we never could attain to previously, nor ever before had thought of."[54]

After they emerged from the waters of the Susquehanna, Joseph laid his hands on Oliver's head and ordained him to the Aaronic Priesthood, and Oliver laid his hands on Joseph's head and ordained him to the same priesthood.[55]

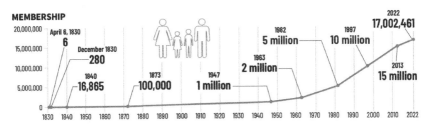

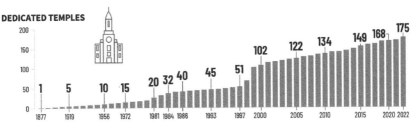

Church growth by numbers of members. Church membership reached over 17 million members in 2022. Aaron Thorup, Church News. © By Intellectual Reserve, Inc.

Oliver cherished this experience and recounted the following:

While the veil was parted and the angel of God came down clothed with glory and delivered the anxiously looked for message, and the keys of the gospel of repentance. What joy! what wonder! what amazement! . . . Our eyes beheld—our ears heard, as in the "blaze of day"; yes, more—above the glitter of the May sunbeam, which then shed its brilliancy over the face of nature! Then his voice, though mild, pierced to the center, and his words, "I am thy fellow-servant," dispelled every fear. We listened, we gazed, we admired! 'Twas the voice of the angel from glory, 'twas a message from the Most High! And as we rejoiced, while His love enkindled upon our souls, and we were wrapped in the vision of the Almighty! Where was room for doubt? Nowhere: uncertainty had fled, and doubt had sunk no more to rise, while fiction and deception had fled forever![56]

Joseph and Oliver kept their visit from John the Baptist a secret due to the persecution that persisted in the Harmony area. Joseph and

Oliver asked Mr. Hale for protection, who by inspiration from God held off the angry mobs in Harmony.[57]

SAMUEL SMITH RECEIVES BAPTISM

A few days passed, and Joseph and Oliver's urge to share their remarkable experience could no longer be restrained; they joyfully shared parts of their experience with neighbors and friends. About this time, Joseph's younger brother, Samuel, arrived in Harmony. With the excitement of the previous week, Joseph and Oliver spoke openly and freely of their experiences and showed Samuel some of the manuscript they had translated. They made efforts to persuade him that the gospel of Jesus Christ had been revealed in its fulness. Samuel was not easily persuaded but sincerely pondered the meaning of their words. After much inquiry and explanation by Joseph and Oliver, Samuel retired to the woods so that he could know of himself whether these things were true. Like Joseph and Oliver, Samuel also followed the "Ask Principle." The Lord responded to his sincere prayer and through personal revelation confirmed to him that Joseph and Oliver's message was true. On May 25, 1829, Oliver baptized Samuel. Samuel returned to Palmyra glorifying and praising God, being filled with the Holy Ghost. Samuel is considered to be one of the first convert baptisms of the Church and is credited with placing copies of the Book of Mormon in the hands of several people who were eventually responsible for the conversion of Brigham Young and others.[58]

HYRUM SMITH VISITS HARMONY

Only days later, Hyrum Smith, Joseph's older brother, visited Harmony.[59] Hyrum requested that Joseph ask through the Urim and Thummim what the Lord would have him do to assist in the work.[60] The Lord told Hyrum not to seek for riches but for wisdom and knowledge that lead to eternal life, for "he that hath eternal life is rich." Hyrum was to study and obtain knowledge first, and then he could preach the gospel by "the power of God unto the convincing of men."[61] Hyrum and his wife Jerusha were later baptized on June 4, 1829, in Seneca Lake in Seneca County, New York, by Joseph.[62] Other than Joseph Smith, no one knew the origins of the Church and its doctrine better than Hyrum, and no one was more trusted by Joseph than him.[63] Hyrum died alongside his brother Joseph as a martyr in Carthage, Illinois, on June 27, 1844.

Joseph Knight Sr. Again Provides Assistance

Joseph and Oliver traveled to Colesville to ask for some provisions from Joseph Knight Sr., who was not at home, so they left him a message of their need for assistance. Upon returning home, Joseph Knight Sr. received the message and immediately set off for Harmony, armed with provisions. He traveled in a wagon loaded with some nine or ten bushels of grain, five or six bushels of potatoes, a barrel of mackerel, and a pound of tea. He also brought lined paper for writing and money to purchase more.[64] Joseph Knight Sr. recalled:

> Joseph and Oliver were gone to see if they could find a place to work for provisions, but found none. They returned home and found me there with provisions, and they were glad, for they were out. Their family consisted of four, Joseph and wife, Oliver and . . . [Joseph's] brother Samuel. Then they went to work, and had provisions enough to last till the translation was done.[65]

Joseph Knight Jr. and his father often traveled to Harmony to deliver provisions and supplies.[66] Joseph Knight Sr. was always willing to assist Joseph. Joseph praised him for his donations and dedication, which enabled the work to progress when otherwise they would have been forced to find gainful full-time employment.[67] After delivering needed provisions on one occasion, Joseph Knight Sr. asked Joseph what the Lord expected him to do to assist in the work.[68] Joseph received a revelation in which Joseph Knight Sr. was told that as long as he followed the commandments, he would be called to assist in the work of the Lord.[69]

The Restoration of the Melchizedek Priesthood

Inspired by his revelation from the Lord, Joseph Knight Sr. requested that Joseph and Oliver go to Broome County, New York, to preach with him in the neighborhood. Joseph and Oliver embraced the opportunity and made the twenty-eight mile journey from Harmony to Colesville. As word spread of Joseph and Oliver's presence in Colesville, a mob quickly assembled to oppose them. Without recourse against the mob, Joseph and Oliver were forced to flee into the night for Harmony. They wandered through the dense evergreen forest all night in mud up to their knees, following along the banks of the Susquehanna River. Oliver became exhausted as the night progressed, and Joseph put his arm around him to support him. As the sun began to rise in the early morning, Oliver's strength failed him entirely. Joseph leaned up against a fence and cried to the Lord to know how long the suffering would continue.[70]

Restoration of the Melchizedek Priesthood by New Testament Apostles
Peter, James, and John by Kenneth Riley

In this moment of desperation, Peter, James, and John, three of Jesus's original Apostles, appeared. Joseph wrote in his journal that he and Oliver heard "the voice of Peter, James and John, in the wilderness between Harmony, Susquehanna County, and Colesville, Broome County, on the Susquehanna river; declaring themselves as possessing the keys of the kingdom, and of the dispensation of the fullness of times."[71] Peter, James, and John conferred upon Joseph and Oliver the Melchizedek Priesthood, or the higher priesthood, ordaining them to the holy apostleship as special witnesses of Jesus Christ.[72] Out of respect and reverence for the name of Jesus Christ, and to avoid over-repetition, the higher priesthood was named after the ancient high priest Melchizedek.[73] Although sixteen or seventeen miles still separated Joseph and Oliver from the comfort of their home in Harmony, Oliver ceased his complaints. The visitation had renewed his strength and boosted his morale.[74] Oliver reveled in the experience, knowing that he stood in the presence of Peter and received the Melchizedek Priesthood under the hands of those who received it from Jesus Christ while He dwelled in the flesh upon the earth.[75]

NOTES

1. History, circa June 1839–circa 1841 [Draft 2], 13, josephsmithpapers. org; B. H. Roberts, *A Comprehensive History of the Church of Jesus Christ of Latter-day Saints* (Salt Lake City, UT: Deseret News, 1948–57), 1:32; Larry E. Morris, "The Conversion of Oliver Cowdery," *Journal of Book of Mormon Studies* 16, no. 1. (Provo, UT: Maxwell Institute, 2007), 7–8. Oliver's brother Lyman first applied to teach school in the Manchester district but backed out at the last minute and sent twenty-two-year-old Oliver in his place. Lucy Mack Smith, History, 1844–1845, book 7, 12, josephsmithpapers.org; Lucy Mack Smith, *Lucy's Book: A Critical Edition of Lucy Mack Smith's Family Memoir*, ed. Lavina Fielding Anderson (Salt Lake City, UT: Signature Books, 2001), 432 (manuscript version); Morris, "The Conversion of Oliver Cowdery," 6.

2. Manuscript, Manchester Commissioners of Common Schools, report "To the Superintendent of Common Schools of the State of New York," July 1, 1829, Manchester Town Office, Clifton Springs, New York, Public School Records, 1828–1915; Morris, "The Conversion of Oliver Cowdery," 7.

3. Lucy Mack Smith, History, 1844–1845, book 7, 12, to book 8, 1, josephsmith-papers.org; Smith, *Lucy's Book*, 432 (manuscript version).

4. Lucy Mack Smith, History, 1844–1845, book 8, 3, josephsmithpapers.org; Smith, *Lucy's Book*, 437 (manuscript version). In 1828, while in Palmyra,

Oliver first met David Whitmer, who was on a business trip from Fayette Township, which is thirty miles east of Palmyra. The two men quickly created a friendship, building on their mutual interest in Joseph Smith. David stated, "Cowdery and I, as well as others, talk[ed] about the [plates], but at the time I paid but little attention to it, supposing it to be only the idle gossip of the neighborhood." "Mormonism," *Kansas City Daily Journal*, June 5, 1881, 1; Morris, "The Conversion of Oliver Cowdery," 7

5. "Mormonism," 1; Morris, "The Conversion of Oliver Cowdery," 14. While at the Whitmers' home, Oliver probably met David's sister Elizabeth Ann, the woman he would marry four years later. Possibly during a subsequent visit by David Whitmer to the Palmyra area, Oliver told David he intended to travel to Harmony to investigate the plates. "Mormonism," 1.

6. "Mormonism," 1; Lyndon W. Cook, ed., *David Whitmer Interviews: A Restoration Witness* (Orem UT: Grandin Book, 1991), 61; Morris, "The Conversion of Oliver Cowdery," 14. Joseph's parents, when they were traveling from Manchester to Pennsylvania to visit Joseph, had stopped to stay overnight at the Whitmers' home. While there, the Smiths gave the Whitmers a brief history of the plates and Joseph's mission. Lucy Mack Smith, *Biographical Sketches of Joseph Smith the Prophet and His Progenitors for Many Generations* (Liverpool: S. W. Richards, 1853), 137; Smith, *Lucy's Book*, 450 (Pratt version).

7. Lucy Mack Smith, History, 1844–1845, book 8, 3, josephsmithpapers.org; Smith, *Lucy's Book*, 437–38 (manuscript version); Richard Lloyd Anderson, "Gold Plates and Printer's Ink," *Ensign*, Sept. 1976, 75. Oliver Cowdery played an important role in the growth and development of the Church as "a scribe for the Book of Mormon translation, the foremost spokesman for the Church after its organization, the leader of the first major mission, the editor of Church publications, a counselor to Joseph Smith, a prominent recorder of Church records, and a member of the Kirtland High Council." Richard Lloyd Anderson, "Personal Writings of the Book of Mormon Witnesses," in Noel B. Reynolds, ed., *Book of Mormon Authorship Revisited: The Evidence for Ancient Origins* (Provo, UT: F.A.R.M.S., 1997), 2.

8. Lucy Mack Smith, History, 1844–1845, book 8, 3–4, josephsmithpapers.org; Smith, *Lucy's Book*, 438 (manuscript version); History, circa June 1839–circa 1841 [Draft 2], 13, josephsmithpapers.org; Roberts, *History of the Church*, 1:32. In the following three months, Oliver recorded the entire Book of Mormon and a dozen of Joseph's revelations. He also made a copy of the entire Book of Mormon later that fall and spring. Michael Hubbard MacKay and Gerrit J. Dirkmaat, *From Darkness unto Light: Joseph Smith's Translation and Publication of the Book of Mormon* (Provo, UT: BYU Religious Studies Center, 2015), 119.

9. Lucy Mack Smith, History, 1844–1845, book 8, 4, josephsmithpapers.org; Smith, *Lucy's Book*, 438–9 (manuscript version).

10. Agreement with Isaac Hale, 6 April 1829, josephsmithpapers.org; Deed Book 8, 59–60, located in the Susquehanna County Courthouse, Montrose, PA;

Morris, "The Conversion of Oliver Cowdery," 16; "Oliver Cowdery, Norton, OH, to William W. Phelps, 7 Sept. 1834," *Latter Day Saints' Messenger and Advocate* (Kirtland, OH), 1834, 14.

11. Agreement with Isaac Hale, 6 April 1829, josephsmithpapers.org.

12. History, circa Summer 1832, 6, josephsmithpapers.org; "Historical Introduction," Agreement with Isaac Hale, 6 April 1829, josephsmithpapers.org. The Smiths completed payments on the property in the summer of 1830 and left shortly thereafter, but they did not sell their property until June 28, 1833, to Joseph McKune Jr., for $300. Mr. McKune owned Joseph Smith's farm at the time of Joseph's death. Deed Book 8, 59–60; Rhamanthus M. Stocker, *Centennial History of Susquehanna County, Pennsylvania*, 2nd ed. (Baltimore, MD: Regional Publishing Company, 1974), 554; Larry C. Porter, *A Study of the Origins of the Church of Jesus Christ of Latter-day Saints in the States of New York and Pennsylvania, 1816–1831* (Provo, UT: BYU Studies, 2000), 51; *Commemorative Biographical Record of Northeastern Pennsylvania,* [. . .] (Chicago: J. H. Beers & Co., 1900), 1085, 1900.

13. History, circa June 1839–circa 1841 [Draft 2], 13, josephsmithpapers.org; Roberts, *History of the Church*, 1:32–33. "Joseph and Oliver probably started writing at or shortly after Mosiah 1." John W. Welch, "The Miraculous Translation of the Book of Mormon," in John W. Welch, ed., *Opening the Heavens*: *Accounts of Divine Manifestations, 1820–1844* (Provo, UT: Brigham Young University Press, 2005), 90, fn. 110 (setting forth reasons why it is plausible that Joseph and Oliver started translating in the Book of Mosiah). The manuscript that Oliver used to write the translation is known today as the "original manuscript." About 28 percent of the manuscript has survived and is located in the Church Historian's Office of the Church. Gospel Topics Essays, "Book of Mormon Translation," Gospel Library.

14. Emma said, "Oliver Cowdery and [Joseph Smith] wrote in the room where I was at work." Joseph Smith III, "Last Testimony of Sister Emma," *The Saints' Herald* 26 (Oct. 1 1879): 289–90.

15. A. W. B., "Mormonites," *Evangelical Magazine and Gospel Advocate* 2 (Apr. 19, 1831): 120; Gospel Topics Essays, "Book of Mormon Translation," Gospel Library.

16. Personal Statement of S. W. Richards, 25 May 1907, at L. Tom Perry Special Collections, Harold B. Lee Library, Brigham Young University, Provo, Utah.

17. Revelation, April 1829–A [D&C 6], 14–17, josephsmithpapers.org; Doctrine and Covenants 6:22–24, 33–34.

18. History, circa Summer 1832, 6, josephsmithpapers.org; History, circa June 1839–circa 1841 [Draft 2], 15, josephsmithpapers.org; Roberts, *History of the Church*, 1:35.

19. History, circa Summer 1832, 6, josephsmithpapers.org.

20. History, circa June 1839–circa 1841 [Draft 2], 15, josephsmithpapers.org; Roberts, *History of the Church*, 1:35.

21. History, circa June 1839–circa 1841 [Draft 2], 15, josephsmithpapers.org; Roberts, *History of the Church*, 1:35. According to David Whitmer, Oliver wrote David a letter about this experience, stating that Joseph "had told him secrets of his life that he knew could not be known to any person but himself, in any other way than by revelation from the Almighty." James H. Hart, "About the Book of Mormon," *Deseret News* (Salt Lake City, UT), Apr. 9, 1884, 190; "Historical Introduction," Revelation, April 1829–A [D&C 6], josephsmithpapers.org.

22. Revelation, April 1829–A [D&C 6], 14–17, josephsmithpapers.org; Doctrine and Covenants 6:25.

23. Revelation, April 1829–A [D&C 6], 15, josephsmithpapers.org; Doctrine and Covenants 6:14.

24. Book of Commandments, 1833, 22–27, josephsmithpapers.org. John Whitmer copied this revelation [ca. Mar. 1831] into Revelation Book 1, but the pages on which the first part of the revelation was copied were removed at some point from that volume and are no longer intact. The version found in the Book of Commandments is the complete version. See also Doctrine and Covenants 10. For an in-depth discussion and analysis of the possible dates that this revelation was received, see Revelation Book 1, josephsmithpapers.org.

25. Joseph Fielding Smith, *Essentials in Church History*, 23rd ed. (Salt Lake City, UT: Deseret Book, 1969), 56; James B. Allen and Glen M. Leonard, *Story of the Latter-day Saints*, 2nd ed. (Salt Lake City, UT: Deseret Book, 1992), 48; Sidney B. Sperry, "What the Book of Mormon Is," *Journal of Book of Mormon Studies* 4, vol. 1 (Spring 1995): 6.

26. Preface to Book of Mormon, circa August 1829, josephsmithpapers.org; Revelation, Harmony Township, Susquehanna Co., PA, [ca. Apr. 1829], 24–25; Doctrine and Covenants 10:38–45; Joseph Fielding Smith, *Essentials in Church History*, 56.

27. History, circa June 1839–circa 1841 [Draft 2], 15, josephsmithpapers.org; Roberts, *History of the Church*, 1:35.

28. Revelation, April 1829–B [D&C 8], josephsmithpapers.org; Doctrine and Covenants 8:1.

29. Revelation, April 1829–B [D&C 8], josephsmithpapers.org; Doctrine and Covenants 8:2–3. The revelation mentioned Oliver's "gift of working with sprout." Oliver used a "sprout" or divining rod to find pockets of water or ore under the ground. MacKay and Dirkmaat, *From Darkness unto Light*, 122.

30. History, circa June 1839–circa 1841 [Draft 2], 15, josephsmithpapers.org. The impetus of the disagreement was John 21:18–23 in which Jesus prophesied of the Apostle Peter's death. In response to Peter's question about what happened to John the Apostle, Jesus said, "If I will that he should tarry till I come, what

is that to thee?" "Historical Introduction," Account of John, April 1829–C [D&C 7], josephsmithpapers.org.

31. History, circa June 1839–circa 1841 [Draft 2], 15, josephsmithpapers.org; Account of John, April 1829–C [D&C 7], josephsmithpapers.org. This revelation was said to be made from parchment written by John himself, but there is no evidence that Joseph had the actual parchment in his possession. It has been suggested that Joseph received an English translation of the parchment through the Urim and Thummim. "Historical Introduction," Account of John, April 1829–C [D&C 7], josephsmithpapers.org, fn. 9, josephsmithpapers.org.

32. History, circa June 1839–circa 1841 [Draft 2], 15–16, josephsmithpapers.org; Roberts, *History of the Church*, 1:36. The revelation also states that Peter desired to go back to God. Account of John, April 1829–C [D&C 7], josephsmithpapers.org; Doctrine and Covenants 7: 4–5.

33. Revelation, April 1829–D [D&C 9], josephsmithpapers.org; Doctrine and Covenants 9:7–9.

34. "Oliver Cowdery, Norton, OH, to William W. Phelps, 7 Sept. 1834," 14.

35. "Testimonies of Oliver Cowdery and Martin Harris," *The Latter Day Saints' Millennial Star* 21 (Aug. 20, 1859), 544; Mark L. McConkie, *Remembering Joseph: Personal Recollections of Those Who Knew the Prophet Joseph Smith* (Salt Lake City, UT: Deseret Book, 2003), 610.

36. "Historical Introduction," Agreement with Isaac Hale, 6 April 1829, josephsmithpapers.org; Mark Lyman Staker, "Joseph and Emma Smith's Susquehanna Home: Expanding Mormonism's First Headquarters," *Mormon Historical Studies* 16, no. 2 (Fall 2015): 98.

37. Joseph Jr. Knight, Autobiographical Sketch, 1862, Church History Library, Salt Lake City.

38. Agreement with Isaac Hale, 6 April 1829, fn. 7, josephsmithpapers.org.

39. "Oliver Cowdery, Norton, OH, to William W. Phelps, 7 Sept. 1834," 15; Porter, *Origins of the Church*, 58.

40. History, circa June 1839–circa 1841 [Draft 2], 17–18, josephsmithpapers. org; Roberts, *History of the Church*, 1:39, 41. Historian Mark Staker has concluded that the evidence suggests that Joseph and Oliver "elected to go in the sugar bush on the north end of Joseph's property where he kept golden plates hidden from his neighbors" to pray and inquire concerning baptism. Mark Lyman Staker, "Where Was the Aaronic Priesthood Restored?: Identifying the Location of John the Baptist's Appearance, May 15, 1829," *Mormon Historical Studies* 12, no. 2 (2011): 155. According to Staker, the historical evidence militates against John the Baptist's visit occurring on the banks of the Susquehanna because the south end of Joseph's property, which abuts the Susquehanna River, was likely a pasture in an underwater floodplain in May 1829 and would not have had any woods. Staker, 151–53.

41. Patriarchal Blessing Book, No. 1, 2 Oct. 1835, 12, Church History Library, Salt Lake City; Joseph F. Smith, "Restoration of the Melchizedek Priesthood," *Improvement Era*, Oct. 1904, 942; Larry C. Porter, "The Restoration of the Aaronic and Melchizedek Priesthoods," *Ensign*, Dec. 1996, 30.

42. There is no question that the Susquehanna has played an integral role in Pennsylvania's history and origin. According to Holly Frederick of the Wyoming Valley Watershed Coalition, "The Susquehanna River is an important and under-appreciated resource in northeast Pennsylvania. Educating people on its value is a vital step to securing its future." Ralph Nardone, "Is the Susquehanna River the Nation's Most Endangered River?," *Northeast Pennsylvania Business Journal, High Impact Issues* (July 2005): 36. Author Otto Reimherr believes that the Susquehanna River is of such importance to the Mormon faith that it should be designated as the "'Jordan' of Mormonism." Otto Reimherr, "The Susquehanna: Mormonism's Jordan," *Susquehanna University Studies* XI, no. 2 (1980): 87.

43. Susan Q. Stranahan, *Susquehanna, River of Dreams* (Baltimore and London: The Johns Hopkins University Press, 1993), 1.

44. Richmond E. Myers, *The Long Crooked River: The Susquehanna* (Boston: The Christopher Publishing House, 1949), xi.

45. R. G. Rincliffe, *"Conowingo!" The History of a Great Development on the Susquehanna* (New York, San Francisco, and Montreal: The Newcomen Society in North America, 1953), 9.

46. Staker, "Where Was the Aaronic Priesthood Restored?," 147–51. Joseph and Oliver likely remained on Joseph's property because trespassing on another's property "without permission would have given Joseph's neighbors cause to accuse him of unethical if not illegal activity . . . [and] local opposition to [Joseph] was at its height." Staker, 148.

47. History, circa June 1839–circa 1841 [Draft 2], 18, josephsmithpapers.org; Roberts, *History of the Church*, 1:40; Porter, "The Restoration of the Aaronic and Melchizedek Priesthoods," 30.

48. History, circa June 1839–circa 1841 [Draft 2], 17, josephsmithpapers.org; Roberts, *History of the Church*, 1:39; Doctrine and Covenants 13. The earliest account of this event was recorded by Oliver Cowdery in "Oliver Cowdery, Norton, OH, to William W. Phelps, 7 Sept. 1834," 14. "Keys" refers to the permission to direct the administration of the priesthood.

49. "After the children of Israel came out of Egypt and while they were sojourning in the wilderness, Moses received a commandment from the Lord to take Aaron and his sons and ordain them and consecrate them as priests for the people (Exodus 28). At that time the males of the entire tribe of Levi were chosen to be the priests instead of the firstborn of all the tribes, and Aaron and his sons were given the presidency over the Priesthood thus conferred. Since that time it has been known as the Priesthood of Aaron, including the

Levitical Priesthood." Joseph Fielding Smith, *Church History and Modern Revelation* (Salt Lake City, UT: Deseret Book, 1946), 1:63.

50. History, circa June 1839–circa 1841 [Draft 2], 18, josephsmithpapers.org; Roberts, *History of the Church*, 1:39.

51. Lucy Mack Smith, History, 1844–1845, book 4, 8, josephsmithpapers.org; Smith, *Lucy's Book*, 439 (manuscript version); Staker, "Where Was the Aaronic Priesthood Restored?," 153–54.

52. History, circa June 1839–circa 1841 [Draft 2], 18, josephsmithpapers.org; Roberts, *History of the Church*, 1:40. The Aaronic Priesthood is the authority by which John the Baptist prepared the way for Jesus Christ and taught faith, repentance, and baptism for the remission of sins. The Aaronic Priesthood does not have the power to confer the Holy Ghost. "Aaronic Priesthood," *Encyclopedia of Mormonism*, ed. Daniel H. Ludlow (New York: Macmillan, 1992), 2:1–4. One key of the Aaronic Priesthood is "ministering of angels," which means that holders of the Aaronic Priesthood are eligible to have angels minister to them. The priesthood also has the key of the preparatory gospel, which is "the gospel of repentance and of Baptism, and the remission of sins, and the Law of carnal commandments." Revelation, 22–23 September 1832 [D&C 84], josephsmithpapers.org; Doctrine and Covenants 84:27; "Aaronic Priesthood," *Encyclopedia of Mormonism*, 2:1–4.

53. History, circa June 1839–circa 1841 [Draft 2], 18, josephsmithpapers.org; Roberts, *History of the Church*, 1:39; Staker, "Where Was the Aaronic Priesthood Restored?," 153–55. Staker concludes that due to the boat traffic on the Susquehanna River at that time, and Nathanial Lewis's unobstructed view of the river near Joseph's property, Joseph and Oliver "likely waited until evening to perform the baptisms." Staker, 154.

54. History, circa June 1839–circa 1841 [Draft 2], 18, josephsmithpapers.org; Roberts, *History of the Church*, 1:42–43.

55. History, circa June 1839–circa 1841 [Draft 2], 18, josephsmithpapers.org; Roberts, *History of the Church*, 1:40. The reason that Joseph and Oliver received baptism followed by ordination to the priesthood by an angel is explained as follows: "First, to confer the Priesthood before baptism, is contrary to the order of the organized Church, therefore they were commanded to confer the Priesthood upon each other in the regular way, after they were baptized. Second, the angel did for them that which they could not do for themselves. There was no one living in mortality who held the keys of this Priesthood, therefore it was necessary that this messenger, who held the keys of the Priesthood in the Dispensation of the Meridian of Time, should be sent to confer this power." Joseph Fielding Smith, *Essentials in Church History*, 58.

56. "Oliver Cowdery, Norton, OH, to William W. Phelps, 7 Sept. 1834," 14–16; History, circa June 1839–circa 1841 [Draft 2], 18, josephsmithpapers.org; Roberts, *History of the Church*, 1:42–44; Porter, *Origins of the Church*, 58.

57. History, circa June 1839–circa 1841 [Draft 2], 18, josephsmithpapers.org; Roberts, *History of the Church*, 1:43–44.

58. History, circa June 1839–circa 1841 [Draft 2], 18–19, josephsmithpapers.org; Roberts, *History of the Church*, 1:44; "Harmony Pennsylvania," *Encyclopedia of Mormonism*, 2:573. Samuel H. Smith was born in Tunbridge, Vermont, on March 13, 1808. He was the fourth son of Joseph and Lucy Smith. Roberts, *History of the Church*, 1:44. He is considered to be the first missionary of the church, called to serve about two months after the Church was organized. Allen and Leonard, *Story of the Latter-day Saints*, 56..

59. History, circa June 1839–circa 1841 [Draft 2], 19, josephsmithpapers.org; Roberts, *History of the Church*, 1:44–45. Hyrum Smith was born in Tunbridge, Vermont, on February 9, 1800. He was the second son of Joseph and Lucy Smith and at this time the oldest son living. Roberts, *History of the Church*, 1:45.

60. History, circa June 1839–circa 1841 [Draft 2], 19, josephsmithpapers.org; Pearson H. Corbett, *Hyrum Smith, Patriarch* (Salt Lake City, UT: Deseret Book, 1963), 48. Hyrum wanted to know "his place in the great work of the restoration." Corbett, *Hyrum Smith*, 48.

61. Revelation, May 1829–A [D&C 11], 28–30, josephsmithpapers.org; Doctrine and Covenants 11:3, 10. This revelation was likely received in late May 1829. "Historical Introduction," Revelation, May 1829–A [D&C 11], josephsmithpapers.org.

62. History, circa June 1839–circa 1841 [Draft 2], 23, josephsmithpapers.org; Roberts, *History of the Church*, 1:51; Larry C. Porter, "From a Book Coming Forth," *Ensign*, July 1988, 42.

63. Anderson, "Personal Writings of the Book of Mormon Witnesses," 5.

64. "Joseph Knight Sr., Reminiscences," no date, Church History Library, Salt Lake City; Joseph Knight Sr., "Joseph Knight's Recollection of Early Mormon History," ed. Dean Jessee, *BYU Studies* 17, no. 1 (1976); *Church History in the Fullness of Times Student Manual* (2000), 54; History, circa June 1839–circa 1841 [Draft 2], 20–21, josephsmithpapers.org; Roberts, *History of the Church*, 1:47; Larry C. Porter, "Joseph Smith's Susquehanna Years," *Ensign*, Feb. 2001, 46.

65. "Joseph Knight Sr., Reminiscences" (spelling modernized); Knight, "Joseph Knight's Recollection," 36; William G. Hartley, *Stand by My Servant Joseph: The Story of the Joseph Knight Family and the Restoration* (Salt Lake City, UT: Deseret Book, 2003), 49.

66. "Father and I often went to see him and carry him something to live upon: at last Oliver Cowdery came to write for him, then he got along faster." Knight, Autobiographical Sketch, 1862; "Historical Introduction," Revelation, May 1829–B [D&C 12], josephsmithpapers.org.

67. History, circa June 1839–circa 1841 [Draft 2], 21, josephsmithpapers.org; Roberts, *History of the Church*, 1:47.

68. Hartley, *Stand by My Servant Joseph*, 51.

69. Revelation, May 1829–B [D&C 12], 31, josephsmithpapers.org; Doctrine and Covenants 12. It is possible that this revelation was received at the same time as or before the revelation provided to Hyrum Smith in Harmony. "Historical Introduction," Revelation, May 1829–B [D&C 12], josephsmithpapers.org. Some historians believe that this revelation to Joseph Knight Sr. was received shortly before the restoration of the Aaronic Priesthood. John D. Giles, "Restoration of the Melchizedek Priesthood," *Improvement Era*, 1945, 4.

70. Letter of Addison Everett to Joseph F. Smith, 16 Jan. 1882, Joseph F. Smith Collection, Church History Library, Salt Lake City; Brian Q. Cannon, "Priesthood Restoration Documents," *BYU Studies* 35, no. 4 (1995–96): 199.

71. Journal, December 1841–December 1842, josephsmithpapers.org; Roberts, *History of the Church*, 1:40. Joseph spoke of the restoration of the Melchizedek Priesthood in a letter to the Church on September 6, 1842 (see Doctrine and Covenants 128:20). Oliver made the following statement about receiving the Melchizedek Priesthood: "After this [the reception of the Aaronic Priesthood], we received the high and holy priesthood; but an account of this will be given elsewhere, or in another place." Patriarchal Blessing Book; Joseph F. Smith, "Restoration of the Melchizedek Priesthood," 942. Oliver also referred to the priesthood in a public address in the fall of 1848: "I was . . . present with Joseph when the higher or Melchisedek Priesthood was conferred by the holy angel from on high. This Priesthood, we then conferred on each other, by the will and commandment of God." "Last Days of Oliver Cowdery," *Deseret Evening News*, Apr. 13, 1859, 48.

72. The Lord referred to this event in a revelation given to Joseph Smith concerning the sacrament, found in Doctrine and Covenants 27. See Revelation, circa August 1830 [D&C 27], 180, josephsmithpapers.org; Doctrine and Covenants 27:12; Roberts, *History of the Church*, 1:40; Larry C. Porter, "Dating the Restoration of the Melchizedek Priesthood," *Ensign*, June 1979, 7. The keys of all dispensations were bestowed upon the Prophet Joseph Smith. "Was the Melchizedek Priesthood conferred upon Joseph Smith and Oliver Cowdery by Peter, James and John? Restoration of the Melchizedek Priesthood," *Improvement Era*, Oct. 1904, 942.

73. Doctrine and Covenants, 1835, 82, josephsmithpapers.org; Doctrine and Covenants 107:1–4.

74. Letter of Addison Everett to Joseph F. Smith, 16 Jan. 1882. Elder Erastus Snow, who was a member of the Quorum of the Twelve Apostles, gave a similar account: "In the due course of time, as we read in the history which he [Joseph] left, Peter, James, and John appeared to him—it was at a period when they were being pursued by their enemies and they had to travel all night, and in the dawn of the coming day when they were weary and worn, who should

appear to them but Peter, James and John, for the purpose of conferring upon them the Apostleship, the keys which they themselves had held while upon the earth, which had been bestowed upon them by the Savior. The Priesthood conferred upon them by those three messengers embraces within it all offices of the Priesthood from the highest to the lowest." Erastus Snow, in *Journal of Discourses*, 23:183; Porter, "Dating the Restoration," 10.

75. Joseph F. Smith, "Restoration of the Melchizedek Priesthood," 941–942; McConkie, *Remembering Joseph*, 260. Larry C. Porter makes a compelling analysis placing the restoration of the Melchizedek Priesthood sometime within a thirteen day period—between the 16th and the 28th of May in 1829. Porter, "The Restoration of the Aaronic and Melchizedek Priesthoods," 30. Oliver commented on the two priesthoods as follows: "John the Baptist, holding the keys of the Aaronic Priesthood; Peter, James and John, holding the keys of the Melchizedek Priesthood, have also ministered for those who shall be heirs of salvation, and with these ministrations ordained men to the same Priesthoods. These Priesthoods, with their authority, are now, and must continue to be, in the body of the Church of Jesus Christ of Latter-day Saints." Letter from Oliver Cowdery to Elder Samuel W. Richards, Jan. 13, 1849, in *Deseret Evening News*, vol. 17, Mar. 22, 1884; Cannon, "Priesthood Restoration Documents," 185. Questions still persist as to why Joseph and Oliver so completely recorded the restoration of the Aaronic Priesthood and not the Melchizedek Priesthood.

CHAPTER 8

Pennsylvania Protects Liberty of Conscience

———— ⟨∞⟩ ————

Chapters 8 and 9 recount in detail the religious protections
afforded by Pennsylvania's Constitution of 1790 and the decisions
of the Supreme Court of Pennsylvania, which were the governing
laws during Joseph Smith's time in Harmony. They also explain the
role these laws played in censuring Joseph's persecutors in Harmony.

THE PENNSYLVANIA CONSTITUTIONS OF 1776 AND 1790 AFFIRMED William Penn's commitment to Liberty of Conscience and adopted his doctrine that civil and spiritual law are derived from God.

THE PENNSYLVANIA CONSTITUTION OF 1776

The Constitution of 1776 preamble states that God is the "Author of existence" who bestowed "natural rights and other blessings" on the inhabitants of Pennsylvania. The preamble establishes God as the "great Governor of the Universe . . . who alone knows to what degree of earthly happiness mankind may attain, by perfecting the arts of government."[1]

The Bill of Rights to the Pennsylvania Constitution of 1776 declared, "That all men have a natural and unalienable right to worship Almighty God, according to the dictates of their own consciences and understanding," and that no one "can be compelled to attend any religious worship . . . against his own free will and consent." Indeed, anyone "who acknowledges the being of a God [cannot] be justly deprived or abridge of any civil right as a citizen, on account of his religious sentiments, or peculiar mode of religious worship," and no power or authority shall "in any case interfere with, or in any manner control the right of conscience in the free exercise of religious worship."[2]

Members of the Pennsylvania legislature were required to make the following declaration before taking office: "I do believe in one God, the creator and governor of the universe, the rewarder of the good and the punisher of the wicked. And I do acknowledge the Scriptures of the Old and New Testament to be given by Divine inspiration."[3]

Section 45 of the Constitution secured further protections for religious societies: "All religious societies or bodies of men heretofore united or incorporated for the advancement of religion or learning, or for other pious and charitable purposes, shall be encouraged and protected in the enjoyment of the privileges, immunities and estates which they were accustomed to enjoy, or could of right have enjoyed, under the laws and former constitution of this state." Finally, the Constitution encouraged virtue and the prevention of vice: "Laws for the encouragement of virtue, and the prevention of vice and immorality, shall be made and constantly kept in force, and provision shall be made for their due execution."[4]

THE PENNSYLVANIA CONSTITUTION OF 1790

The Pennsylvania Constitution of 1790 arguably conferred more protections of Liberty of Conscience than the Constitution of 1776.[5] The Pennsylvania Constitution of 1790 removed the requirement that a person acknowledge God in order to enjoy civil rights, thus extending civil rights to all inhabitants. The 1790 Constitution unconditionally declared, for both believers and non-believers, the following:

- That all men have a natural and indefeasible right to worship Almighty God according to the dictates of their own consciences;
- That no man can of right be compelled to attend, erect or support any place of worship, or to maintain any ministry against his consent;

- That no human authority can, in any case whatever, control or interfere with the rights of conscience; and
- That no preference shall ever be given by law to any religious establishments or modes of worship.[6]

RIDDLE V. STEVENS

In 1816 the Supreme Court of Pennsylvania declared in the case *Riddle v. Stevens* that church laws were not subject to state laws or state authority, thus affirming William Penn's fundamental principle of Liberty of Conscience. The Supreme Court was presented with a dispute between a minister and members of a Presbyterian congregation. The members of the congregation had dismissed the minister based on violations of church rules, and the minister filed a lawsuit claiming that after his discharge, he was owed money under his written contract.[7]

At trial, the jury found in favor of the minister, but the members of the congregation appealed, claiming the trial was in error because they were not permitted to introduce evidence from the church disciplinary proceedings concerning the alleged "improper conduct [of the minister] in his private capacity." The Supreme Court held that the church disciplinary proceedings could not be introduced as evidence for improper conduct of the minister during the trial because "discipline is confined to spiritual affairs; it operates on the mind and conscience, without pretending to temporal authority." In other words, church rules and discipline were not subject to state authority and had no place in the civil context. The state would not interfere with church law and respected the laws of the church.[8]

UPDEGRAPH V. THE COMMONWEALTH

In 1824, the year before Joseph Smith first arrived in Pennsylvania and three years before he and Emma moved permanently to Pennsylvania, the Supreme Court of Pennsylvania handed down the landmark decision *Updegraph v. The Commonwealth*, which enshrined Liberty of Conscience in Pennsylvania law.[9] Mr. Updegraph was charged and indicted by the Commonwealth of Pennsylvania with criticizing the "Christian religion" and "the scriptures of truth" in violation of a Pennsylvania blasphemy statute passed in 1700. The blasphemy statute imposed a fine of ten pounds for "whosoever shall willfully, premeditatedly and despitefully blaspheme, and speak loosely and *profanely* of Almighty God, Christ Jesus, the Holy Spirit, or the Scripture of Truth."[10] Mr. Updegraph was tried before a jury and convicted of possessing "a malicious intention . . . to vilify the Christian religion and the scriptures."[11]

Mr. Updegraph objected to his conviction by challenging the constitutionality of Christianity as part of the common law of Pennsylvania. Mr. Updegraph also argued that his indictment was improper because he was not charged with speaking profanely, as required by the blasphemy statute. The Pennsylvania Supreme Court rejected Mr. Updegraph's challenge to the constitutionality of Christianity, holding that "Christianity is part of the common law of [Pennsylvania]" and that "it is the purest system of morality, the firmest auxiliary, and the only stable support of all human laws."[12] The "laws and institutions" of Pennsylvania were "built on the foundation of reverence for Christianity" and a "complete liberty of conscience."[13]

The Supreme Court pronounced the Charter of the Province of Pennsylvania, the document from Charles II to William Penn conveying the land today known as Pennsylvania, as "the first legislative act in the colony as the recognition of the Christian religion, and establishment of liberty of conscience."[14] The charter was bequested to William Penn "by gentle and just measures, to the love of civil society, and the Christian religion."[15] The Supreme Court reasoned that "Christianity was one of the considerations of the Royal Charter, and the very basis of its great founder, William Penn; not Christianity founded on any particular religious tenets; not Christianity with an established church, and tithes and spiritual courts; *but Christianity with liberty of conscience to all men.*"[16]

The Supreme Court defined Christianity broadly as affording Liberty of Conscience to *all* men, not only the Christian faith or one particular religion. It stated, "No preference is given by law to any particular religious persuasion; protection is given to all by our laws. . . . By general Christianity is not intended the doctrine of any particular church or sect; the law leaves these disputes to theologians;

it is not known as a standard by which to decide political dogmas. The worship of the Jews is under the protection of the laws."[17]

The Supreme Court also relied on the Great Law of Pennsylvania, passed on December 7, 1682, which mandated that the government "make and establish such laws as shall best preserve the Christian and civil liberty."[18] The Great Law of Pennsylvania further proclaimed the "Almighty God, being only Lord of conscience . . . and the author as well as object of all divine knowledge, faith and worship, who only can enlighten the minds, and peruse and convince the understandings of people in due reverence to his sovereignty over the souls of mankind."[19] The Supreme Court, however, ultimately overturned the conviction of Mr. Updegraph on a technicality because the indictment did not charge Mr. Updegraph with speaking profanely, as required by the blasphemy statute. But the court nonetheless emphasized that "man should [not] have the right publicly to vilify the religion of his neighbors of the country."[20]

In summary, the Supreme Court upheld the constitutionality of Liberty of Conscience for all citizens as part of the common law of Pennsylvania and proclaimed Pennsylvania's "complete" liberty of conscience. Referencing William Penn's founding documents and the Pennsylvania charter that William sacrificed so much to protect, the Supreme Court declared, "Our own free constitution secures liberty of conscience and freedom of religious worship to all."[21]

NOTES

1. "Preamble," *The Constitution of the Common-Wealth of Pennsylvania, as Established by the General Convention Elected for that Purpose, and Held at Philadelphia, July 15th, 1776, and Continued by Adjournments to September 28, 1776.*

2. "Bill of Rights," *The Constitution of the Common-Wealth of Pennsylvania [1776].*

3. "Section 10," *The Constitution of the Common-Wealth of Pennsylvania [1776].*

4. "Section 45," *The Constitution of the Common-Wealth of Pennsylvania [1776].*

5. Gary S. Gilden, "Coda to William Penn's Overture: Safeguarding Non-Mainstream Religious Liberty Under The Pennsylvania Constitution," *Journal of Constitutional Law* 4, no. 1 (2001): 107.

6. *Constitution of the Commonwealth of Pennsylvania: 1790*, Historical Society of Pennsylvania, Philadelphia; Gilden, "Coda to William Penn's Overture," 107.

7. 2 Serg. & Rawle 537, 537–38.

8. 2 Serg. & Rawle 537, 543.

9. 11 Serg. & Rawle 394 (Pa. Sept. 13, 1824).

10. 11 Serg. & Rawle 394, 398 (emphasis added).

11. 11 Serg. & Rawle 394, 400.

12. 11 Serg. & Rawle 394, 407.

13. 11 Serg. & Rawle 394, 402.

14. 11 Serg. & Rawle 394, 402.

15. *Charter of the Province of Pennsylvania: Granted by Charles II to William Penn: 1682*, Historical Society of Pennsylvania, Philadelphia.

16. 11 Serg. & Rawle 394, 408 (emphasis added).

17. 11 Serg. & Rawle 394, 408.

18. 11 Serg. & Rawle 394, 402.

19. 11 Serg. & Rawle 394, 402.

20. 11 Serg. & Rawle 394, 408.

21. 11 Serg. & Rawle 394, 408.

CHAPTER 9

JOSEPH SMITH'S PERSECUTORS
ARE CENSURED

———— ∾◎↝ ————

PENNSYLVANIA'S CONSTITUTION OF 1790, AND THE PENNSYLVANIA Supreme Court decisions in *Riddle* and *Updegraph*, ultimately contributed to Joseph Smith's persecutors being censured. The reason Joseph came to Harmony is in fact the same reason he eventually left. Contention began to intensify in the neighborhood, originating in large part with Reverend Nathaniel Lewis.[1] Reverend Lewis and his sons were openly antagonistic toward Joseph, questioning the gold plates and his character.[2] Reverend Lewis did not believe Joseph's message, nor would he accept Joseph's heavenly visits as true. He later commented, "These circumstances and many others of a similar tenor, embolden me to say that Joseph Smith Jr. is not a man of truth and veracity; and that his general character in this part of the county, is that of an imposter, hypocrite and liar."[3]

Others in Harmony agreed with Reverend Lewis's opinion. Levi Lewis thought Joseph to be "a liar," and Alva Hale considered "Joseph Smith Jr., to be an imposter, and a liar, and [knew] Martin Harris to be a liar likewise." Joshua McKune, Joseph's neighbor, considered Joseph and Martin to be "artful seducers."[4] Even Emma's extended family apparently harbored "unprovoked prejudices" against Joseph.[5]

Removal to the Whitmer Farm

Oliver maintained contact with David Whitmer of Fayette during his time in Harmony.[6] He had written David shortly after arriving in Harmony, apprising him of the progress of translation. Later Oliver wrote another letter to him that included a few lines of translated text and assurances that a record of a people that inhabited the American continents indeed existed.[7] Joseph received inspiration that he and Oliver should write another letter to David and ask for help.[8] Oliver wrote the letter, asking David to come to Pennsylvania with a team of horses and take Joseph and Oliver to his farm in New York so they could finish the translation without persecution.[9]

In late May 1829 David prepared to travel to Harmony with a two-horse wagon in order to bring Joseph and Oliver to Fayette.[10] However, he had considerable farm work to do before he could free himself to travel; the field needed harrowing and the plaster of paris sowing. David miraculously harrowed his field in a different manner than he had ever done before and accomplished two days' worth of work in one day. The next morning, when David went to sow the plaster, it was already done. No one knew who had performed the work except his sister who lived across from the field. She said that the day before, her children had called her to watch three strangers spread the plaster with remarkable skill.[11] His work being completed, David immediately left for Harmony.[12]

After a two- or three-day journey, David arrived in Harmony. Oliver and Joseph were waiting for him and met him some distance from their house.[13] David Whitmer later wrote, "Oliver told me that Joseph had informed him when I started from home, where I stopped the first night, how I read the sign at the tavern, where I stopped the next night, etc., and that I would be there that day for dinner, and this is why they had come out to meet me. All of which was exactly as Joseph had told Oliver, at which I was greatly astonished."[14]

David, Oliver, and Joseph quickly left for Fayette, arriving on the first of June.[15] They found the Whitmers and their eight children to be very friendly and eager to learn more about the work.[16] Emma joined Joseph at the Whitmer home shortly thereafter.[17] David arranged for

Joseph and Oliver to board free of charge and for one of his brothers to write for Joseph, and David volunteered his own assistance.[18]

Joseph and Oliver found the people of Seneca County to be of an open and willing disposition. Many of the people opened their doors to Joseph and Oliver and allowed them to teach and instruct them. Joseph wrote, "We met with many from time to time who were willing to hear us, and who desired to find out the truth as it is in Christ Jesus, and apparently willing to obey the Gospel, when once fairly convinced and satisfied in their own minds . . . and some were baptized whilst we continued to instruct and persuade as many as applied for information."[19]

CENSURE OF PERSECUTORS IN HARMONY

If the Pennsylvania Constitution of 1790 and the Supreme Court's decisions in *Riddle* and *Updegraph* protected Joseph and his Liberty of Conscience, then why did Joseph leave Harmony for New York to continue translation of the gold plates? After he and Oliver completed the translation of the gold plates, Joseph and Emma returned to their permanent residence in Harmony. Joseph then wrote a letter to Oliver, dated October 4, 1829, offering key insights as to why he may have left Pennsylvania to complete the translation. He wrote, in part:

> I found all well the people [in Harmony] all friendly to us except a few who are in opposition to evry thing unless it is some thing that is exactly like themselves and two of our most formidable persacutors are now under censure and cited to a trial in the church for crimes which if true are worse than all the Gold Book business. We do not rejoice in the affliction of our enimies but we shall be glad to have truth prevail.[20]

Joseph specifically mentions that "two of our most formidable persacutors are now under censure." The identity of the two persecutors is unclear. They may have been members of the Nathaniel Lewis family, who are often referred to as the source of opposition in Harmony, or they may have been other members of the Harmony community. Regardless of their identity, the persecutors were placed "under censure and cited to trial" for crimes.

These "crimes" may have been related to the persecution of Joseph and Oliver. Joseph expressly calls the two persons "persacutors" and also states that he was "glad to have truth prevail," which may suggest that Joseph knew of the persecutors' crimes against him or against others, and the persecutors previously had not been charged with crimes. Maybe these persecutors—motivated by religious prejudice—had escalated their actions from contention to death threats, arson threats, stealing, or some other crimes in violation of church code.

Apparently Mr. Hale's protection and influence in Harmony could not protect Joseph and Oliver from these two persecutors, or else they may have stayed in Harmony to complete translation of the gold plates. Joseph noted that the two persecutors were "cited to a trial in the church," which means they were subject to a church trial as opposed to a trial before a Pennsylvania state court. Church trials were common in Pennsylvania, and trials before the state court were rare.[21] The Supreme Court of Pennsylvania's decision in *Riddle v. Stevens* in 1816 found that "discipline is confined to spiritual affairs; it operates on the mind and conscience, without pretending to temporal authority."[22] Church discipline was not subject to state authority, and churches had full power and authority to address violations of religious codes without state intervention.

Joseph seems to add humor to his letter when he states that the two persecutors' crimes "are worse than all the Gold Book business." Joseph uses the words "Gold Book business," probably referring to the allegations of his persecutors that he was not doing the work of God by translating the gold plates but that he was fabricating the story to achieve financial gain. Joseph also highlights the hypocrisy of his persecutors by recognizing that their crimes were much worse than his supposed crime.

If the crimes of the persecutors were directed toward Joseph and Oliver, the crimes likely violated Pennsylvania law or church law. Four years earlier, the Pennsylvania Supreme Court had decided *Updegraph v. The Commonwealth*, which unequivocally secured "complete" Liberty of Conscience in Pennsylvania for Joseph and others and also affirmed Pennsylvania's blasphemy statute. It likely was common understanding in Harmony that (1) the Constitution of Pennsylvania "secures liberty of conscience and freedom of religious worship to all," and (2) "[no] man should have the right publicly to vilify the religion of his neighbors of the country."²³ Vilifying Joseph Smith for his alleged "Gold Book business" may have been a violation of the blasphemy statute, while Joseph exercising Liberty of Conscience was absolutely protected.

In summary, Joseph and Oliver probably left Pennsylvania to continue translation of the plates in part because of these two persecutors who likely were attempting to commit crimes against Joseph and Oliver. Because the persecutors were censured under church law or Pennsylvania law, Joseph was probably able to return to Pennsylvania after the translation was completed, with the intention to live permanently in Pennsylvania. Joseph's letter to Oliver illustrates that Pennsylvania's laws protecting "complete" Liberty of Conscience enabled Joseph's "formidable persacutors" to be censured and afflicted.

THE TRANSLATION CONTINUES

Upon settling in at the Whitmers' home, Joseph continued the translation in the upstairs room, probably starting with the small plates of Nephi.²⁴ While Oliver served as Joseph's principal scribe, David, John, Peter Jr., and Christian Whitmer were devoted assistants, willing to start working early in the morning until late at night.²⁵ "It was a laborious work for the weather was warm, and the days were long and they worked from morning till night," said David Whitmer.²⁶

As Joseph translated, apparently his ability and understanding increased, making him a more efficient translator.²⁷ Sometime before June 11, 1829, Joseph applied for a copyright for the Book of Mormon.²⁸

David Whitmer described his experience in translating the plates as follows:

Joseph Smith would put the seer stone into a hat, and put his face in that hat, drawing it closely around his face to exclude the light; and in the darkness the spiritual light would shine. A piece of something resembling parchment would appear, and on that appeared the writing. One character at a time would appear, and under it was the interpretation in English. Brother Joseph would read off the English to Oliver Cowdery, who was his principal scribe, and when it was written down and repeated it to Brother Joseph to see if it was correct, then it would disappear, and another character with the interpretation would appear. Thus the Book of Mormon was translated by the gift and power of God, and not by any power of man.[29]

Scribe	Tasks
Martin Harris	The 116 pages of manuscript that were later lost
Oliver Cowdery	Principal scribe of the Book of Mormon who wrote more pages than all of the other scribes combined
Emma Hale Smith	A few passages while awaiting the arrival of Oliver Cowdery, who arrived in Harmony, Pennsylvania on April 5, 1829, and maybe other passages
Samuel Smith	A few passages likely in summer of 1829
Reuben Hale	Assisted in Harmony, Pennsylvania
Christian Whitmer	Assisted in Fayette, New York
David Whitmer	Assisted in Fayette, New York
Unknown scribes	Assisted throughout the translation process

At least seven scribes assisted Joseph in translating the Book of Mormon.[30]

According to David Whitmer, Joseph could only translate when he was humble, faithful, and clear of conscious. He recalled, "At times when Brother Joseph would attempt to translate . . . he found he was spiritually blind and could not translate. He told us his mind dwelt too much on earthly things, and various causes would make him incapable of proceeding with the translation. When in this condition he would go out and pray, and when he became sufficiently humble before God, he could then proceed with the translation."[31] One such experience stood out in David's mind:

> One morning when [Joseph] was getting ready to continue the translation, something went wrong about the house and he was put out about it. Something that Emma, his wife, had done. Oliver and I went up stairs and Joseph came up soon after to continue the

Book of Mormon original manuscript of 1 Nephi 3
© By Intellectual Reserve, Inc.

translation, but he could not do anything. He could not translate a single syllable. He went down stairs, out into the orchard and made supplication to the Lord; was gone about an hour—came back to the house, asked Emma's forgiveness and then came up stairs where we were and the translation went on all right. He could do nothing save he was humble and faithful.[32]

David Whitmer later said that Joseph "had to trust in God" in order to translate the plates.[33] He said Joseph was "but little versed in Biblical lore, was oftimes compelled to spell the words out, not knowing the correct pronunciation . . . [and he] did not even know that Jerusalem was a walled city."[34] Hiram Page, who later assisted Joseph, stated that "to say that a man of Joseph's ability, who at that time did not know how to pronounce the word Nephi, could write a book of six hundred pages, as correct as the Book of Mormon, without supernatural power . . . would be treating the God of heaven with contempt."[35]

While in Harmony, Joseph and Oliver likely started translating in the Book of Mosiah (the beginning of the plates of Mormon).[36] They would have continued until the beginning of June, completing the plates of Mormon, including the writings of Mormon, Ether, and Moroni and the title page.[37] The text for the title page (the last leaf of the plates of Mormon) was used as the book's description on the copyright form filed by Joseph on June 11, 1829, in the United States Federal Court of the Northern District of New York, which is consistent with Joseph and Oliver finishing the plates of Mormon in early June.[38]

Once in Fayette, New York, at the Whitmers' home, Joseph probably started translating the small plates of Nephi (1 Nephi to Omni) and the Words of Mormon, which would have taken him until the end of June.[39] It is estimated that Joseph and Oliver completed the entire translation of the Book of Mormon in around sixty-three days—essentially dictating 3,500 words per day.[40] It is miraculous that the translation was completed in such a remarkably short time period.[41]

Pennsylvania was the ideal state for safeguarding the plates because of its exceptional protection of religious liberty. Despite the numerous detailed accounts of the translation of the Book of Mormon, many people did not believe that Joseph, a young man with little formal education, could accomplish such a monumental task. Joseph

Smith later wrote that the translation of the Book of Mormon was made possible only by the "gift and power of God." Joseph's scribes agreed that he was only able to translate by the power of God.[42]

Time Period*	Portion of Book of Mormon Translated
April 12 to June 14, 1828	The Book of Lehi from Mormon's abridgment of the large plates of Nephi
January to March 1829	A few passages from the Book of Mosiah contained in the large plates
April 7 to June 1, 1829	The remaining portion of the large plates (the plates of Mormon), including the writings of Mormon, Ether, and Moroni and the title page
After June 1 until the end of June	The small plates of Nephi (1 Nephi to Omni) and the Words of Mormon

*Time periods are estimates and not exact;
the specific dates included in the chart are for ease of reference.*

Time line of the translation of Book of Mormon.

THE ELEVEN WITNESSES OF THE GOLD PLATES

Oliver Cowdery, David Whitmer, and Martin Harris desired to view the plates themselves.[43] In June 1829, with this purpose in mind, Joseph and the three men retired to the woods adjacent to the Whitmer home and knelt in humble prayer.[44] After much prayer and no result, Martin Harris withdrew himself from the group to another location in the forest, believing that his presence was preventing communication with God. The others continued in prayer, and moments later an angel appeared to them with the gold plates in his hands.

They saw the plates with their own eyes. The men heard a voice say, "These plates have been revealed by the power of God, and they have been translated by the power of God; the translation of them which you have seen is correct, and I command you to bear record of what you now see and hear."[45] David described the plates as "about eight inches wide and six or seven inches long, as they appeared a little wider than long, and three rings to keep the plates together: one above, one in the middle, and one below, so the angel could turn every leaf entirely over. He said the gold plates were about the thickness of a common sheet of tin."[46] Joseph then joined Martin Harris in a place not too far away, and the angel again displayed the plates to both of them in the same manner as the others.

After showing the plates to Oliver, Martin, and David (sometimes called the Three Witnesses), Joseph told his parents that an extraordinary burden had been lifted from him:

> Father, mother, you do not know how happy I am: the Lord has now caused the plates to be shown to three more besides myself. They have seen an angel, who has testified to them, and they will have to bear witness to the truth of what I have said, for they know for themselves, that I do not go about to deceive the people, and I feel as if I was relieved of a burden which was almost too heavy for me to bear; and it rejoices my soul, that I am not any longer to be entirely alone in the world.[47]

Martin Harris was overcome with joy and cried out, "'Tis enough; 'Tis enough; mine eyes have beheld; mine eyes have beheld!" Jumping up in the air, he shouted "Hosannah" and praised the Lord. According to Lucy Smith, David and Oliver responded similarly: "No tongue could express the joy in their hearts, and the greatness of the things which they had both seen and heard."[48] This experience fulfilled the law of witnesses contained in 2 Corinthians 13:1, which reads, "In the mouth of two or three witnesses shall every word be established."[49]

A few days later, Joseph showed the plates to eight other men (sometimes called the Eight Witnesses): Christian Whitmer, Jacob Whitmer, Peter Whitmer Jr., John Whitmer, Hiram Page, Joseph Smith Sr., Hyrum Smith, and Samuel H. Smith.[50] They were permitted to handle and see the plates. This fulfilled a prophecy in the Book of Nephi of the Book of Mormon, which foretold that not only three witnesses would view the plates but "more witnesses" as well (2 Nephi

11:3). Though many of the witnesses eventually left the Church, not one denied his testimony of the Book of Mormon.[51]

A replica of the Book of Mormon gold plates.
© By Intellectual Reserve, Inc.

All eleven witnesses left personal restatements of their experience and apparently shared their testimonies often.[52] All testified not only that they saw the plates but also that the teachings of the Book of Mormon were significant and important to the modern world.[53] They believed that all who read and hear their testimonies will be accountable for their acceptance or rejection of the Book of Mormon and the teachings of Jesus Christ contained therein.[54]

The Testimonies of Martin Harris, David Whitmer, and Oliver Cowdery

Martin Harris, David Whitmer, and Oliver Cowdery, all witnesses of the plates and scribes for the translation of the Book of Mormon, affirmed their testimonies later in their lives. Martin Harris gave his testimony of the gold plates and Joseph's work, saying, "I was the right-hand man of Joseph Smith, and I know he was a Prophet of God. I know the Book of Mormon is true." Then, pounding his fist on the table, he said, "And you know that I know that it is true. I know that the plates have been translated by the gift and power of God, for his voice declared it unto us; therefore I know of a surety that the work is true."[55]

David Whitmer later affirmed his witness of the gold plates:

That the world may know the truth, I wish now, standing as it were, in the very sunset of my life, and in the fear of God, once and for all to make this public statement. That I have never at any time denied that testimony or any part therefore, which has so long since been published with that book, as one of the three witnesses. Those who know me best, well know that I have always adhered to that testimony. And that no man may be misled or doubt my present views in regard to the same, I do again affirm the truth of all of my statements, as then made and published. He that hath an ear to hear, let him hear; it was no delusion! What is written is written, and he that readeth, let him understand.[56]

Oliver Cowdery later testified as to the restoration of the priesthood of God:

In fulfillment of the sacred scriptures, the everlasting gospel was proclaimed by the mighty angel (Moroni) who, clothed in the authority of his mission, gave glory to God in the highest. This gospel is the 'stone taken from the mountain without hands.' John the Baptist, holding the keys of the Aaronic Priesthood; Peter, James and John, holding the keys of the Melchizedek Priesthood, have also ministered for those who shall be heirs of salvation, and with these administrations, ordained men to the same priesthoods. These priesthoods, with their authority, are now, and must continue to be, in the body of The Church of Jesus Christ of Latter-day Saints.[57]

Three and Eight Witnesses of the Book of Mormon gold plates,
Printer's Manuscript of the Book of Mormon, circa August 1829–circa
January 1830. © By Intellectual Reserve, Inc.

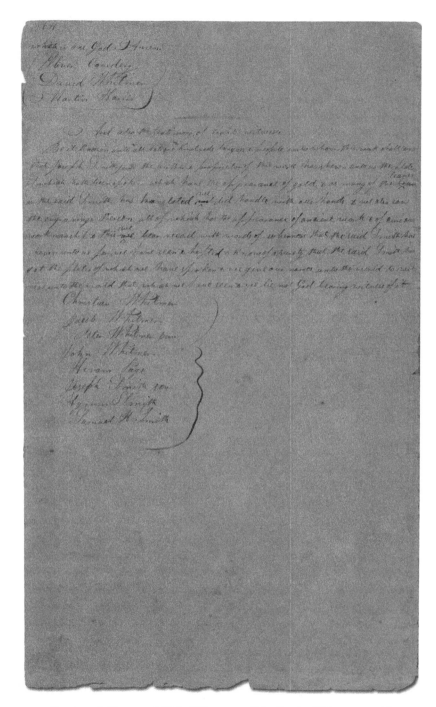

Continued: Three and Eight Witnesses of the Book of Mormon gold plates, Printer's Manuscript of the Book of Mormon, circa August 1829–circa January 1830. © By Intellectual Reserve, Inc.

Notes

1. Larry C. Porter, "The Book of Mormon: Historical Setting for Its Translation and Publication," in *Joseph Smith: The Prophet, The Man*, ed. Susan Easton Black and Charles D. Tate Jr. (Provo, UT: BYU Religious Studies Center, 1993), 49. Apparently Nathaniel Lewis, Emma's uncle, was the most opposed to Joseph. Susan Easton Black, "Isaac Hale: Antagonist of Joseph Smith," in *Regional Studies in Latter-day Saint Church History: New York* (Provo, UT: BYU Department of Church History and Doctrine, 1992), 7. Historian Mark Staker has commented, "In fact, Emma's uncle, Methodist minister Nathaniel Lewis [was] Joseph's greatest opponent in Harmony." Mark Lyman Staker, "Where Was the Aaronic Priesthood Restored?: Identifying the Location of John the Baptist's Appearance, May 15, 1829," *Mormon Historical Studies* 12, no. 2 (2011): 154.

2. *Modified Register for Nathaniel Lewis: First Generation*, Descendants of Nathaniel Lewis, Aug. 6, 2005, 1, Susquehanna Historical Society, Montrose, PA; Stanley James Thayne, "In Harmony? Perceptions of Mormonism in Susquehanna, Pennsylvania," *Journal of Mormon History* (Fall 2007): 118, fn. 11. Nathaniel Lewis's preaching style made him the religious authority of the family. *Modified Register for Nathaniel Lewis*, 1.

3. Statement of Nathaniel C. Lewis, Mar. 20, 1834, published in *The Susquehanna Register* (Montrose, PA), May 1, 1834; Larry C. Porter, *A Study of the Origins of the Church of Jesus Christ of Latter-day Saints in the States of New York and Pennsylvania, 1816–1831* (Provo, UT: BYU Studies, 2000), 63; Susan Easton Black, "Isaac Hale: Antagonist of Joseph Smith," in *Regional Studies in Latter-day Saint Church History: New York* (Provo, UT: BYU Department of Church History and Doctrine, 1992), 9.

4. Statement of Joshua McKune, Mar. 20, 1834, published in *The Susquehanna Register* (Montrose, PA), May 1, 1834. See statements of Joshua McKune, Alva Hale, Levi Lewis, and Sophia Lewis in Howe, in E. D. Howe, *Mormonism Unvailed* (Painesville, OH: 1834), 263; Rhamanthus M. Stocker, *Centennial History of Susquehanna County, Pennsylvania*, 2nd ed. (Baltimore, MD: Regional Publishing Company, 1974), 266–269.

5. Lorenzo Wasson to Emma Hale Smith, Undated [ca. December 1840–April 1841], L. Tom Perry Special Collections, Harold B. Lee Library, Brigham Young University, Provo, Utah; Mark L. Staker, "A Comfort unto My Servant, Joseph," in *Women of Faith in the Latter Days: Volume 1, 1775–1820*, ed. Richard E. Turley Jr. and Brittany A. Chapman (Salt Lake City, UT: Deseret Book, 2011), 343–362. Lorenzo Wasson, Emma's nephew, later in his life admitted that he had been raised to believe incorrect things about his uncle Joseph. Staker, "A Comfort unto My Servant, Joseph," 343–362.

6. "Historical Introduction," Revelation, June 1829–A [D&C 14], josephsmith-papers.org.

7. Larry C. Porter, "From a Book Coming Forth," *Ensign*, July 1988, 42.

8. Lucy Mack Smith, History, 1844–1845, book 8, 8, josephsmithpapers.org; Lucy Mack Smith, *Lucy's Book: A Critical Edition of Lucy Mack Smith's Family Memoir*, ed. Lavina Fielding Anderson (Salt Lake City, UT: Signature Books, 2001), 446 (manuscript version).

9. "Mormonism," *Kansas City Daily Journal*, June 5, 1881, 1.

10. History, circa June 1839–circa 1841 [Draft 2], 21, josephsmithpapers.org; B. H. Roberts, *A Comprehensive History of the Church of Jesus Christ of Latter-day Saints* (Salt Lake City, UT: Deseret News, 1948–57), 1:48–49. The Whitmer farm is about twenty-seven miles southeast of Palmyra, between Seneca Lake and Lake Cayuga. The Whitmers were Pennsylvania Germans who had moved to Fayette around 1809, purchased a farm, and joined the German Reformed Church. The town elected Peter Whitmer Sr. as overseer of highways and as school trustee. The entire family took an interest in Joseph's translation. Fayette is "where Joseph Smith and Oliver Cowdery completed the translation of the gold plates, the site of twenty revelations to the Lord's prophet, and the location where the first and second elders of the Restoration determined to organize the Church." Michael Hubbard MacKay, *Sacred Space: Exploring the Birthplace of Mormonism* (Provo, UT: BYU Religious Studies Center, 2016), viii (foreword).

11. Lucy Mack Smith, History, 1844–1845, book 8, 8–9, josephsmithpapers.org; Smith, *Lucy's Book*, 447–49 (manuscript version).

12. Lucy Mack Smith, History, 1844–1845, book 8, 9, josephsmithpapers.org; Smith, *Lucy's Book*, 449 (manuscript version).

13. "Mormonism," 1..

14. "Report of Elders Orson Pratt and Joseph F. Smith," *The Latter-Day Saints' Millennial Star* 40 (Dec. 9, 1878): 772.

15. During the journey, Joseph and Oliver saw a man who appeared alongside their wagon. When they invited him to ride with them, he said pleasantly, "No, I am going to Cumorah." He had on his back a sort of knapsack with something in it shaped like a book. It was most likely the messenger Moroni, who had apparently taken the plates from Joseph just prior to leaving Harmony. "Report of Elders," 772–73. See also Joseph F. Smith, New York City, NY, to John Taylor et al., [Salt Lake City, Utah Territory], 17 Sept. 1878, draft, Joseph F. Smith Papers, Church History Library, Salt Lake City.

16. History, circa June 1839–circa 1841 [Draft 2], 22, josephsmithpapers.org; Roberts, *History of the Church*, 1:49. Joseph Smith received revelations for David, John, and Peter Whitmer while in Fayette. These revelations are now located in the current version of the Doctrine and Covenants under sections 14, 15, and 16. See Revelation, June 1829–A [D&C 14], Revelation, June 1829–C [D&C 15], and Revelation, June 1829–D [D&C 16], josephsmithpapers.org; History, circa June 1839–circa 1841 [Draft 2], 22–23, josephsmithpapers.org; Roberts, *History of the Church*, 1:49–51. In early June Joseph also

received a revelation containing the duties of twelve future leaders of the Church. Revelation, June 1829–B [D&C 18], josephsmithpapers.org.

17. Smith, *Lucy's Book*, 450, fn. 230 (manuscript version).

18. Mrs. Mary Musselman Whitmer had the opportunity to see the plates while Joseph stayed at Fayette. David Whitmer recalled, "She was met out near the yard by the same old man (judging by her description of him) who said to her: 'You have been very faithful and diligent in your labors, but you are tired because of the increase of your toil, it is proper therefore that you should receive a witness that your faith may be strengthened.' Thereupon he showed her the plates. My father and mother had a large family of their own, in addition to it therefore of Joseph, his wife Emma and Oliver very greatly increased the toil and anxiety of my mother. And although she never complained she had sometimes felt that her labor was too much, or at least she was perhaps beginning to feel so. This circumstance, however, completely removed all such feelings and nerved her up for her increased responsibilities." "Report of Elders Orson Pratt and Joseph F. Smith," 772–73.

19. History, circa June 1839–circa 1841 [Draft 2], 23, josephsmithpapers.org; Roberts, *History of the Church*, 1:51; "Report of Elders Orson Pratt and Joseph F. Smith," 772–73.

20. Letter to Oliver Cowdery, 22 October 1829, 9, josephsmithpapers.org.

21. J. William Frost, *A Perfect Freedom: Religious Liberty in Pennsylvania* (University Park, PA: Pennsylvania State University Press, 1993), 34; Emily C. Blackman, *History of Susquehanna County, Pennsylvania* (Philadelphia: Claxton, Remsen & Haffelfinger, 1873), 582.

22. 2 Serg. & Rawle 537 (Pa. Sept., 1816), 543.

23. 11 Serg. & Rawle 394 (Pa. Sept. 13, 1824), 408.

24. Historian Dean Jessee suggests that Joseph and Oliver began translating in the book of Mosiah in Harmony and started the small plates of Nephi around the time he and Joseph arrived in Fayette, New York. He believes the plates of Nephi—comprising First Nephi to Mosiah—were translated after the completion of the plates of Mormon. Dean. C. Jessee, "The Original Book of Mormon Manuscript," *BYU Studies* 10, no. 3 (1970): 12–13. The evidence supports Dean Jessee's theory that Oliver and Joseph commenced with the Book of Mosiah. In the original manuscript of the Book of Mormon, John Whitmer's work as scribe only dealt with material from the small plates. If Oliver and Joseph had started translating the small plates of Nephi, they would have discussed the promised Three Witnesses while in Harmony (instead of Fayette), and John Whitmer likely would have served as scribe for material on the large plates.

25. Porter, "The Book of Mormon: Historical Setting," 49. This is not a comprehensive list of scribes or a list of those believed to be scribes. For a discussion of the transcription performed by various scribes, both known and unknown, see Royal Skousen, "Oliver Cowdery as Book of Mormon Scribe," in *Days Never*

to Be Forgotten: Oliver Cowdery, ed. Alexander L. Baugh (Provo, UT: BYU Religious Studies Center, 2009), 51–70.

26. James H. Hart, "About the Book of Mormon," *Deseret News* (Salt Lake City, UT), Apr. 9, 1884, 190; "Historical Introduction," Book of Mormon Manuscript Excerpt, circa June 1829 [1 Nephi 2:2b–3:18a], josephsmithpapers.org.

27. Tim Rathbone and John W. Welch, "Translation of the Book of Mormon by Joseph Smith," in Daniel H. Ludlow, S. Kent Brown, and John W. Welch, *To All the World: The Book of Mormon Articles from the Encyclopedia of Mormonism* (Provo, UT: F.A.R.M.S., 2000); William E. Berrett, *The Restored Church* (Salt Lake City, UT: Deseret Book, 1969), 34.

28. Copyright for Book of Mormon, 11 June 1829, josephsmithpapers.org; Richard L. Bushman, "The Recovery of the Book of Mormon," in Noel B. Reynolds, ed., *Book of Mormon Authorship Revisited: The Evidence for Ancient Origins* (Provo, UT: F.A.R.M.S., 1997), 28. By this time, Joseph had finished the plates of Mormon and had translated Mormon's title page.

29. David Whitmer, *An Address to All Believers in Christ: By a Witness to the Divine Authenticity of the Book of Mormon* (Richmond, MO: by the author, 1887), 12.

30. "Printer's Manuscript of the Book of Mormon," Joseph Smith Papers, accessed Mar. 22, 2024, https://www.josephsmithpapers.org/intro/introduction-to-revelations-and-translations-volume-3.

31. Whitmer, *An Address to All Believers*, 30.

32. "Letter From Elder W. H. Kelley," *The Saints' Herald*, Mar. 1, 1882, 68.

33. "David Whitmer, interview by William H. Kelley and George A. Blakeslee, Sept. 15, 1881," *The Saints' Herald*, Mar. 1, 1882, 68.

34. "The Book of Mormon," *Chicago Daily Tribune*, Dec. 17, 1885, 3. It is true that the Smiths were poor and generally ignorant in common learning. It was said of Joseph, "Joseph Smith is a person of very limited abilities in common learning—but his knowledge of *divine things* . . . has astonished many." "Letter of W. W. Phelps to E. D. Howe, Jan. 15, 1831," in *Mormonism Unvailed*, 274.

35. "Hiram Page Letter to William E. McLellin, written 30 May 1847," *The Ensign of Liberty of the Church of Christ* (Kirtland, OH) 1 (Jan. 1848): 63.

36. "Historical Introduction," Book of Mormon Manuscript Excerpt, circa June 1829 [1 Nephi 2:2b–3:18a], fn. 2, josephsmithpapers.org; John W. Welch, "The Miraculous Translation of the Book of Mormon," in John W. Welch, ed., *Opening the Heavens: Accounts of Divine Manifestations, 1820–1844* (Provo, UT: Brigham Young University Press, 2005), 100, fn. 110.

37. Joseph Smith recorded that the title page was "taken from the very last leaf, on the left hand side of the collection or book of plates," which may have been the last page of the plates. History, circa June 1839–circa 1841 [Draft 2], 34, josephsmithpapers.org; "Historical Introduction," Title Page of Book of Mormon, circa Early June 1829, fn. 2, josephsmithpapers.org.

38. Copyright for Book of Mormon, 11 June 1829, josephsmithpapers.org; "Historical Introduction," Title Page of Book of Mormon, circa Early June 1829, josephsmithpapers.org. Some scholars believe that it is likely that Joseph did not complete all the requirements in order to secure a copyright for the Book of Mormon. The process for obtaining a copyright of the Book of Mormon was likely performed by Martin Harris. Michael Hubbard MacKay and Gerrit J. Dirkmaat, *From Darkness unto Light: Joseph Smith's Translation and Publication of the Book of Mormon* (Provo, UT: BYU Religious Studies Center, 2015), 165.

39. Smith, *Lucy's Book*, 451, fn. 232 (manuscript version).

40. Welch, "Miraculous Translation of the Book of Mormon," 79, 102 (collecting and analyzing 202 original documents pertaining to the translation of the Book of Mormon).

41. Welch, "Miraculous Translation of the Book of Mormon," 79–82. In this article, Professor Welch has provided a helpful time line of the events surrounding the translation of the Book of Mormon.

42. Preface to Book of Mormon, circa August 1829, iii, josephsmithpapers.org; Gospel Topics Essays, "Book of Mormon Translation," Gospel Library. Joseph once stated, "It was not intended to tell the world all the particulars of the coming forth of the Book of Mormon." Minute Book 2, 10–15, josephsmithpapers.org

43. "Historical Introduction," Revelation, June 1829–E [D&C 17], josephsmithpapers.org. Joseph inquired of the Lord and received a revelation that the three men would see the plates by their faith in order to "testify of them by the power of God." Revelation, June 1829–E [D&C 17], 119, josephsmithpapers.org.

44. Martin Harris had traveled from his home in Palmyra to the Whitmers' home in order to visit Joseph. Andrew Jenson, *Latter-Day Saint Biographical Encyclopedia* (Salt Lake City, UT: Deseret News, 1941), 1:272. Historians suggest that two passages in the Book of Mormon, Ether 5:2–4 and 2 Nephi 27:12, prompted the men to ask if others, apart from Joseph, could see the plates. "Historical Introduction," Revelation, June 1829–E [D&C 17], josephsmithpapers.org; Bushman, "The Recovery of the Book of Mormon," 16. These scriptures foretell that three witnesses shall see the plates and testify of their authenticity.

45. "Mormonism," 1; Richard Lyman Bushman, *Joseph Smith: Rough Stone Rolling* (New York: Alfred A. Knopf, 2005), 78.

46. P. W. Poulson to editors of the Deseret News, Aug. 13, 1878, cited in *Deseret News*, Aug. 16, 1878, 2. One hundred and forty-four original manuscript leaves of the Book of Mormon are currently filed in the Church Historian's Office in Salt Lake City, Utah. (Of the 144 pages, 124 are in the handwriting of Oliver Cowdery, and 11 were probably written by John Whitmer.) Jessee, "The Original Book of Mormon Manuscript," 12. The three men also saw the

breastplate, the Urim and Thummim, the sword of Laban, and the Liahona. Bushman, *Joseph Smith: Rough Stone Rolling*, 77. David later recalled, "About half the book was sealed. Those leaves which were not sealed, about the half of the first part of the book, were numerous, and the angel turned them over before our eyes." P. W. Poulson to editors, 2.

47. Lucy Mack Smith, *Biographical Sketches of Joseph Smith the Prophet and His Progenitors for Many Generations* (Liverpool: S. W. Richards, 1853), 139; Lucy Mack Smith, *Lucy's Book: A Critical Edition of Lucy Mack Smith's Family Memoir*, ed. Lavina Fielding Anderson (Salt Lake City, UT: Signature Books, 2001), 451 (Pratt version); Joseph Fielding Smith, *Essentials in Church History*, 23rd ed. (Salt Lake City, UT: Deseret Book, 1969), 64–65.

48. Lucy Mack Smith, History, 1844–1845, book 8, 11, josephsmithpapers.org; Smith, *Lucy's Book*, 453 (manuscript version); Joseph Fielding Smith, *Essentials in Church History*, 64–65.

49. "Visions of Joseph Smith," *Encyclopedia of Mormonism*, ed. Daniel H. Ludlow (New York: Macmillan, 1992), 4:1512.

50. James B. Allen and Glen M. Leonard, *Story of the Latter-day Saints*, 2nd ed. (Salt Lake City, UT: Deseret Book, 1992), 52. For Hyrum Smith, this was a never-to-be-forgotten moment. Pearson H. Corbett, *Hyrum Smith, Patriarch* (Salt Lake City, UT: Deseret Book, 1963), 53. The Three Witnesses' experience differed from that of the Eight Witnesses. An angel showed the Three Witnesses the plates and turned the pages for them, while the Eight Witnesses were shown the plates by Joseph himself and were able to touch and feel them. Terryl L. Givens, *By the Hand of Mormon: The American Scripture that Launched a New World Religion* (New York: Oxford University Press, 2002), 40.

51. Richard Lloyd Anderson, "Personal Writings of the Book of Mormon Witnesses," in Noel B. Reynolds, ed., *Book of Mormon Authorship Revisited: The Evidence for Ancient Origins* (Provo, UT: F.A.R.M.S., 1997), 2. In that same month of June, Joseph baptized Hyrum Smith, David Whitmer, and Peter Whitmer Jr. in Seneca Lake. *Times and Seasons* (Nauvoo, IL), Sept. 1, 1842, vol. 3, no. 21, 897.

52. MacKay and Dirkmaat, *From Darkness unto Light*, 154.

53. The testimony of the eleven witnesses (two separate testimonies—one testimony by the first Three Witnesses and the other by the later Eight Witnesses) was published at the end of the first edition of the Book of Mormon. Appendix 4: Testimony of Three Witnesses, Late June 1829, josephsmithpapers.org.

54. John Whitmer, History, 1831–ca. 1847, as found in "The Book of John, Whitmer kept by Comma[n]d," ca. 1838–ca. 1847, handwriting of John Whitmer, 25, Community of Christ Library Archives, Independence, MO; Anderson, "Personal Writings of the Book of Mormon Witnesses," 8. "Faithful scholars have turned up evidence that refutes most of the criticisms [of the Book of Mormon] and they have found mountains of turned up evidence

for the book's ancient origins—evidence that is rarely confronted squarely by critics." Noel B. Reynolds, "Introduction," in Noel B. Reynolds, ed., *Book of Mormon Authorship Revisited: The Evidence for Ancient Origins* (Provo, UT: F.A.R.M.S., 1997), 2.

55. "Testimonies of Oliver Cowdery and Martin Harris," *Latter-Day Saints' Millennial Star* 21 (Aug. 20, 1859): 545. Martin Harris "clung tenaciously to his testimony of the Book of Mormon." Susan Easton Black and Larry C. Porter, *Martin Harris: Uncompromising Witness of the Book of Mormon* (Provo, UT: Brigham Young University, 2018), xiii (foreword). Martin also "risked his financial standing in Palmyra and marital accord to finance the Book of Mormon publication" and "put his reputation on the line as year after year he testified of the truthfulness of the Book of Mormon." Black and Porter, *Martin Harris*, xiv (foreword).

56. Whitmer, *An Address to All Believers,* 8–9. David Whitmer, in speaking of the Three Witnesses, further stated, "It is recorded in the American Cyclopaedia and the Encyclopaedia Brittanica, that I David Whitmer, have denied my testimony as one of the three witnesses to the divinity of the Book of Mormon; and that the other two witnesses, Oliver Cowdery and Martin Harris, denied their testimony or any part thereof. I also testify to the world, that neither Oliver Cowdery nor Martin Harris, ever at any time denied their testimony. They both died reaffirming the truth of the divine authenticity of the Book of Mormon. I was present at the deathbed of Oliver Cowdery, and his last words were, Brother David, be true to your testimony to the Book of Mormon. He died here in Richmond, Missouri, on March 3rd, 1850. Many witnesses yet live in Richmond who will testify to the truth of these facts, as well as to the good character of Oliver Cowdery." Whitmer, 8.

57. "Testimonies of Oliver Cowdery and Martin Harris," 545–46.

CHAPTER 10

PENNSYLVANIA COMPARED
TO OTHER COLONIES

———— ∞◎∞ ————

*This chapter compares the Pennsylvania Constitution with
the constitutions of other colonies and shows that it offered the
highest protection of religious liberty. Chapters 11 and 12 recount
Joseph Smith's arrests in New York and his accomplishments of
publishing the Book of Mormon, organizing the Church, and
receiving significant revelations, all while maintaining his home in
Harmony.*

WILLIAM PENN PIONEERED PROTECTIONS OF LIBERTY OF CONSCIENCE
in early America. He made Liberty of Conscience and toleration of
eclectic beliefs the hallmark of Pennsylvania's laws and system of government.[1] The Pennsylvania Constitution provided the most protection of religion and religious worship among the colonial constitutions of the era.[2] Thomas Jefferson called Pennsylvania's approach to
Liberty of Conscience a religious "experiment" of toleration that flourished "infinitely" in order to "preserve peace and order."[3] For Thomas
Jefferson, Pennsylvania was "the cradle of toleration and freedom of
religion."[4] James Madison wrote that Pennsylvania's "alliance between
law and religion" was a safe practice and a sound theory.[5]

Between 1776 and 1789, twelve of the thirteen original colonies drafted constitutions. Rhode Island was governed by a Royal
Charter and was the only exception.[6] Of the twelve colonies, only

eight colonies included a Declaration of Rights, or a statement of rights similar to the Bill of Rights of the United States Constitution. Pennsylvania included a Declaration of Rights making religion and religious worship its primary focus.[7] Constitutions of the colonial era, including Pennsylvania, addressed religion and religious worship in six ways: (1) a declaration of right to worship God; (2) protection of freedom of worship; (3) freedom from compelled religious attendance; (4) freedom from compelled financial contribution; (5) regulation of religious establishments; and (6) religious tests for civil rights and political office.

A Declaration of the Right to Worship God

The colony of Pennsylvania's Declaration of Rights provides that "all men have a natural and unalienable right to worship Almighty God according to the dictates of their own conscience and understanding."[8] Only four other colonies—Delaware, North Carolina, Vermont, and New Hampshire—provided the same protection, while the other three colonies with Declarations of Rights—Virginia, Maryland, and Massachusetts—emphasized individual religious duties instead of natural rights. A natural right that was derived from the existence of humanity is a more compelling statement of law than an individual religious duty and in theory would offer more protection to individuals.[9] In contrast, New York did not enact a separate Declaration of Rights with its constitution.[10] Thus, Pennsylvania followed the most liberal approach of the colonies to protecting religious worship in its Declaration of Rights.

Protection of Freedom of Worship

The Pennsylvania Constitution of 1776 absolutely, without qualification, protected "the right of conscience in the free exercise of religious worship." It also prohibited the state from interfering with this right. This is the strongest legal statement and protection of this right. Only Vermont and Delaware used similar language. In contrast, New Jersey, Maryland, North Carolina, Georgia, Massachusetts, New Hampshire, and New York qualified the right to worship, or provided exceptions to the right. For example, New York excluded religious worship that consisted of "acts of licentiousness" or was "inconsistent with the peace or safety of this State."[11] Thus, the New York Constitution provides grounds on which the state could outlaw religious acts. In other words, this exception in the New York Constitution could be interpreted broadly and abused by a state authority.[12] South Carolina's constitution did not guarantee a right to worship, and Virginia's constitution delegated how worship would be protected to legislative action. In short, Pennsylvania was among the colonies that offered "a more complete protection for the freedom to worship."[13]

FREEDOM FROM COMPELLED RELIGIOUS ATTENDANCE

Some state constitutions provided that individuals could not be compelled to attend religious worship against their will. For example, Pennsylvania's Constitution of 1776 stated, "No man . . . can be compelled to attend any religious worship . . . against, his own free will and consent."[14] Five other states—New Jersey, Delaware, Maryland, North Carolina, and Vermont—provided a similar protection. In contrast, Massachusetts, New Hampshire, Georgia, Virginia, South Carolina, and New York did not recognize the right not to worship.[15] Thus, Pennsylvania was among the colonies that offered the greatest protection against compelled religious attendance.

FREEDOM FROM COMPELLED FINANCIAL CONTRIBUTION

Many state colonial era constitutions protected individuals from being required to financially support religion. Every state except Virginia included legal rules governing financial support to religion. The Pennsylvania Constitution of 1776 banned religious taxes: "No man . . . can be compelled . . . to support any place of worship . . . against, his own free will and consent."[16] This was an absolute prohibition without exceptions. Delaware and Vermont adopted similar language in their constitutions. New York also prohibited compelled religious support but adopted different language. In contrast, Maryland, Massachusetts, and New Hampshire authorized their legislatures to tax citizens to support religion. Four other constitutions—that of New Jersey, North Carolina, Georgia, and South Carolina—could be interpreted as permitting a tax on individuals but only to support an individual's chosen religion.[17] Thus, Pennsylvania was among the colonies that provided the most protection against compelled financial contribution.

Laws Respecting an Establishment of Religion

No state constitution absolutely banned religious laws respecting an establishment of religion. The Pennsylvania Constitution of 1776 contained no specific language addressing laws regarding religious establishments, but it did affirmatively protect religious societies, stating that "all religious societies . . . . shall be encouraged and protected in the enjoyment of [their] privileges, immunities and estates"[18] Virginia, Maryland, Georgia, and Vermont followed the same approach. New Jersey, Delaware, and North Carolina provided that there was to be no establishment of any one religious sect with the state in preference to any other religious sect. Massachusetts and New Hampshire had similar laws. New York rejected any English law or existing law that established "any particular denomination of Christians or their ministers" but did not absolutely ban religious laws. In a unique approach, South Carolina declared that "the Christian Protestant religion" was the established religion of the state. Thus, although Pennsylvania did not prohibit laws respecting religious establishments—as New Jersey, Delaware, and North Carolina did—Pennsylvania affirmatively protected its religious societies.[19]

Religious Tests for Civil Rights and Political Office

Colonial era constitutions used religion to both deny and grant civil and political rights. At the time, nondiscrimination in civil and political rights did not appear to be necessary for religious liberty at the state level. Except for Virginia, every state used religion as a basis to limit or grant civil or political rights. Most states limited political and civil rights to Protestants. Pennsylvania followed the unique approach of limiting civil rights and political office to those who believed in God. In fact, those who wanted to take political office in Pennsylvania were required to acknowledge that the Old Testament and New Testament were given by divine inspiration. The opposite approach was taken by New York, Delaware, Massachusetts, North

Carolina, Georgia, and South Carolina, which prohibited religious ministers from holding office. In short, Pennsylvania encouraged religion and belief in God by limiting certain specifically enumerated protections to those who believed in God.[20]

SUMMARY

Overall, Pennsylvania embraced the highest protections for religion and afforded religious worship more protection than the other twelve colonies. In the six ways that colonial era constitutions protected religion and religious worship, Pennsylvania took the most protective approach in each case, except when addressing laws regarding religion, which Pennsylvania addressed by protecting its religious societies. In short, the Pennsylvania Constitution of 1776 (1) declared the right to worship God a natural right; (2) granted its citizens absolute freedom of worship without exception; (3) absolutely prohibited compelled religious attendance; (4) absolutely prohibited compelled financial contributions; (5) did not prohibit laws respecting an establishment of religion but affirmatively protected its religious societies; and (6) encouraged citizens to believe in God by requiring a belief in God and the Bible for political office and making specific civil rights contingent on a belief in God.

MAINTAINING THE PLATES IN PENNSYLVANIA

Protecting the plates was a key part of the Restoration of the gospel of Jesus Christ and founding of the Church. Had the plates been captured by the enemy, the Book of Mormon, the keystone of the Church, could have been undermined and maybe lost forever. The importance of safeguarding the plates cannot be emphasized enough!

With the translation completed, Joseph no longer had use for the plates and looked forward to leaving the contention that accompanied them. The angel Moroni appeared to Joseph and took possession of the plates. Joseph later explained, "By the wisdom of God, they [the plates] remained safe in my hands, until I accomplished by them what was required at my hand. When, according to arrangement, the messenger called for them, I delivered them up to him, and he has them in his charge until this day."[21] According to David Whitmer, the plates are now in a cave not far from the Hill Cumorah. It has been said that the sealed portion of the plates will be translated when the work of God is finished and Jesus Christ returns to the earth.[22]

Returning the plates to Moroni removed an enormous burden from Joseph. His charge to maintain the plates was daunting and challenging and left no room for error. Almost immediately after securing the plates, forces and pressures from every direction tried to capture the plates, including mobs, soothsayers, money diggers, and all types of deceiving and evil persons. Joseph may have recalled the angel Moroni's charge concerning the plates: "I should be responsible for them. That if I should let them go carelessly or <through> any neglect of mine I should be cut off, but that if I would use all my endeavours to preserve them."[23]

Accounts indicate that Joseph maintained the plates in his possession for a period of roughly twenty-one months. He first acquired the plates at the Hill Cumorah on September 22, 1827, and returned the plates to the angel Moroni after completing the translation of the Book of Mormon, likely sometime at the end of June or in early July 1829.[24] The angel Moroni removed the plates from Joseph's possession for short periods during this time.

After obtaining the plates on September 22, 1827, Joseph stayed in New York for about two months and then relocated to Harmony due to the intense persecution that accompanied the plates. He maintained the plates in Harmony from November or December 1827 until the end of May 1829, when he and Oliver journeyed to Fayette, New York, to continue translating for another month. Thus, during at least eighteen of the twenty-one months, it appears that the plates stayed in Harmony with Joseph.

When the persecution was the most extreme and there was a threat of being "cut off," Joseph resorted to his home in Harmony for protection. Pennsylvania provided the protective environment for Joseph and the gold plates. Liberty of Conscience in Harmony, along with Mr. Hale's inspired protection, provided Joseph a safe harbor while he transcribed the characters on the plates, learned to translate the plates, and translated the majority of the Book of Mormon.

Time Period*	Location of Book of Mormon Gold Plates
September 22, 1827	Joseph Smith received the plates from the angel Moroni in New York
End of November or December 1827 [25]	Joseph Smith departed Palmyra, New York, for Harmony, Pennsylvania
July 1828 [26]	The angel Moroni temporarily removed the gold plates from Joseph Smith's possession while he resided in Pennsylvania
End of May / June 1, 1829 [27]	Joseph Smith departed Harmony, Pennsylvania, for Fayette, New York
End of June or July 1829 [28]	Joseph Smith returned the plates to Moroni
Estimated time possessing the plates [29]	21 months: 3 months in New York / 18 months in Pennsylvania

*Time periods are estimates and not exact;
the specific dates included in the chart are for ease of reference.

Time line of Joseph Smith's possession of the plates.

NOTES

1. J. William Frost, *A Perfect Freedom: Religious Liberty in Pennsylvania* (University Park, PA: Pennsylvania State University Press, 1993), 3.

2. Vincent Phillip Munoz, "Church and State in the Founding-Ear State Constitutions," *American Political Thought: A Journal of Ideas, Institutions, and Culture* 4 (Winter 2015): 10–11.

3. Thomas Jefferson, *Notes of the State of Virginia* (New York: Harper Torch Books, 1964), 154.

4. Letter from Thomas Jefferson to Thomas Cooper (Nov. 2, 1922), in Andrew A. Lipscomb, ed., *Writings of Thomas Jefferson* (Washington, DC: Thomas Jefferson Memorial Association, 1905), 15:40.

5. James Madison, Religion in Public Schools, in *Writings of James Madison*, 3:305, cited in William Addison Blakely, *American State Papers Bearing on Sunday Legislation* (Washington, DC: Religious Liberty Association, 1911), 205.

6. Rhode Island was governed by a Royal Charter from England until 1842.

7. Ohio, Missouri, and Illinois did not become states until the 1800s.

8. "Bill of Rights," *The Constitution of the Common-Wealth of Pennsylvania, as Established by the General Convention Elected for that Purpose, and Held at Philadelphia, July 15th, 1776, and Continued by Adjournments to September 28, 1776.* The First Amendment of the United States Constitution follows the form of Delaware, Pennsylvania, and Vermont because it focuses on the limits of state power and does not specify an individual right.

9. Munoz, "Church and State," 10. Notably, however, individual religious duties during the founding era may have suggested it was a natural right.

10. Munoz, 10–11.

11. Munoz, 12, 14–15.

12. Munoz, 12, 14–15

13. Munoz, 17.

14. "II," *The Constitution of the Common-Wealth of Pennsylvania [1776].*

15. Munoz, "Church and State," 17.

16. "II," *The Constitution of the Common-Wealth of Pennsylvania [1776].*

17. Munoz, "Church and State," 20–23.

18. "Section 45," *The Constitution of the Common-Wealth of Pennsylvania [1776].*

19. Munoz, "Church and State," 24.

20. Munoz, 27, 30.

21. History, circa June 1839–circa 1841 [Draft 2], 8, josephsmithpapers.org; B. H. Roberts, *A Comprehensive History of the Church of Jesus Christ of Latter-day Saints* (Salt Lake City, UT: Deseret News, 1948–57), 1:18. Martin Harris spoke of the return of the plates to Moroni: "They were returned to the angel Moroni, from whom they were received to be brought forth again in the due time of the Lord." Letter from Martin Harris Sr. to Hanna B. Emerson, Jan. 1871, Smithfield, Utah Territory, published in *The True Latter-Day Saints' Herald* 22 (Oct. 15, 1875): 630. According to Leman Copley, who recorded a conversation between Joseph Smith and Joseph Knight Jr., Joseph buried the plates in the side of a mountain. E. D. Howe, *Mormonism Unvailed* (Painesville, OH: 1834), 277. William Smith also said that Joseph Smith "buried up the

plates again in the same manner; which he accordingly did." William Smith, "The Old Soldier's Testimony," *The Saints' Herald*, Oct. 4, 1864, 643–44.

22. P. W. Poulson to editors of the Deseret News, Aug. 13, 1878, cited in *Deseret News*, Aug. 16, 1878, 2.

23. History, circa June 1839–circa 1841 [Draft 2], 8, josephsmithpapers.org; Roberts, *History of the Church*, 1:18.

24. History, circa June 1839–circa 1841 [Draft 2], 8, josephsmithpapers.org; Roberts, *History of the Church*, 1:18.

25. History, circa June 1839–circa 1841 [Draft 2], 8, josephsmithpapers.org.

26. History, circa Summer 1832, 5, josephsmithpapers.org.

27. "Historical Introduction," Revelation, July 1828 [D&C 3], josephsmithpapers.org; Doctrine and Covenants 3:3–8, 10; Smith, *Biographical Sketches*, 125; Smith, *Lucy's Book*, 424–25 (Pratt version).

28. "Report of Elders Orson Pratt and Joseph F. Smith," *The Latter-Day Saints' Millennial Star* 40 (Dec. 9, 1878): 772–73. See also Joseph F. Smith, New York City, NY, to John Taylor et al., [Salt Lake City, Utah Territory], 17 Sept. 1878, draft, Joseph F. Smith, Papers, Church History Library, Salt Lake City.

29. History, circa June 1839–circa 1841 [Draft 2], 8, josephsmithpapers.org.

CHAPTER 11

Publication of the
Book of Mormon

Printing the Book of Mormon

Around June 1829 Joseph traveled from Harmony to Palmyra in search of a printer for the Book of Mormon manuscript.[1] Joseph and Martin first spoke of the project to Egbert B. Grandin, the owner of a local print shop, who likely refused to print the Book of Mormon due to public skepticism of its validity.[2] Mr. Grandin may also have been concerned that Martin Harris was being defrauded.[3] Joseph and Martin then approached Jonathan A. Hadley, an editor of a Palmyra newspaper. Mr. Hadley not only refused to publish the Book of Mormon but later published a critical and negative article about Joseph Smith entitled "Golden Bible."[4] Mr. Hadley may have then referred Joseph to a more reputable printer in nearby Rochester, New York, named Thurlow Weed, who was the former editor and publisher of the *Rochester Telegraph*.[5] Mr. Weed declined to publish the Book of Mormon, later writing, "I thought the man [Joseph] either crazed or a very shallow imposter, and therefore declined to become a publisher."[6] Mr. Weed was apparently also concerned with depriving Martin Harris of "his hard earnings."[7] Joseph then solicited another printer in Rochester, Mr. Elihu F. Marshall, who was a more

237

experienced publisher than Mr. Grandin and Mr. Hadley. After some negotiations, Mr. Marshall agreed to publish the book.[8]

With one printer now willing to publish the Book of Mormon, Joseph and Martin returned to Palmyra and renewed their request to Mr. Grandin to publish it.[9] Joseph likely preferred a local printer so he could maintain control over the manuscript and avoid the travel costs to Rochester.[10] This time, Mr. Grandin agreed to publish five thousand copies (an enormous printing job for that day) for the price of three thousand dollars, a huge sum of money for Joseph and Martin.[11] Mr. Grandin had acquired a state-of-the art printing press called a "Smith Press," delivered by the recently completed Erie Canal.[12] The Smith Press could handle more complex and lengthy print jobs than the standard hand press and was one of the only presses of its kind.

Smith Patented Improved Press used by E. B. Grandin
to print the first 5,000 copies of the Book of Mormon.
© By Intellectual Reserve, Inc.

Mr. Grandin insisted on full payment up front in the form of property, which required Martin to pledge 151 acres of his 240-acre farm to satisfy him.[13] Martin promised to pay Mr. Grandin three thousand dollars within a time period of eighteen months. If Martin defaulted, Mr. Grandin was entitled to sell Mr. Harris's farm at a public auction to pay the debt.[14] The publication agreement was consummated on August 25, 1829, and printing began in September 1829.[15]

Joseph charged Martin Harris and Oliver Cowdery with overseeing the printing of the Book of Mormon, and he returned to Emma in Harmony in the beginning of October.[16] Oliver and Joseph corresponded by letter as Oliver reported on the progress of the printing.[17] While in Harmony, Joseph used early printed sheets of the Book of Mormon to spread the gospel and showed certain parts to his relatives.[18]

Precautions were taken in order to protect the manuscript. Oliver prepared a handwritten copy of the manuscript for the printer, called the "printer's manuscript," and safeguarded the original at the Smith home.[19] Hyrum carried the first twenty-four pages of the printer's manuscript to Grandin's printing office, the manuscript secured under his vest with his coat closely buttoned over it. That night, Hyrum retrieved the manuscript and with the same precaution carried it away.[20] For several months, Hyrum made daily trips to the printing office in this manner, during which he was accompanied by a guard. Another guard was also stationed at the Smiths' home to protect the other manuscript.[21]

Joseph wrote a letter to Oliver dated October 22, 1829, explaining that the printing of the Book of Mormon was exciting the locals in Harmony.[22] Oliver responded to Joseph on November 6, 1829, the day after receiving his letter. Oliver wrote that the printing was moving rather slowly because one of the people assisting with the printing process had been sick, but he thought the printing would be completed by February 1.[23]

Through his involvement in the printing, Oliver learned the printing business and set some of the type for some of the pages with his own hands. He again wrote to Joseph on December 28, 1829, stating, "It may look rather strange to you to find that I have so soon become a printer."[24] Sometimes Oliver spotted errors as the pages rolled from the press and stopped to make corrections. This resulted in differences among the copies of the first edition.[25]

The printing process was slowed by frequent stops to punctuate the manuscript. John Gilbert, Grandin's foreman printer and chief compositor, once called a grammatical error to Martin's and Hyrum's attention and asked whether he should correct it. Martin consulted with Hyrum a short time and responded, "The old testament is ungrammatical, set it as it is written."[26]

The original Book of Mormon manuscript was without traditional punctuation, such as periods, commas, or question marks. Joseph considered the dictated manuscript to be his final work and not a work in progress as with most dictated drafts.[27] Later in his life, John Gilbert wrote about the translation process:

> Every Chapter, if I remember correctly, was one solid paragraph, without a punctuation mark from beginning to end. Names of persons and places were generally capitalized, but sentences had no end. The character or short &, was used almost invariably where the word and, occurred, except at the end of a chapter. I punctuated it to make it read as I supposed the Author intended, and but very little punctuation was altered in proof-reading. The [Mormon] Bible was printed 16 pages at a time, so that one sheet of paper made two copies of the 16 pages each, requiring 2,500 sheets of paper for each form of 16 pages. There were 37 forms of 16 pages each, 570 pages in all.[28]

The original manuscript, except for some minor adjustments, became the text of the first copy of the Book of Mormon.[29] The printing of the Book of Mormon became a focus of Joseph's aggressors. One Sunday afternoon, Hyrum Smith had "peculiar feelings [that] led him to believe that something was going wrong at the printing office."[30] Hyrum and Oliver traveled into town to the printing office and discovered that a man by the name of Abner Cole secretly used the printing press on Sunday afternoons and evenings when no one was present and copied excerpts of the Book of Mormon. Under the pseudonym of Obadiah Dogberry Jr., he printed the stolen excerpts in the *Reflector*, a local newspaper in Palmyra.[31]

Oliver and Hyrum informed Joseph Smith Sr., who took off immediately for Harmony to warn Joseph. After he arrived in Harmony, he and Joseph immediately departed for Palmyra to confront Mr. Cole in person despite the heavy winter storms.[32] Upon arriving at the printing press, Joseph presented the copyright he had obtained for the Book of Mormon to Mr. Cole and ordered him to stop. Mr. Cole threw off his coat, rolled up his sleeves, and came toward Joseph, smacking his fists together with vengeance and stating, "Do you want to fight, sir? Do you want to fight?"[33] Joseph had no intention of fighting Mr. Cole and persuaded him to desist and calm down and to submit the issue of printing to arbitration.[34] Mr. Cole published three issues of the *Reflector* with portions of the Book of Mormon and then stopped, apparently because of Joseph's authority under the copyright.[35]

While Joseph was in Palmyra, he likely signed an agreement with Martin Harris, providing Martin "equal privilege" to sell copies of the Book of Mormon up to the value of the 151 acres of Martin's farm that had been pledged for the printing of the Book of Mormon.[36] The agreement gave Martin comfort that he may be able to protect his farm.

THE PUBLICATION OF THE BOOK OF MORMON

It took seven months to print the Book of Mormon, from August 25, 1829, to March 26, 1830.[37] On March 26, 1830, the Book of Mormon was published and made available to the public.[38] *The Wayne Sentinel* in Palmyra ran an advertisement that day indicating that the Book of Mormon would be for sale. Joseph and Joseph Knight Sr. drove to Palmyra to attend the long-anticipated event. Joseph later commented on the Book of Mormon's publication:

> It was accounted as a strange thing. No small stir was created by its appearance; great opposition and much persecution followed the believers of its authenticity; but it had now come to pass that truth had sprung out of the earth; and righteousness had looked down from heaven—so we feared not our opponents, knowing that we had both truth and righteousness on our side; that we had both the Father and the Son, because we had the doctrines of Christ, and abided by them; and therefore continued to preach, and to give information to all who were willing to hear.[39]

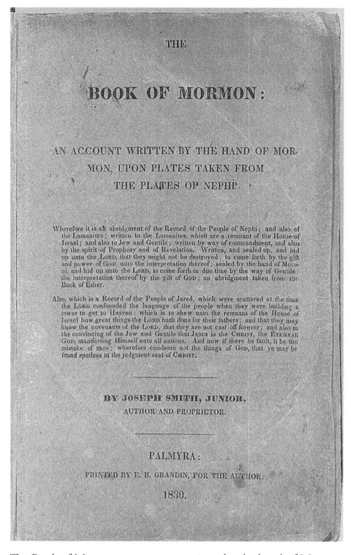

The Book of Mormon; an account written by the hand of Mormon upon plates taken from the plates of Nephi. By Joseph Smith, Jr. Palmyra [N.Y.] Printed by E. B. Grandin for the author, 1830. Image from the US Library of Congress Rare Book and Special Collections Division.

Other local newspapers did not greet the publication with the same zealousness as Joseph and his companions. The *Rochester Daily Advertiser and Telegraph* headline stated, "'Blasphemy': The Book of Mormon has been placed in our hands. A viler imposition was never practiced. It is an evidence of fraud, blasphemy, and credulity shocking both to Christians and moralists."[40] And the *Pennsylvania Inquirer* of Wayne County printed the following:

> A fellow by the name of Joseph Smith, who resides in the upper part of Susquehanna county, has been, for the last two years we are told, employed in dedicating as he says, by inspiration, a new bible. He pretended that he had been entrusted by God with a golden bible which had been always hidden from the world. Smith would put his face in a hat in which he had a white stone, and pretend to read from it, while his coadjutor transcribed. The book purports to give an account of the "Ten Tribes" and strange as it may seem, there are some who have full confidence in his Divine commission.[41]

Later, in April 1831, in order to fulfill the outstanding debt for the Book of Mormon, Martin sold 151 acres of his farm at a private sale for $3,000.[42] He ultimately recouped all his money and even more as a result of financing the publication of the Book of Mormon. It is recorded that he later said, "I never lost one cent. Mr. Smith . . . paid me all that I advanced, and more too."[43]

The Book of Mormon is in fact a collection writings of ancient prophets who lived on the American continents and testified of Jesus Christ. Two groups of people, and their descendants, are discussed in the book of scripture. The first group left Jerusalem in 600 BC under the leadership of a prophet named Lehi and traveled to the American continents. The other group of people, called the Jaredites, traveled to the American continents after the fall of the tower of Babel. The Book of Mormon consists of the history of these peoples over a period of hundreds of years and discusses their faith and challenges. Through these experiences, God makes His character, will, and designs known. In short, the Book of Mormon presents God's character and His love for His children.[44] The culminating event recorded in the book is Jesus Christ's visit to the people of Lehi in the Americas. After his death and Resurrection, Jesus appeared to the descendants of Lehi and taught them His gospel and established His Church among them. The Book of Mormon contains a transcription of the words of Christ by a prophet in the Americas.

The Book of Mormon is intricate and dynamic. It develops complex relationships; maintains three independent dating systems; quotes religious sermons; refers to official records, sermons, letters, monument inscriptions, and church records; lays out complex geographic data and names; forms sentences through the art of chiasmus; and consistently mentions a variety of political traditions. In addition, hundreds of individual characters are introduced and tracked. Comprehending and analyzing these elements of the Book of Mormon has taken scholars years, while Joseph, an uneducated young man from the early 1800s, translated the entire record in just over two months.[45]

The Book of Mormon in published form did not sell as well as expected. Joseph intended to sell the book for one dollar and seventy-five cents, but the price soon fell to one dollar and twenty-five cents.[46] Joseph's mother recorded that people in the surrounding counties resolved "never to purchase one of our books."[47] But as people opened their hearts and sincerely read the Book of Mormon, many came to a spiritual understanding that it is the word of God.[48]

From the date of its publication, the popularity and readership of the Book of Mormon has dramatically increased and continues to grow. The Book of Mormon has spread throughout the world and has been translated into over 125 languages. Over 150 million printed copies of the Book of Mormon are in circulation as of this publication.[49]

JOSEPH EXPANDS HIS HARMONY HOME

During the period of the publication of the Book of Mormon, Joseph made frequent trips between Palmyra and Harmony.[50] He spent much of his time that winter working outside in freezing temperatures and thick snow to almost triple the size of his Harmony home.[51] Joseph added a lean-to addition to his home and a previously constructed two-story saltbox home.[52] The lean-to addition may have served as a buttery to produce cheese and butter for the market.[53] The two-story saltbox home would have greatly increased the square footage of the home. The large addition may have been to accommodate Joseph's family and Oliver Cowdery, who were living in the small log cabin in New York.[54] The home may also have served as a base for missionaries spreading the gospel.[55] Joseph probably intended to stay in Harmony long-term for several reasons: (1) his father-in-law provided him inspired protection; (2) Emma was close to her family; (3) some of his persecutors were charged with crimes under church law and may have been an example and deterrence to others; (4) his home was now large enough to accommodate the affairs of the Church; and (5) Pennsylvania's laws and polices fostered Liberty of Conscience.

THE ORGANIZATION OF THE CHURCH OF JESUS CHRIST OF LATTER-DAY SAINTS

Eleven days after the publication of the Book of Mormon, on Tuesday, April 6, 1830, The Church of Jesus Christ of Latter-day Saints was officially organized.[56] The first official worship service was held in a one-and-a-half-story log home on the Peter Whitmer farm in Fayette, New York.[57] More than fifty people attended, twenty of whom made the 100-mile journey from Colesville, New York.[58] At least three members needed to be present to form the Church, and potentially six elders of the Church attended the meeting.[59] Once assembled in the small room, the members consented by unanimous vote to many propositions.[60] Joseph Smith and Oliver Cowdery were sustained as teachers of the gospel of Jesus Christ. Joseph ordained Oliver as an elder of The Church of Jesus Christ of Latter-day Saints and Oliver did likewise for Joseph. The members at the meeting participated in the ordinance of the sacrament. They took bread and wine, blessed it, and distributed it. The Holy Ghost was poured out upon those who attended—some members prophesied and everyone praised the Lord.[61]

At the conclusion of the meeting, many in attendance decided to be baptized, which included Joseph's parents and Martin Harris.[62] Joseph stood on the banks of the lake and watched his father's baptism. When his father emerged from the water, Joseph took him in his arms and exclaimed with tears of happiness, "Have I lived to see my own father baptized into the true church of Jesus Christ!"[63]

Organizing the Church and seeing his parents baptized deeply moved Joseph. Joseph Knight Sr. recalled:

> He went out into the lot and appeared to want to get out of site of everybody and would sob and cry and seemed to be so full that he could not live. Oliver and I went after him and came to him and after a while he came in. But he was the most wrought upon that I ever saw any man. But his joy seemed to be full. I think he saw the great work he had begun and was desirous to carry it out.[64]

CONVERTS AND ARRESTS IN COLESVILLE, NEW YORK

During the period in which the Church was organized and the Book of Mormon was published, Joseph maintained his residence in Harmony. Following the organization of the Church, sometime in April, Joseph again traveled to the Knights' home in Colesville. He recorded:

> Mr. Knight and his family were Universalists, but were willing to reason with me upon my religious views, and were, as usual, friendly and hospitable. We held several meetings in the neighborhood; we had many friends, and some enemies. Our meetings were well attended, and many began to pray fervently to Almighty God, that He would give them wisdom to understand the truth. Amongst those who attended our meetings regularly, was Newel Knight, son of Joseph Knight.[65]

While in Colesville, Newel Knight's wife asked Joseph to help her husband. Newel was suffering mentally and physically. When Joseph found him, his face and limbs were distorted and twisted, and he tossed about on the floor of the apartment. As Joseph held him, Newel asked him to cast the devil out of him. Joseph replied, "If you know that I can, it shall be done." He then rebuked the devil. Joseph later said, "And it was done not by man, nor by the power of man, but it was done by God, and by the power of godliness."[66]

The first official conference of the Church was held in Fayette, New York, on June 9, 1830. Following the conference, Joseph returned home to Emma in Harmony and likely arranged for another payment on his farm.[67] On May 1, 1830, Joseph was obligated under his agreement with Mr. Hale to pay the remaining eighty-six dollars owing on his farm. But he missed the date because he was focused on organizing the Church and was thus subject to the $400 penalty.[68] The agreement does not indicate that Mr. Hale enforced the $400 penalty, but it does indicate that Joseph made an interest-only payment, up to the date of June 21, 1830.[69] Although Joseph and Mr. Hale had a strained relationship, Mr. Hale seems to have shown compassion toward Joseph in accepting an interest payment rather than demanding the $400 penalty payment. Having addressed the payment issue, little time passed and Joseph and Emma departed for

Colesville to visit Joseph Knight Sr. and administer to those who had attended the organization of the Church and desired baptism.[70]

Joseph scheduled a meeting with the people of Colesville on Sunday, June 27, 1830. On Saturday afternoon, June 26, the Saints piled rocks and logs in a nearby stream to create a pool of water for the performing of baptisms the following morning.[71] Later, under the cover of night, a mob from the town crossed the fields and destroyed the dam. The mob was instigated by sectarian priests of the neighborhood who considered their congregations in danger and planned to stop the baptisms.[72]

The next morning, on Monday, June 28, a meeting was held in which Oliver Cowdery preached and others bore testimony of the Book of Mormon.[73] Among those present at the meeting were those who had torn down the dam the night before.[74] Unbeknownst to the mob, however, the Saints partially rebuilt the dam so that Joseph and Oliver could perform baptisms. Thirteen people were baptized in all, which included Joseph's wife, Emma; Hezekiah Peck and his wife, Martha Long Peck; Joseph Knight Sr. and his wife, Polly Peck Knight; William Stringham and his wife, Esther Knight Stringham; Joseph Knight Jr.; Aaron Culver and his wife, Esther Peck Culver; Levi Hall; Polly Knight; and Julia Stringham.[75] These baptisms were performed in a stream that flowed from Pickerel Pond (which was located on the farm of Joseph Knight Sr.) to the Susquehanna River.[76]

Before the baptisms concluded, a mob of fifty men began to assemble nearby. Joseph and Oliver sought refuge from the mob in Joseph Knight Sr.'s home, but the mob quickly surrounded the home and they escaped to Newel Knight's home. The mob continued to pursue them, and as recorded by Joseph, "it was only by the exercise of great prudence on our part, and reliance on our Heavenly Father that they [the mob] were kept from laying violent hands upon us."[77] That evening, before the meeting started in which those recently baptized were to be confirmed, Ebenezer Hatch, a constable of Chenango County, interrupted. He charged Joseph with being a disorderly person and causing "an uproar by preaching from the Book of Mormon."[78] He served Joseph with an arrest warrant, took him into custody, and drove him to the town of South Bainbridge in Chenango County, barely outpacing the mob of fifty men that had assembled. Joseph recounted, "Whilst driving in great haste one of the wagon wheels came off, which left us once more very nearly surrounded by [the mob], as they had come on in close pursuit. However, we managed to replace the wheel and again left them behind us."[79]

Once in Chenango County, the constable placed Joseph in the upper room of a tavern and stayed with him during the night. The constable laid with his feet against the door and kept a loaded musket by his side. Joseph occupied a bed close by. The constable declared that if they were unlawfully molested, he would fight to his utmost ability for Joseph. No one dared disturb the constable that night.[80]

The constable ultimately saved Joseph's life. Before executing the arrest the night before, he had been told by the mob of its plan to ambush Joseph and had agreed to deliver Joseph into their hands. Upon exiting the house where the meeting occurred, the mob encircled the wagon, but the constable "gave the horse whip" and drove through the mob. The constable had changed his mind, finding Joseph "to be a different sort of person from what . . . had been represented to him."[81]

Joseph's hearing began at 10 a.m. the next morning in front of Justice of the Peace Joseph Chamberlain.[82] A crowd of spectators gathered and generally seemed to believe that Joseph was guilty. Joseph Knight Sr. engaged two men for Joseph's defense—James Davidson and John Reid. Although not lawyers, they were well-respected and intelligent farmers who knew the law.[83] Many witnesses were called, including Josiah Stowell and two of his daughters. Josiah Stowell was examined as follows:

> Q: Did not the prisoner Joseph Smith have a horse of you?
> A: Yes.
> Q: Did not he go to you and tell you, that an angel had appeared unto him, and authorized him to get the horse from you?
> A: No, he told me no such story.
> Q: Well, How had he the horse of you?
> A: He bought him of me, as any other man would do.
> Q: Have you had your pay?
> A: That is not your business.[84]

The prosecuting attorney persisted in the same line of questions, to which Josiah Stowell said, "I hold his note from the price of the horse, which I consider as good as the pay—for I am well acquainted with Joseph Smith Jr., and know him to be an honest man; and if he wishes I am ready to let him have another horse on the same terms." The hearing lasted through the day and into the evening, concluding at 2 a.m. the following morning. Joseph was provided breakfast before the hearing but was deprived of any food during the day and evening. No credible evidence was brought against Joseph, and he was acquitted.[85]

No sooner had Joseph been acquitted and was exiting the tavern than the constable from neighboring Broome County served another warrant on him. The arresting constable of Broome County was not as pleasant as the constable of Chenango County, rushing Joseph on a fifteen-mile journey without food or drink. He brought Joseph to a tavern full of ill-mannered men who abused, ridiculed, and insulted him. "They spit on him and pointed their fingers at him, saying 'Prophesy! Prophesy!'" wrote Newel Knight. Joseph wished to be granted bail in order to be with his wife and family that evening, but bail was denied. The constable allowed him to eat a few crusts of bread and drink water that evening. Upon retiring to bed, the constable laid himself next to Joseph and placed his arm around him. If Joseph moved at all during the night, the constable clenched him fast, fearing his escape. Joseph recalled, "And in this very disagreeable manner did we pass the night."[86]

The hearing took place the following morning in front of Justice of the Peace Joel K. Noble.[87] Joseph Smith was charged with "a breach of the peace, against the good people of the state of New York, by looking through a certain stone to find hid[den] treasures."[88] About twenty witnesses were examined, as was done at the previous hearing. Some witnesses testified to blatant falsehoods but contradicted themselves so plainly that the judge would not admit their testimony.[89] James Davidson and John Reid again vigorously defended Joseph. They directly tackled the prosecution's accusations against Joseph and demonstrated their utter futility and misapplication. They scrutinized each piece of evidence and silenced the prosecution.[90]

Newel Knight was called and sworn in during the hearing.[91] The prosecution, led by William Seymour, questioned, "Did the prisoner, Joseph Smith Jr. chase the devil out of you?" Newel admitted that a devil was cast out of him and that Joseph had a part in it, but he insisted it was the work of the Lord. When asked to describe the appearance of the devil, Newel responded, "I believe, I need not answer that question, but I will do it if I am allowed to ask you one, and you can answer it." Mr. Seymour agreed, and Newel asked, "Do you, Mr. Seymour, understand the things of the spirit?"

"No, I do not pretend to such big things," answered Mr. Seymour.

"Well, then, it would be of no use to tell you what the devil looked like, for it was a spiritual sight and spiritually discerned; and of course you would not understand it were I to tell you of it."[92]

Due to the lack of credible evidence, Justice Noble found Joseph innocent of the charges and acquitted him.[93] Joseph Knight Sr. recorded, "It continued all day till midnight. But they could find nothing against him, therefore he was dismissed."[94] It was said that the trial lasted twenty-three hours.[95] The constable who had arrested Joseph and treated him so poorly apologized and asked for forgiveness. He also warned Joseph that the mob planned to tar and feather him if he was acquitted and that he could help him escape to safety.[96] Joseph left the tavern through the back door and traveled to Emma's sister's house, where Emma awaited him with much anxiety.[97] The next morning, Emma and Joseph returned to Harmony.[98]

Later John Reid shared how he came to defend Joseph at the two hearings. When he was asked to defend Joseph, he declined because he had never met him before. But then Reid heard a voice say, "You *must* go and deliver the Lord's Anointed." Reid assumed that the person next to him said this and replied, "The Lord's Anointed? What do you mean by the Lord's Anointed?" The person was surprised at Reid's question and asked, "What do you mean sire? I said nothing about the Lord's Anointed." Reid believed the person was telling the truth and experienced a peculiar feeling, causing him to immediately go to the place of the trial. When he spoke during the hearings, he said he was inspired with an eloquence that was altogether new to him and which was overpowering and irresistible.[99] He affirmed the moral and trustworthy character of Joseph: "His character was irreproachable; that he was well known for truth and uprightness . . . [and] was often spoken of as a young man of intelligence, and good morals."[100]

Following the two hearings and a visit to Emma's sister, Joseph and Emma returned to Harmony and rested a few days, happy to be among friends but disappointed in the failure of the law to protect Joseph's constitutional rights.[101] They may have spoken of the number of arrests and lawsuits they had experienced in New York and been grateful to be back in Pennsylvania. Unfortunately, they experienced contention and hostility from local citizens in both states.

Joseph and Oliver later set off again for Colesville, sometime in July, to perform the confirmations, but they heard of a gathering mob and thought it was prudent to return to Harmony.[102] One month later, in late August 1830, Joseph and Hyrum, along with David and John Whitmer, made yet another visit to Colesville to perform the long-awaited confirmations. Joseph's enemies in Colesville offered a five-dollar reward to anyone who notified them that Joseph was in the neighborhood.[103] Joseph and his brethren supplicated God in mighty prayer that they could perform the confirmations and that their enemies would not see them. As recorded by Newel Knight, "Their prayers were not in vain. A little distance from my house they encountered a large company of men at work upon the public road, among whom were found some of our most bitter enemies who looked earnestly at the brethren but not knowing them, the brethren passed on unmolested."[104] Under the protection of God, Joseph and the others performed the confirmations and returned home to Harmony without being detected.[105]

NOTES

1. "Historical Introduction," Revelation, circa Summer 1829 [D&C 19], josephsmithpapers.org.

2. *Wayne Sentinel*, June 26, 1829.

3. Pomeroy Tucker, *Origin, Rise, and Progress of Mormonism* (New York: Appleton & Company, 1867), 50–51. Larry C. Porter, "The Book of Mormon: Historical Setting for Its Translation and Publication," in *Joseph Smith: The Prophet, The Man*, ed. Susan Easton Black and Charles D. Tate Jr. (Provo, UT: BYU Religious Studies Center, 1993), 50.

4. "Golden Bible," *Palmyra Freeman*, Aug. 11, 1829.

5. Michael Hubbard MacKay and Gerrit J. Dirkmaat, *From Darkness unto Light: Joseph Smith's Translation and Publication of the Book of Mormon* (Provo,

UT: BYU Religious Studies Center, 2015), 168. Hadley was an apprentice of Thurlow Weed.

6. Harriet A. Weed, ed., *Life of Thurlow Weed Including His Autobiography And A Memoir* (Boston: Houghton, Mifflin and Company, 1884), 1:359; Porter, "The Book of Mormon: Historical Setting," 50.

7. "Recent Progress of the Mormons," *Albany Evening Journal*, July 31, 1854; MacKay and Dirkmaat, *From Darkness unto Light*, 171.

8. Tucker, *Origin, Rise, and Progress*, 52.

9. Tucker, 52.

10. MacKay and Dirkmaat, *From Darkness unto Light*, 175.

11. History, circa June 1839–circa 1841 [Draft 2], 32, josephsmithpapers.org; B. H. Roberts, *A Comprehensive History of the Church of Jesus Christ of Latter-day Saints* (Salt Lake City, UT: Deseret News, 1948–57), 1:71.

12. John Gilbert's 1892 Memorandum, 2, cited in Royal Skousen, "Worthy of Another Look: John Gilbert's 1892 Account of the 1830 Printing of the Book of Mormon," in *Journal of the Book of Mormon and Other Restoration Scripture* 21, no. 2 (2012): 70–72 (contains complete transcription of original memorandum); Porter, "The Book of Mormon: Historical Setting," 50–51. The Smith Press was a single pull press with old-fashioned balls.

13. Indenture, Martin Harris to Egbert B. Grandin, Wayne Co., NY, 25 Aug. 1829, Wayne Co., NY, Mortgage Records, vol. 3, 325–326, microfilm 479, 556, US and Canada Record Collection, Family History Library, Salt Lake City; Preston Nibley, 156. fn. 1. Mr. Grandin apparently was doubtful that the Book of Mormon would sell for a profit and did not believe in the gold plates. MacKay and Dirkmaat, *From Darkness unto Light*, 180. Thomas Rogers, second assignee on the original mortgage agreement between Martin Harris and Grandin, certified before the commissioner of deeds for Wayne County, Truman Hemingway, on January 28, 1832, that "said mortgage is redeemed paid off, satisfied and discharged." The long-standing debt was duly retired. Susan Easton Black and Larry C. Porter, "For the Sum of Three Thousand Dollars," *Journal of Book of Mormon Studies* 14, no. 2 (2005): 11.

14. John W. Welch, "The Miraculous Translation of the Book of Mormon," in John W. Welch, ed., *Opening the Heavens: Accounts of Divine Manifestations, 1820–1844* (Provo, UT: Brigham Young University Press, 2005), 98; Wayne Culter Gunnell, "Martin Harris—Witness and Benefactor to the Book of Mormon" (master's thesis, Brigham Young University, 1955), 37–38. There is some historical confusion surrounding the financing of the Book of Mormon, as Lucy Mack Smith recalled that Mr. Grandin took Martin's farm as a security and the Book of Mormon would be paid for through sales of the book. But historians have concluded that it was unlikely that Mr. Grandin was relying on sales from the Book of Mormon for financing because he did not believe the book would sell. MacKay and Dirkmaat, *From Darkness unto Light*, 187–193.

15. Wayne County Mortgage Book, 3:325–26; John H. Gilbert, Memorandum, 8 Sept. 1892, 2, Church History Library, Salt Lake City. In the summer of 1829 Joseph received a revelation from the Lord directed to Martin Harris, commanding Martin to "not covet thine own property, but impart it freely to the printing of the book of Mormon." Revelation, circa Summer 1829 [D&C 19], 41, josephsmithpapers.org; Doctrine and Covenants 19:26.

16. "Historical Introduction," Letter to Oliver Cowdery, 22 October 1829, josephsmithpapers.org; Mark Lyman Staker, "Joseph and Emma Smith's Susquehanna Home: Expanding Mormonism's First Headquarters," *Mormon Historical Studies* 16, no. 2 (Fall 2015): 69. Joseph may have visited the printing office on a few occasions, according to Lucy Smith, Pomeroy Tucker, and Stephen Harding. Richard Lyman Bushman, *Joseph Smith: Rough Stone Rolling* (New York: Alfred A. Knopf, 2005), 581, fn. 89. Pomeroy Tucker worked in the Palmyra printing office.

17. In one letter, Oliver wrote Joseph about the "type founder" at the printing press being sick and about Thomas B. Marsh, a future bishop of the early Church, showing an interest in the Book of Mormon. Letter from Oliver Cowdery, 6 November 1829, 6–8, josephsmithpapers.org.

18. Tucker, *Origin, Rise, and Progress*, 56; MacKay and Dirkmaat, *From Darkness unto Light*, 200. During this period, Lucy, Hyrum, and Samuel Smith were suspended from the Presbyterian Church for neglecting their public worship. "Records of the Session of the Presbyterian Church in Palmyra," vol. 2, 11–12, Western Presbyterian Church, Palmyra, NY; Porter, "The Book of Mormon: Historical Setting," 60.

19. Gospel Topics Essays, "Book of Mormon Translation," Gospel Library.

20. John Gilbert's 1892 Memorandum, 2.

21. Lucy Mack Smith, *Biographical Sketches of Joseph Smith the Prophet and His Progenitors for Many Generations* (Liverpool: S. W. Richards, 1853), 143; Lucy Mack Smith, *Lucy's Book: A Critical Edition of Lucy Mack Smith's Family Memoir*, ed. Lavina Fielding Anderson (Salt Lake City, UT: Signature Books, 2001), 459 (Pratt version); Dean. C. Jessee, "The Original Book of Mormon Manuscript," *BYU Studies* 10, no. 3 (1970): 2.

22. Letter to Oliver Cowdery, 22 October 1829, 9, josephsmithpapers.org; Richard Lloyd Anderson, "Gold Plates and Printer's Ink," *Ensign*, Sept. 1976, 76.

23. Letter from Oliver Cowdery, 6 November 1829, 8, josephsmithpapers.org.

24. Letter from Oliver Cowdery, 28 December 1829, 5, josephsmithpapers.org; Bushman, *Joseph Smith: Rough Stone Rolling*, 80. This letter was either mailed or delivered by Joseph Smith Sr. who traveled to Harmony, Pennsylvania, around this time. The reason for Joseph Smith Sr.'s trip to Harmony is unknown. "Historical Introduction," Letter from Oliver Cowdery, 28 December 1829, josephsmithpapers.org.

25. In 1841 Joseph deposited the original manuscript in the cornerstone of the Nauvoo House in Nauvoo, Illinois. William G. Hartley, *Stand by My Servant Joseph: The Story of the Joseph Knight Family and the Restoration* (Salt Lake City, UT: Deseret Book, 2003), 56–57.

26. John Gilbert's 1892 Memorandum, 2; Pearson H. Corbett, *Hyrum Smith, Patriarch* (Salt Lake City, UT: Deseret Book, 1963), 54.

27. Gospel Topics Essays, "Book of Mormon Translation," Gospel Library.

28. John Gilbert's 1892 Memorandum, 3.

29. Gospel Topics Essays, "Book of Mormon Translation," Gospel Library. Punctuation, formatting, and other elements of typesetting were performed on the manuscript as well as minor corrections to copying and scribal errors.

30. Lucy Mack Smith, History, 1844–1845, book 9, 9, josephsmithpapers.org; Smith, *Lucy's Book*, 470 (manuscript version); MacKay and Dirkmaat, *From Darkness unto Light*, 206.

31. Smith, *Biographical Sketches*, 148–49; Smith, *Lucy's Book*, 471–72 (Pratt version).

32. Lucy Mack Smith, History, 1844–1845, book 9, 9, josephsmithpapers.org; Smith, *Lucy's Book*, 473 (manuscript version); MacKay and Dirkmaat, *From Darkness unto Light*, 211.

33. Smith, *Biographical Sketches*, 149; Smith, *Lucy's Book*, 474 (Pratt version).

34. Smith, *Biographical Sketches*, 150; Smith, *Lucy's Book*, 474–75 (Pratt version); Bushman, *Joseph Smith: Rough Stone Rolling*, 81; MacKay and Dirkmaat, *From Darkness unto Light*, 212. Joseph also may have threatened Mr. Cole with a lawsuit. Smith, *Biographical Sketches*, 150; Smith, *Lucy's Book*, 474–75 (Pratt version).

35. Copyright for Book of Mormon, 11 June 1829, josephsmithpapers.org.

36. Agreement with Martin Harris, 16 January 1830, josephsmithpapers.org.

37. John Gilbert's 1892 Memorandum; Anderson, "Gold Plates and Printer's Ink," 76. During this time, according to David Whitmer, Joseph gave a seer stone to Oliver Cowdery. David Whitmer, *An Address to All Believers in Christ: By a Witness to the Divine Authenticity of the Book of Mormon* (Richmond, MO: by the author, 1887), 32.

38. Book of Mormon, 1830, i, josephsmithpapers.org; Richard L. Bushman, "The Recovery of the Book of Mormon," in Noel B. Reynolds, ed., *Book of Mormon Authorship Revisited: The Evidence for Ancient Origins* (Provo, UT: F.A.R.M.S., 1997), 36. The publication of the Book of Mormon is said to be "the spark that set a great fire blazing." Richmond E. Myers, *The Long Crooked River: The Susquehanna* (Boston: The Christopher Publishing House, 1949), 341.

Some theorize that Joseph Smith copied the Book of Mormon from Solomon Spaulding of Pittsburgh, Pennsylvania. See *Pennsylvania, A Guide to the Keystone State (American Guide)* (New York: Oxford University Press,

1940), 593. They claim that while Mr. Spaulding was living in Conneaut, Ohio, he found the opening of an Indian mound, which inspired him to write a novel about the Indian population of America and its descendants from the lost tribes of Israel. He entitled his story "The Manuscript Found" and left the manuscript in the printing office of Patterson & Lambdin. He died in 1816. Some claim that Sidney Rigdon—a Baptist minister from Allegheny County, Pennsylvania, who converted to the Church—found the manuscript and gave it to Joseph Smith. *Pennsylvania, A Guide*, 593.

The theory, however, has no evidentiary support. "It cannot be accurately stated just when, where, and how [Spaulding] met Joseph Smith." Frederic G. Mather, "The Early Days of Mormonism," *Lippincott's Magazine of Popular Literature and Science* 26 (Aug. 1880): 205; Larry E. Morris, "The Conversion of Oliver Cowdery," *Journal of Book of Mormon Studies* 16, no. 1. (2007): 81, fn. 3. No records have been located that indicate that Sidney Rigdon knew Joseph Smith before 1830, and Sidney Rigdon himself certified that he first learned of the Book of Mormon when it was presented to him by Parley P. Pratt in the fall of 1830. In fact, Sidney Rigdon, a restorationist preacher, partly condemned the Book of Mormon and was surprised to see it. M. S. C. [Matthew S. Clapp], "Letter to the Editor," *Painesville Telegraph*, Feb. 15, 1831. It was only with much persuasion and argument that Parley P. Pratt convinced Sidney Rigdon to read it. Sidney Rigdon's son, John Wickliffe Rigdon, stated that Sidney Rigdon repeatedly insisted that he never saw the Book of Mormon until Parley Pratt presented it to him and never saw the Spaulding manuscript in his lifetime.

Lucy Mack Smith's account of events further undermines the Spaulding theory. She stated, "The Book of Mormon had been translated and published some time before Parley P. Pratt had united with the Church before I knew Sidney Rigdon or heard of him. At the time the Book of Mormon was translated there was no church organized and Rigdon did not become acquainted with Joseph and me till after the Church was established in 1830. How long after that I do not know, but it was some time." Joseph Smith III, "Last Testimony of Sister Emma," *The Saints' Herald* 26 (Oct. 1, 1879), 289–90. Notably, even most of Joseph's critics dismiss the Spaulding theory.

Kent P. Jackson performed a detailed review of the manuscript, entitled "Manuscript Found," and concluded it has nothing in common with the Book of Mormon. Solomon Spaulding, *Manuscript Found: The Complete Original "Spaulding Manuscript,"* ed. Kent P. Jackson (Provo, UT: BYU Religious Studies Center, 1996). He noted, "In reality, 'Manuscript Found' is a fictional historical romance that has nothing in common with the Book of Mormon, aside from the fact that its setting is among Native Americans of a past generation." Spaulding, *Manuscript Found*, editor's introduction.

For a more in-depth discussion of this topic, see Spaulding, *Manuscript Found*, and Matthew Roper and Paul J. Fields, "The Historical Case against Sidney Rigdon's Authorship of the Book of Mormon," *Mormon Studies Review* 23, no. 1 (2011): 113–25.

39. History, circa June 1839–circa 1841 [Draft 2], 41, josephsmithpapers.org.

40. "BLASPHEMY -- 'BOOK OF MORMON,' alias THE GOLDEN BIBLE," *Rochester Daily Advertiser And Telegraph* (Rochester, NY), Apr. 2, 1830, published in Francis W. Kirkham, *A New Witness for Christ in America: The Book of Mormon, vol. 2, Contemporary Historical Data concerning Its "Coming Forth" and Publication* (Independence, MO: Zion's Printing, 1942), 40, 129–37, 146–52; Bushman, "The Recovery of the Book of Mormon," 36. Richard Bushman remarked that Joseph did not give the newspapers any notice of the publication, as he had not translated the book to win acclaim in the newspapers. Bushman, 36.

41. *Wayne County, Pennsylvania Inquirer*, ca., May 1830, reprinted in the *Cincinnati Advertiser* and *Ohio Phoenix*, June 2, 1830; Larry E. Morris, "'I Should Have an Eye Single to the Glory of God': Joseph Smith's Account of the Angel and the Plates," *FARMS Review* 17, 1 (2005): 49.

42. Gunnell, "Martin Harris," 37–38. The Lord sorely rebuked Martin Harris for coveting his own property and admonished him to impart it freely for printing the Book of Mormon. Revelation, circa Summer 1829 [D&C 19], 40, josephsmithpapers.org; Doctrine and Covenants 19:26; Black and Porter, "For the Sum," 11.

43. "Additional Testimony of Martin Harris," *Latter Day Saints' Millennial Star*, Aug. 20, 1859, 21:545; "Historical Introduction," Agreement with Martin Harris, 16 January 1830, josephsmithpapers.org.

44. Sidney B. Sperry, "What the Book of Mormon Is," *Journal of Book of Mormon Studies* 4, vol. 1 (Spring 1995): 1–2.

45. Noel B. Reynolds, "Introduction," in Noel B. Reynolds, ed., *Book of Mormon Authorship Revisited: The Evidence for Ancient Origins* (Provo, UT: F.A.R.M.S., 1997).

46. "Historical Introduction," Agreement with Martin Harris, 16 January 1830, josephsmithpapers.org.

47. Lucy Mack Smith, History, 1844–1845, book 9, 12, josephsmithpapers.org; Smith, *Lucy's Book*, 475 (manuscript version).

48. Parley P. Pratt, one of the first converts to the Church, obtained a copy of the Book of Mormon and wrote, "I open it with eagerness, and read its title page. I then read the testimony of several witnesses in relation to the manner of its being found and translated. After this I commenced its contents by course. I read all day; eating was a burden, I had no desire for food; sleep was a burden when the night came, for I preferred reading to sleep." Parley P. Pratt, ed., *Autobiography of Parley P. Pratt* (Salt Lake City, UT: Deseret Book, 1985), 22.

49. "Book of Mormon Reaches 150 Million Copies," *Church News*, Apr. 20, 2011, https://www.churchofjesuschrist.org/church/news/book-of-mormon-reaches-150-million-copies.

50. Lucy Mack Smith, History, 1844–1845, book 9, 12, josephsmithpapers.org; Smith, *Lucy's Book*, 475 (manuscript version).

51. Staker, "Joseph and Emma Smith's Susquehanna Home," 69.

52. Staker, 99.

53. Staker, 100.

54. Staker, 107.

55. Historian Mark Staker notes that the census of August 1830 listed four adult males (age 20–30) and one adult female (age 20–30) and a young boy (age 10–15) living in the home during the year. Staker, "Joseph and Emma Smith's Susquehanna Home," 107. Apparently during the 1820s graceful symmetric homes became popular, and shed-like structures attached to homes became an indication of poor style and a lack of sophistication. Staker, 107.

56. William W. Phelps, "Rise and Progress of the Church of Christ," April 1833, 4, josephsmithpapers.org. Within one year of the organization of the Church, 125 members were living in Pennsylvania. "Pennsylvania," in S. Kent Brown, Donald Q. Cannon, and Richard H. Jackson eds., *Historical Atlas of Mormonism* (New York: Simon & Schuster, 1994), 2.

57. History, circa June 1839–circa 1841 [Draft 2], 37, josephsmithpapers.org; Roberts, *History of the Church*, 1:76–77. During the month of April, Joseph made a special missionary visit to the home of Joseph Knight Sr. He conducted several meetings in the neighborhood. History, circa June 1839–circa 1841 [Draft 2], 39–40, josephsmithpapers.org; Roberts, *History of the Church*, 1:81–82.

    Historian Michael Hubbard MacKay performs a compelling analysis of original sources pertaining to the location of the organization of the Church. MacKay points to three documents attributed to Smith and/or Cowdery that indicate that the Church was established in Fayette, New York, and not Manchester, New York: (1) *The Evening and Morning Star*; (2) two deeds that Cowdery signed for Smith in 1834; and (3) drafts of Joseph Smith's history. Michael Hubbard MacKay, *Sacred Space: Exploring the Birthplace of Mormonism* (Provo, UT: BYU Religious Studies Center, 2016), 59, 86.

58. Larry C. Porter, "From a Book Coming Forth," *Ensign*, July 1988, 42; Kenneth L. Alford and Craig K. Manscill, "Hyrum Smith's Liberty Jail Letters," in *Foundations of the Restoration* (Provo, UT: BYU Religious Studies Center, 2016), 6. For an in-depth discussion of the first meeting and organization of the Church, see Larry C. Porter, "Organizational Origins of the Church of Jesus Christ, 6 April 1830," in Larry C. Porter, Milton V. Backman Jr., and Susan Easton Black, eds., *Regional Studies in Latter-day Saint History: New York* (Provo: BYU Department of Church History and Doctrine, 1992), 149–162.

59. History, circa June 1839–circa 1841 [Draft 2], 37, josephsmithpapers.org; Roberts, *History of the Church*, 1:76. Joseph Smith, Oliver Cowdery, Hyrum Smith, Peter Whitmer Jr., David Whitmer, and Samuel H. Smith potentially were the six elders who organized the Church. Corbett, *Hyrum Smith*, 65.

60. History, circa June 1839–circa 1841 [Draft 2], 37, josephsmithpapers.org; Roberts, *History of the Church*, 1:77–78. Porter, "Organizational Origins of the Church," 149–162. At the time of its organization on April 6, 1830, the Church was named "the Church of Christ." Revelation, 6 April 1830 [D&C 21], 28–29, josephsmithpapers.org. At a conference held on May 3, 1834, the name was changed to "The Church of the Latter Day Saints." "Communicated," *The Evening and the Morning Star*, May 1834, 160. Finally, in 1838, the Lord told Joseph in a revelation dated April 2, 1838, that the Church should be named "The Church of Jesus Christ of Latter-day Saints." Journal, March–September 1838, 32, josephsmithpapers.org; Doctrine and Covenants 115:4; Ivan J. Barrett, *Joseph Smith and the Restoration* (Provo, UT: Brigham Young University Press, 1970), 87. For a complete history of the changes to the name of the Church, see Richard Lloyd Anderson, "What Changes Have Been Made in the Name of the Church?," *Ensign*, Jan. 1979, 13–14.

61. History, circa June 1839–circa 1841 [Draft 2], 37, josephsmithpapers.org; Roberts, *History of the Church*, 1:77–78.

62. "Joseph Knight Sr., Reminiscences," no date, Church History Library, Salt Lake City; Joseph Knight Sr., "Joseph Knight's Recollection of Early Mormon History," ed. Dean Jessee, *BYU Studies* 17, no. 1 (1976): 37; History, circa June 1839–circa 1841 [Draft 2], 38, josephsmithpapers.org; Roberts, *History of the Church*, 1:79. Many of the individuals in attendance had received baptism for the remission of sins through the Aaronic Priesthood but had not received the gift of the Holy Ghost, a province of the Melchizedek Priesthood. Porter, "Organizational Origins of the Church," 9.

63. These are Joseph's words as recorded by his mother. Smith, *Biographical Sketches*, 151; Smith, *Lucy's Book*, 477 (Pratt version).

64. "Joseph Knight Sr., Reminiscences"; Knight, "Joseph Knight's Recollection," 37; History, circa June 1839–circa 1841 [Draft 2], 38, josephsmithpapers. org; Roberts, *History of the Church*, 1:79. Orson Pratt, who later served as an Apostle of the Church, stated it is generally believed by those who have studied the matter that Christ was born in April. It is stated that according to the best of their judgment from the research they have made, Christ was crucified on April 6. Orson Pratt, in *Journal of Discourses*, 15:253; B. H. Roberts, *Outline of Ecclesiastical History* (Salt Lake City, UT: George Q. Cannon & Sons, 1893), 17.

65. History, circa June 1839–circa 1841 [Draft 2], 39–40, josephsmithpapers.org; Roberts, *History of the Church*, 1:81–82.

66. History, circa June 1839–circa 1841 [Draft 2], 40–41, josephsmithpapers. org; see Roberts, *History of the Church*, 1:82–83. This is considered the first miracle that was done in the Church. Milton V. Backman and Richard O. Cowan, "Encouragement and Instruction," in *Joseph Smith and the Doctrine and Covenants* (Salt Lake City, UT: Deseret Book, 1992).

67. History, circa June 1839–circa 1841 [Draft 2], 42, josephsmithpapers.org; Roberts, *History of the Church*, 1:86.

68. Agreement with Isaac Hale, 6 April 1829, josephsmithpapers.org; Staker, "Joseph and Emma Smith's Susquehanna Home," 114.

69. Agreement with Isaac Hale, 6 April 1829, josephsmithpapers.org.

70. History, circa June 1839–circa 1841 [Draft 2], 42, josephsmithpapers.org; Roberts, *History of the Church*, 1:86.

71. History, circa June 1839–circa 1841 [Draft 2], 42, josephsmithpapers.org; Roberts, *History of the Church*, 1:86; Newel Knight's Journal Manuscript, 57, Church History Library, Salt Lake City; "Newel Knight's Journal," *Classic Experiences and Adventures* (Salt Lake City, UT: Bookcraft, 1969), 46–104. This book contains two citations to Newel Knight's journal for ease of reference, the original manuscript as well as an often-referenced publication of the manuscript.

72. History, circa June 1839–circa 1841 [Draft 2], 42, josephsmithpapers.org; Roberts, *History of the Church*, 1:86; Newel Knight's Journal Manuscript, 57; "Newel Knight's Journal," 46–104.

73. History, circa June 1839–circa 1841 [Draft 2], 42, josephsmithpapers.org; Roberts, *History of the Church*, 1:86.

74. History, circa June 1839–circa 1841 [Draft 2], 43, josephsmithpapers.org; Roberts, *History of the Church*, 1:86–87.

75. History, circa June 1839–circa 1841 [Draft 2], 43, josephsmithpapers.org; Roberts, *History of the Church*, 1:88; Newel Knight's Journal Manuscript, 62–63; "Newel Knight's Journal," 46–104. Joseph's account of the baptisms differs slightly from Newell Knight's account. Joseph places the baptisms on Monday and an additional meeting on Sunday. History, circa June 1839–circa 1841 [Draft 2], 43, josephsmithpapers.org; Roberts, *History of the Church*, 1:87.

76. LaMar C. Berrett and Larry C. Porter, *Sacred Places: A Comprehensive Guide to Early LDS Historical Sites: New York and Pennsylvania* (Salt Lake City, UT: Deseret Book, 2000), 124–25; Larry C. Porter, "The Colesville Branch and the Coming Forth of the Book of Mormon," *BYU Studies* 10, no. 3 (1970): 372–373.

77. History, circa June 1839–circa 1841 [Draft 2], 43–44, josephsmithpapers.org; Roberts, *History of the Church*, 1:88.

78. History, circa June 1839–circa 1841 [Draft 2], 44, josephsmithpapers.org. "Disorderly persons" was defined by New York state law during this time period as "pretending to tell . . . where lost or stolen good may be found." *Of Disorderly Persons, Revised Statutes of the State of New-York* [1827–1828], 1:638, part 1, chap. 20, title 5, sec. 1.

79. History, circa June 1839–circa 1841 [Draft 2], 44, josephsmithpapers.org; Roberts, *History of the Church*, 1:89.

80. History, circa June 1839–circa 1841 [Draft 2], 44, josephsmithpapers.org; Roberts, *History of the Church*, 1:89; Newel Knight's Journal Manuscript, 66–67; "Newel Knight's Journal," 46–104.

81. Newel Knight's Journal Manuscript, 65–66; "Newel Knight's Journal," *Classic Experiences and Adventures*, 46–104.

82. "Some of the Remarks of John S. Reed," *Times and Seasons* (Nauvoo, IL) 5, no. 11 (June 1, 1844): 551.

83. Newel Knight's Journal Manuscript, 68, 84; "Newel Knight's Journal," 46–104. Joseph commented, "In fact, these men, (although not regular lawyers) were upon this occasion able to put to silence their opponents, and convince the court that I was innocent." History, circa June 1839–circa 1841 [Draft 2], 44, josephsmithpapers.org; Roberts, *History of the Church*, 1:93–94.

84. "Persecution and its Causes," *The Saints' Herald* 33 (Sept. 4, 1886): 547.

85. History, circa June 1839–circa 1841 [Draft 2], 44–45, josephsmithpapers.org; Roberts, *History of the Church*, 1:90–91; "Some of the Remarks of John S. Reed," 551.

86. History, circa June 1839–circa 1841 [Draft 2], 45–46, josephsmithpapers. org; Roberts, *History of the Church*, 1:91; Newel Knight's Journal Manuscript, 74–76; "Newel Knight's Journal," 46–104.

87. Trial Report, 28 August 1832 [*State of New York v. JS–C*], josephsmithpapers. org.

88. "Mormonism," *The Evening and the Morning Star*, Nov. 16, 1832, 114.

89. Newel Knight's Journal Manuscript, 77; "Newel Knight's Journal," 46–104. According to a report supposedly from one of the justices of the peace who presided over the trial, Joseph was acquitted on statute of limitations grounds, not on lack of evidence, because "he had not looked in the glass for two years to find money." "Mormonism," 114. The New York law apparently required legal actions to "be commenced within two years after the offence shall have been committed, and not after." *Of the Time of Commencing Actions for Penalties and Forfeitures, Revised Statutes of the State of New-York* [1827–1828], 2:297, part 3, chap. 4, title 2, art. 3, sec. 29.

90. History, circa June 1839–circa 1841 [Draft 2], 47, josephsmithpapers.org; Roberts, *History of the Church*, 1:91. Newel Knight's Journal Manuscript, 78–83; "Newel Knight's Journal," 46–104; Barrett, *Joseph Smith and the Restoration*, 91.

91. Newel Knight was baptized in Seneca Lake by David Whitmer in the last week of May 1830. "Newel Knight's Journal," 46–104; Hartley, *Stand by My Servant Joseph*, 71.

92. History, circa June 1839–circa 1841 [Draft 2], 46, josephsmithpapers.org; Roberts, *History of the Church*, 1:92–93; Newel Knight's Journal Manuscript, 79–82; "Newel Knight's Journal," 46–104.

93. Newel Knight's Journal Manuscript, 82; "Newel Knight's Journal," 46–104; "Historical Introduction," Trial Report, 28 August 1832 [*State of New York v. JS–C*], josephsmithpapers.org.

94. "Joseph Knight Sr., Reminiscences"; Knight, "Joseph Knight's Recollection," 38; Hartley, *Stand by My Servant Joseph*, 83.

95. "Mormonism," 114.

96. History, circa June 1839–circa 1841 [Draft 2], 47, josephsmithpapers.org; Roberts, *History of the Church*, 1:95–96; Newel Knight's Journal Manuscript, 85–86; "Newel Knight's Journal," 46–104.

97. Mark L. Staker, "A Comfort unto My Servant, Joseph," in *Women of Faith in the Latter Days: Volume 1, 1775–1820*, ed. Richard E. Turley Jr. and Brittany A. Chapman (Salt Lake City, UT: Deseret Book, 2011), 343–362. Emma's older sister Elizabeth Hale Wasson lived in Harpursville near the Knight farm. Joseph and Emma stayed there often when visiting the area. Grant E. Carter, "Along the Susquehanna," *Improvement Era*, May 1960, 6.

98. History, circa June 1839–circa 1841 [Draft 2], 47, josephsmithpapers.org; Roberts, *History of the Church*, 1:96; Carter, "Along the Susquehanna," 6. In his history, Joseph gives a detailed accounting of his two arrests and trials. History, circa June 1839–circa 1841 [Draft 2], 44–47, josephsmithpapers.org; Roberts, *History of the Church*, 1:86–96.

99. Lucy Mack Smith, History, 1844–1845, book 10, 1, josephsmithpapers.org.

100. "Some of the Remarks of John S. Reed," 549; Staker, "A Comfort unto My Servant," 343–362.

101. History, circa June 1839–circa 1841 [Draft 2], 46–47, josephsmithpapers.org; Roberts, *History of the Church*, 1:96–97.

102. History, circa June 1839–circa 1841 [Draft 2], 47, josephsmithpapers.org; Roberts, *History of the Church*, 1:97; Larry C. Porter, *A Study of the Origins of the Church of Jesus Christ of Latter-day Saints in the States of New York and Pennsylvania, 1816–1831* (Provo, UT: BYU Studies, 2000), 80.

103. History, circa June 1839–circa 1841 [Draft 2], 51–53, josephsmithpapers.org; Roberts, *History of the Church*, 1:97–101; Porter, *Origins of the Church*, 80; Hartley, *Stand by My Servant Joseph*, 86–87.

104. Newel Knight's Journal Manuscript, 138–39; "Newel Knight's Journal," 46–104.

105. History, circa June 1839–circa 1841 [Draft 2], 51–53, josephsmithpapers.org; Roberts, *History of the Church*, 1:97–101; Porter, *Origins of the Church*, 80; Hartley, *Stand by My Servant Joseph*, 86–87. Newel Knight and his family, however, did not avoid persecution by the mob. He recorded that not long after the brethren left, "the mob began to collect together and threatened and abused us in the most shameful and disgusting manner during the remainder of the day." Newel Knight's Journal Manuscript, 140; "Newel Knight's Journal," 46–104.

CHAPTER 12

Revelations in the Summer of 1830

—— ⟨∞⟩ ——

"I Am with Thee, Even unto the End of Thy Days"

Contention in Harmony intensified against Joseph and Oliver during the summer of 1830. They prayed to the Lord, asking for strength, encouragement, and instruction. The Lord commanded Joseph to continue in the work and consoled him, saying, "Be patient in afflictions for thou shalt have many but endure them for Lo! I am with thee even unto the end of thy days. And in temporal labors thou shalt not have strength for this is not thy calling attend to thy calling and thou shalt have wherewith to magnify thine office, and to expound all scriptures, and continue in laying on of the hands and confirming the churches."[1]

It is likely that following this revelation, in response to the commandment "to expound all scriptures," Joseph commenced a translation of the Bible, starting with an inspired translation of the book of Genesis. As he translated the Bible, he likely learned from the Spirit of Truth and was taught truths for his personal benefit and the benefit of the Church.[2]

Joseph often implored the Lord for guidance by following the "Ask Principle," and by now it was habit and part of his prophetic disposition. Joseph did not know everything about the Church and the gospel of Jesus Christ, but truths were revealed to him step by step and principle upon principle as he inquired and sought answers.[3] Brigham Young later explained:

> When Joseph first received revelation the Lord could not tell him what he was going to do. . . . He could merely reveal to him that the Lord was pleased to bless him and forgive his sins and there was a work for him to perform on the earth and that was about all he could reveal. The first time he sent [an] angel to visit him he could then lead his mind a little further. He could reveal to him there was certain records deposited in the earth to be brought forth for the benefit of [the] inhabitants of the earth. He could reveal after this that Joseph could get them; then he could reveal he should have power to translate the records from the language and characters in which it was written and give it to the people in the English language, but this was not taught him first. . . . He could then reveal to Joseph that he might take Oliver Cowdery into water and baptize him and ordain him to [the] Priesthood.[4]

Scripture Study and Common Consent

The Lord instructed Joseph to devote his efforts to strengthening other branches of the Church due to growing contention in Harmony.[5] He was counseled to study and ponder the scriptures and to conduct Church decisions by common consent. The Lord said, "[You] shall let your time be devoted to the studying [of] the scriptures, and to preaching . . . and all things shall be done by common consent in the Church by much prayer and faith."[6]

Emma Smith: The Lord's Elect Lady

Emma at times wondered what her role should be in the work. The Lord directed a revelation to her, stating she was an "Elect Lady."[7] She was commanded to compile a book of hymns for church worship services,[8] and she was also ordained "to expound Scriptures & exhort the Church."[9] Emma later assembled a hymnbook, relying on her rich Methodist background in music, and produced a pocket-sized hymnbook titled "A Collection of Sacred Hymns for the Church of the Latter-day Saints." It contained ninety hymns, the first being "Know This, That Every Soul Is Free."[10] She also became president of the female Relief Society of Nauvoo, Illinois, a women's organization within the Church that has grown to be one of the largest women's organizations in the world.

Joseph's mother commented on Emma's strength and resilience:

> I have never seen a woman in my life, who would endure every species of fatigue and hardship, from month to month, and from year to year, with that unflinching courage, zeal, and patience, which she has ever done. . . . How often I have parted every bed in the house for the accommodation of the brethren . . . while Joseph and Emma slept upon the . . . floor with nothing but their cloaks for both bed and bedding.[11]

Joseph later spoke of Emma's sacrifice and dedication during their Harmony years:

> With what unspeakable delight, and what transports of joy swelled my bosom, when I took by the hand on that night, my beloved Emma, she that was my wife, even the wife of my youth; and the choice of my heart. Many were the reverberations of my mind when I contemplated for a moment the many scenes we had been called to pass through, the fatigues, and the toils, the sorrows, and sufferings, and the joys and consolations from time to time had strewed our paths and crowned our board. Oh, what a comingling of thought filled my mind for the moment, again she is here, even in the seventh trouble—undaunted, firm, and unwavering—unchangeable, affectionate Emma.[12]

THE SACRAMENT

Early in August 1830 Newel Knight and his wife, Sally Coburn Knight, visited the Smiths in Harmony.[13] Because Sally Knight and Emma had not been confirmed members of the Church, Joseph decided to confirm them and administer the sacrament.[14] In preparation for the sacrament, Joseph set out to procure some wine but had gone only a short distance when a heavenly messenger appeared and gave him the following direction:[15]

> Behold I say unto you it mattereth not what ye shall eat or what ye shall drink when ye partake of the sacrament if it so be that ye do it with an eye single to my glory [r]emembering unto the Father my

Body which [was] laid down for you and my blood which was shed for the Remission of your sins. Wherefore a commandment I give unto you that ye shall not Purchase Wine neither strong drink of your enemies.[16]

In obedience to this revelation, they prepared wine of their own making and partook of the sacrament.[17] Afterward, Sally Knight and Emma Smith were confirmed members of the church. Newel Knight commented, "The Spirit of the Lord was poured out upon us. We praised the God of Israel and rejoiced exceedingly."[18] This was the last summer that Joseph and Emma lived in Harmony.[19]

Later that fall, in September 1830, Joseph received more revelation pertaining to the sacrament and spiritually putting on the armor of God.[20]

ISAAC HALE WITHDRAWS HIS PROTECTION

Reverend Nathaniel Lewis learned that Mr. Hale and his family had promised Joseph protection while he translated the Book of Mormon. In an attempt to turn Mr. Hale against Joseph, Reverend Lewis told him falsehoods, rumors, and lies about Joseph.[21] After much persistence and persuasion, he succeeded in shaking the already fragile relationship between Joseph and his father-in-law. Persuaded by Reverend Lewis' prodding, Mr. Hale withdrew his protection from Joseph.[22] According to Reverend George Peck, Mr. Hale turned against Joseph, considering him an imposter and a knave.[23] Once Mr. Hale withdrew his protection, mobs assembled and intensified their efforts to run Joseph and Oliver out of Harmony.[24] According to Joseph's mother, evil-designing mobs combined forces to steal the gold plates and kill Joseph.[25]

Without Isaac's protection, Joseph was more vulnerable to contention, especially from the local Methodists and Presbyterians who disliked Joseph and his attempts to draw converts away from their congregations.[26] The official organization and existence of the Church seemed only to fuel the contention. Aware of the intensifying persecution in Harmony, Mr. Whitmer invited Joseph and Emma to stay with his family in Fayette.[27] Joseph agreed, and soon thereafter Joseph

Knight Sr. took his team and wagon to Harmony to move Joseph and his family to Fayette.[28]

Although Joseph departed from Harmony in 1830 because of the contention exerted by members of other faiths,[29] he was not arrested, imprisoned, or tried for his religious beliefs while in Harmony. Nor is there any record that Pennsylvania residents brought civil lawsuits against Joseph as a pretext for religious persecution. The protection of Mr. Hale probably helped Joseph avoid entanglements with the law, and the laws and policies of Pennsylvania supported Joseph's cause. It is possible that Pennsylvania law also supported Mr. Hale and enabled him to provide the necessary protection to Joseph and Oliver. Nathaniel Lewis may have influenced Mr. Hale or prevailed on him sooner had it not been for the Pennsylvania Constitution and the decisions of the Pennsylvania Supreme Court in *Riddle v. Stevens* and *Updegraph v. The Commonwealth*.

JOSEPH MAKES THE FINAL PAYMENT ON HIS HOME

Around August 25 or 26, 1830, Joseph obtained full title to his farm and completed the last and final payment on his home to Isaac and Elizabeth Hale.[30] He obtained a loan from George H. Noble, a shopkeeper in nearby Lanesboro, in order to make the final payment.[31] The loan was recorded by the Court of Common Pleas in Montrose, Pennsylvania, as a non-adversarial judgment in favor of George H. Noble.[32] In effect, Mr. Noble paid Mr. Hale the outstanding eighty-six dollars under the agreement and added the eighty-six dollars to Joseph's preexisting $104.95 debt.[33] The judgment was satisfied in full on June 3, 1831.[34] This judgment is the only known recorded legal proceeding in Pennsylvania in which Joseph was named.[35]

Joseph's agreement with Isaac Hale powerfully symbolizes his commitment to the Lord's work and his sacrifice of worldly pursuits. Joseph epitomized William's theme in *No Cross, No Crown*. He pursued the Lord's work and faced the adversity and stigma that accompanied his incredible sacrifice. Joseph likely desired to fulfill the expectations of his father-in-law and develop a strong bond of friendship by securing full-time employment. He also may have been regarded as idle and lazy because he did not work full-time and could not pay for his own home. But Joseph had a greater purpose and learned to rely on others. He exercised his faith in God by focusing on the Lord's work instead of seeking full-time employment, and the Lord provided the means by which Joseph could make the final payment on his contract with his father-in-law. Joseph truly feared God, not the judgments of men.

Only a few days after acquiring full title to his property, Joseph locked the door to the house with the furniture in it, and he and Emma said goodbye to their farm.[36] He only spent a few days in his home as the legal owner due to his sacrifice for the Lord's work. This was the last time Emma would see her parents.[37]

Joseph and Emma arrived in Fayette, New York, amid the joy and congratulations of friends.[38] They resided in Fayette for less than five months. The trials and tribulations they endured while in Harmony prepared them for challenges they would encounter in the future. Shortly after arriving in Fayette, Joseph traveled to Colesville in order to hold prayer meetings with the members.[39] While in Colesville, he made a hurried trip to Harmony to settle some business. This was Joseph's last recorded visit to the Susquehanna area.[40]

Notes

1. Revelation, July 1830–A [D&C 24], 33, josephsmithpapers.org; Doctrine and Covenants 24:8–9.

2. David A. LeFevre, "The Education of a Prophet," in *Foundations of the Restoration: Fulfillment of the Covenant Purposes* (Provo, UT: BYU Religious Studies Center, 2016), 101–102.

3. Anthony R. Sweat, Michael Hubbard MacKay, and Gerrit J. Dirkmaat, "Evaluating Latter-day Saint Doctrine," in *Foundations of the Restoration*, 29.

4. Brigham Young Discourse 25 March 1855, Papers of George D. Watt, MS 4534, box 3, disk 1, images 142–53, Church History Library, Salt Lake City (transcribed by LaJean Purcell Carruth; punctuation and capitalization added); Sweat, MacKay, and Dirkmaat, "Evaluating Latter-day Saint Doctrine," 29–30.

5. Revelation, July 1830–A [D&C 24], 32, josephsmithpapers.org; Doctrine and Covenants 24:1–3

6. Revelation, July 1830–B [D&C 26], 34, josephsmithpapers.org; Doctrine and Covenants 26:1–2.

7. Revelation, July 1830–C [D&C 25], 34, josephsmithpapers.org; Doctrine and Covenants 25:3. When John Whitmer compiled Revelation Book 1, he placed

this revelation after the two other revelations from this period, and this text follows his order. "Historical Introduction," Revelation, July 1830–C [D&C 25], josephsmithpapers.org.

8. History, circa June 1839–circa 1841 [Draft 2], 49–50, josephsmithpapers.org; B. H. Roberts, *A Comprehensive History of the Church of Jesus Christ of Latter-day Saints* (Salt Lake City, UT: Deseret News, 1948–57), 1:103–104. Oliver Cowdery wrote that Emma was "most certainly evinced a decidedly correct mind and uncommon ability of talent and judgment, in a manifest willingness to fulfil, on her part, the passage in sacred writ,-- 'and they twain shall be one flesh.'—by accompanying her husband, against the wishes and advise of her relatives, to a land of strangers . . . her character stands as fair for morality, piety and virtue, as any in the world." History, 1834–1836, 102, josephsmithpapers.org; "Oliver Cowdery Letter VIII," *Latter Day Saints' Messenger and Advocate* (Kirtland, OH), Oct. 1835, 201.

9. Revelation, July 1830–C [D&C 25], 34, josephsmithpapers.org; Doctrine and Covenants 25:7.

10. Collection of Sacred Hymns, 1835, 5, josephsmithpapers.org; Susan Easton Black, *Who's Who in the Doctrine & Covenants* (Salt Lake City, UT: Deseret Book, 1997), 274. Emma completed the first official hymnbook for the Church in 1835 while living in Kirtland, Ohio.

11. Lucy Mack Smith, *Biographical Sketches of Joseph Smith the Prophet and His Progenitors for Many Generations* (Liverpool: S. W. Richards, 1853), 169; Lucy Mack Smith, *Lucy's Book: A Critical Edition of Lucy Mack Smith's Family Memoir*, ed. Lavina Fielding Anderson (Salt Lake City, UT: Signature Books, 2001), 502 (Pratt version).

12. Journal, December 1841–December 1842, 164, josephsmithpapers.org; Larry C. Porter, "Joseph Smith's Susquehanna Years," *Ensign*, Feb. 2001, 48. "Seventh trouble" refers to Job 5:19. Tribulation and affliction were common during Emma's and Joseph's marriage. Jennifer Reeder, *First: The Life and Faith of Emma Smith* (Salt Lake City, UT: Deseret Book, 2021), 21. Even amidst their tribulation and affliction, Emma and Joseph expressed terms of endearment in their correspondence. Reeder, *First*, 22.

13. History, circa June 1839–circa 1841 [Draft 2], 51, josephsmithpapers.org; Roberts, *History of the Church*, 1:106. David Whitmer was also in Harmony at the time. William G. Hartley, *Stand by My Servant Joseph: The Story of the Joseph Knight Family and the Restoration* (Salt Lake City, UT: Deseret Book, 2003), 83.

14. History, circa June 1839–circa 1841 [Draft 2], 51, josephsmithpapers.org; Roberts, *History of the Church*, 1:106. Due to his arrest in June 1830, Joseph had been unable to perform the confirmations of Sally Knight and Emma at the time of their baptism at the Knight farm in Broome County, New York.

15. History, circa June 1839–circa 1841 [Draft 2], 51, josephsmithpapers.org; Roberts, *History of the Church*, 1:106.

16. Revelation, circa August 1830 [D&C 27], 35, josephsmithpapers.org; Doctrine and Covenants 27:2–3.

17. Newel Knight's Journal Manuscript, 125; "Newel Knight's Journal," 46–104. "This is one of the many important revelations given to the Church. The knowledge that it matters not what we can eat or drink, if we partake of the sacrament in the Spirit of the Lord and by divine authority, is the foundation for the present practice in the Church of using water instead of wine, for so the Lord commanded." Joseph Fielding Smith, *Essentials in Church History*, 23rd ed. (Salt Lake City, UT: Deseret Book, 1969), 93.

18. Newel Knight's Journal Manuscript, 126; "Newel Knight's Journal," 46–104.

19. "Harmony, Pennsylvania," *Encyclopedia of Mormonism*, ed. Daniel H. Ludlow (New York: Macmillan, 1992), 2:573. In the summer of 1830, a local boy between the ages of 10 and 15 lived with Joseph and attended Prospect School, the first public schoolhouse in Oakland. Joseph sent the boy there for ten days and paid fifteen cents. George A. Stearns, *The Schools of Susquehanna County Pennsylvania 1795–1945* (Montrose, Pennsylvania: Montrose Publishing Company, 1947), 28; Rhamanthus M. Stocker, *Centennial History of Susquehanna County, Pennsylvania*, 2nd ed. (Baltimore, MD: Regional Publishing Company, 1974), 556.

20. Doctrine and Covenants, 1835, 180–181, josephsmithpapers.org; Doctrine and Covenants 27:15–18.

21. History, circa June 1839–circa 1841 [Draft 2], 53, josephsmithpapers.org; Roberts, *History of the Church*, 1:108; Susan Easton Black, "Isaac Hale: Antagonist of Joseph Smith," in *Regional Studies in Latter-day Saint Church History: New York* (Provo, UT: BYU Department of Church History and Doctrine, 1992), 9.

22. History, circa June 1839–circa 1841 [Draft 2], 53, josephsmithpapers.org; Roberts, *History of the Church*, 1:108; Newel Knight's Journal Manuscript, 126–27; "Newel Knight's Journal," 46–104. Isaac Hale and Nathaniel Lewis seemed to have established a strong bond, which may have influenced Isaac Hale in withdrawing his protection from Joseph later on. Isaac Hale and Nathaniel Lewis cleared land together, built two homes for the wealthy Colonel Timothy Pickering Jr., and interacted often. Isaac Hale attended Mr. Lewis's Methodist congregation. Mark Lyman Staker, "Isaac and Elizabeth Hale in Their Endless Mountain Home," *Mormon Historical Studies* 15, no. 2 (2014): 27.

23. George Peck, *The Life and Times of Rev. George Peck* (New York: Nelson & Phillips, 1874), 68.

24. Larry C. Porter, "The Book of Mormon: Historical Setting for Its Translation and Publication," in *Joseph Smith: The Prophet, The Man*, ed. Susan Easton Black and Charles D. Tate Jr. (Provo, UT: BYU Religious Studies Center, 1993), 49. When Isaac Hale was on his deathbed, he apparently told his family, "You must not believe in Jo Smith or any false doctrines, but believe

in the Holy Bible. In it you will find the words of eternal life." Mark Lyman Staker and Robin Scott Jensen, "New Details about Joseph and Emma Smith, the Hale Family, and the Book of Mormon," *BYU Studies Quarterly* 53, no. 3 (2014): 15 (expanded web version), citing Byron Hale, "Reuben Hale's Obituary," Mar. 21, 1887.

25. Lucy Mack Smith, History, 1844–1845, book 8, 8, josephsmithpapers.org; Smith, *Lucy's Book*, 446 (manuscript version); Stocker, *Centennial History of Susquehanna County*, 556; Porter, The Book of Mormon: Historical Setting," 49; Porter, "Joseph Smith's Susquehanna Years," 46.

26. History, circa June 1839–circa 1841 [Draft 2], 18, josephsmithpapers.org; Roberts, *History of the Church*, 1:44.

27. Lucy states that Joseph received a commandment to move his family to Waterloo (Fayette), New York. Smith, *Biographical Sketches*, 159; Smith, *Lucy's Book*, 487 (Pratt version). In June 1830 Joseph began the translation of the Bible. Kenneth L. Alford and Craig K. Manscill, "Hyrum Smith's Liberty Jail Letters," in *Foundations of the Restoration* (Provo, UT: BYU Religious Studies Center, 2016), 6.

28. History, circa June 1839–circa 1841 [Draft 2], 53, josephsmithpapers.org; Roberts, *History of the Church*, 1:109. According to Newel Knight, he came with his wagon and team to transport the Smiths to Fayette. Newel Knight's Journal Manuscript, 141; "Newel Knight's Journal," 46–104.

29. Author Richmond Myers remarked that Joseph Smith did not encounter "harmony" when he resided in Harmony. Richmond E. Myers, *The Long Crooked River: The Susquehanna* (Boston: The Christopher Publishing House, 1949), 342.

30. Agreement with Isaac Hale, 6 April 1829, josephsmithpapers.org. Joseph likely could not make the full payment for the property by the contract date of May 1, 1830, so he made an "interest" payment of an unspecified amount for the remaining balance on June 21, 1830, and made the full payment on or around August 26, 1830. See footnote 4, Agreement with Isaac Hale.

31. Transcript of Judgment, 26 Aug. 1830, *George H. Noble & Co. v. Joseph Smith* (Susquehanna Co.: C. P., 1830), Susquehanna County Historical Society, Montrose, PA.

32. Transcript of Judgment. "In civil courts, judgments were often entered in favor of creditors against [Joseph] and his partners, but often these obligations were not even contested and were simply being entered into the public record as a regular step in the ordinary debt collection process of that day." Gordon A. Madsen, Jeffrey N. Walker, and John W. Welch, eds., *Sustaining the Law: Joseph Smith's Legal Encounters* (Provo, UT: BYU Studies, 2014), xviii (introduction).

33. Madsen, Walker, and Welch, *Sustaining the Law*, 464.

34. Madsen, Walker, and Welch, 464 ("Legal Chronology").

35. In *Sustaining the Law,* the "Legal Chronology" references the following lawsuit: "State v. Smith: A legal action brought by the state of Pennsylvania against Joseph Smith and Oliver Cowdery, Summer 1829, Harmony, Pennsylvania." This reference is incorrect. It is based on the following statement by Oliver Cowdery: "[P]revious to his [Joseph] obtaining the records of the Nephites, only that while in that country, some very officious person, brought him before the authorities of the country; but there being no cause of action he was honorably acquitted." "Oliver Cowdery Letter VIII," 201. This is a reference to the trial of 1826 in New York. Gordon A. Madsen, "Being Acquitted of a 'Disorderly Person' Charge in 1826," in Gordon A. Madsen, Jeffrey N. Walker, and John W. Welch, eds., *Sustaining the Law: Joseph Smith's Legal Encounters* (Provo, UT: BYU Studies, 2014), 90.

It is unlikely that this occurred in Pennsylvania and more likely that it relates to one of the several lawsuits brought against Joseph in New York. Research in the records of the Montrose County Courthouse and Pennsylvania legal documents have not produced any indication that this legal matter occurred in Pennsylvania. Also, neither Joseph, nor Lucy, nor anyone else mentions a legal proceeding in Pennsylvania. It would be assumed that Lucy would have mentioned this proceeding, as she seemed particularly concerned about Joseph's legal encounters in New York during the same time period. Moreover, had this proceeding occurred in Pennsylvania, it likely would have been an important event and noted by others in the area, including the prominent historian of Susquehanna County, Emily Blackman, who dedicated an entire section of her history to Joseph Smith.

Even if a civil lawsuit had been filed in Pennsylvania based on religious prejudice, the lawsuit may have been dismissed since the church protected against persecution. Letter to Oliver Cowdery, 22 October 1829, josephsmithpapers.org. ("Two of our most formidable persacutors are now under censure and cited to a trial in the church for crimes. . . . We do not rejoice in the affliction of our enemies but we shall be glad to have truth prevail.")

36. Smith, *Biographical Sketches,* 158–59; Smith, *Lucy's Book,* 487 (Pratt version). Joseph and Emma later requested their possessions. Smith, *Biographical Sketches,* 168–69; Smith, *Lucy's Book,* 502 (Pratt version). Joseph had planned to visit the Church members in Colesville in late August, but his transportation did not arrive in time. On August 28 Joseph and John Whitmer wrote a letter while in Harmony encouraging the Church members of Colesville to "fight the good fight of faith" and indicating that he would visit the Saints the following week. Letter to Newel Knight and the Church in Colesville, 28 August 1830, josephsmithpapers.org; Newel Knight, History, 128–136, Church History Library, Salt Lake City.

37. Mark L. Staker, "A Comfort unto My Servant, Joseph," in *Women of Faith in the Latter Days: Volume 1, 1775–1820,* ed. Richard E. Turley Jr. and Brittany A. Chapman (Salt Lake City, UT: Deseret Book, 2011), 343–362. All of the Hales' children eventually left Harmony except for Alva Hale. Staker, "Isaac and Elizabeth Hale," 56. Only after Isaac Hale died did Emma feel she could

write her mother and siblings. She wrote them while living in Nauvoo, Illinois, and invited her family to come live near her, even if they did not accept her religion. Letter to David Hale, 12–19 February 1841, josephsmithpapers.org; Staker, "Isaac and Elizabeth Hale," 57.

On July 14, 1896, the *Scranton Tribune*, a newspaper based in Scranton, Pennsylvania, reported on the Joseph Smith home, which had crumbled and been left in ruins (then owned by the McKune family). The article predicted that the Church would crumble just like the Joseph Smith home: "And so the old house where the book was compiled crumbles back to earth and the winds mourn over its ruins, so are the foundations of Mormonism sinking into dust and the winds of truth are chanting sad requiems as they pass up and down this great land of freedom." "Relics of Mormonism," *Scranton Tribune*, July 14, 1896. Obviously, the author of this article was incorrect and never understood the grandeur of the events that took place in the home.

38. History, circa June 1839–circa 1841 [Draft 2], 25, josephsmithpapers.org; Roberts, *History of the Church*, 1:109; Porter, "Joseph Smith's Susquehanna Years," 48.

39. Sidney Rigdon accompanied Joseph on this visit to Colesville. Hartley, *Stand by My Servant Joseph*, 103.

40. "Joseph Knight Sr., Reminiscences," no date, Church History Library, Salt Lake City; Joseph Knight Sr., "Joseph Knight's Recollection of Early Mormon History," ed. Dean Jessee, *BYU Studies* 17, no. 1 (1976): 38. A considerable following of devoted Church members had developed in Pennsylvania prior to 1860. Sylvester K. Stevens, *Pennsylvania: The Keystone State* (New York: The American Historical Company, Inc., 1956), 333. Even after Joseph and Emma left Harmony, digging for the golden plates, or hidden treasure, continued for some time. Stocker, *Centennial History of Susquehanna County*, 556.

CHAPTER 13

JOSEPH SMITH IN OHIO, MISSOURI, AND ILLINOIS

———— ∽◎∾ ————

This final chapter compares Pennsylvania's Constitution to the constitutions of other states where Joseph Smith resided, showing that Pennsylvania embraced the highest protections of religious liberty. This chapter then recounts the religious persecution Joseph encountered in Ohio, Missouri, Illinois, and New York, and concludes by showing that today Harmony stands as a symbol of religious liberty.

PENNSYLVANIA'S CONSTITUTIONS OF 1776 AND 1790 EMBRACED THE highest protections for religion and afforded religious worship more protection than the other eleven constitutions of the colonial era. They also protected and emphasized religion and freedom of worship more than the post-colonial era constitutions of other states where Joseph Smith resided, specifically Ohio, Missouri, and Illinois.[1] While the constitutions of Ohio, Missouri, and Illinois included a Declaration of Rights that protected religious worship, these constitutions did not make religious liberty their central focus. For example, their preambles did not invoke Deity but focused more on their admittance to the United States. The constitutions of Ohio, Missouri, and Illinois also appear to focus more on the balance of powers between the branches of government, property rights, and other issues rather than religious liberty.

The Ohio Constitution of 1803

The state of Ohio adopted its first constitution in 1803 after becoming as state in 1802.² The preamble to the constitution does not invoke God or Deity. The Declaration of Rights in Ohio's Constitution of 1803 provides similar protections of religion as Pennsylvania's Declaration of Rights: "That all men have a natural and indefeasible right to worship Almighty God according to the dictates of conscience." It also prohibits the state from interfering with the right to worship and protects against compelled financial contribution and religious attendance. No religious test was required to hold office, and civil and political rights were not contingent on belief in God or religious affiliation.

The Ohio Constitution of 1803 also encouraged religious worship: "But religion, morality and knowledge being essentially necessary to good government and the happiness of mankind, schools and the means of instructions shall forever be encouraged by legislative provision not inconsistent with the rights of conscience."³ It also protected "every denomination of religious societies" with profits generated for the support of religion.⁴ Thus, although the Ohio Constitution of 1803 afforded protection to religious worship and encouraged religious worship, similar to the Pennsylvania Constitution, its primary focus does not appear to be God and religious liberty.

The Missouri Constitution of 1820

The state of Missouri adopted its first constitution in 1820 after becoming a state that same year.⁵ The preamble to the constitution does not invoke God or Deity. The Declaration of Rights provides similar protections to that of Pennsylvania: "That all men have a natural and indefeasible right to worship Almighty God according to the dictates of their own consciences." But the right to worship is not absolute and has an exception: "If he do not disturb others in their religious worship." It also protects against compelled financial contribution and religious attendance. No religious test was required to hold office, and civil and political rights were not contingent on belief in God or religious affiliation. It also states that "no religious corporation can ever be established in this state." Notably, the right to religious worship is not the first or second right in the list of rights as in other state constitutions but is listed as the fourth right. The constitution also prohibits bishops, priests, clergymen, or teachers of any religious persuasion from holding political office of the general assembly.[6]

In contrast, the Pennsylvania Constitution emphatically invokes religion and God in its preamble and provides an absolute right to religious worship without exception. It also protects religious societies and does not prohibit preachers and clergy from holding political office. In comparison with the Missouri Constitution of 1820, the Pennsylvania Constitution offers much more protection to religious worship and places much more emphasis on religion.

The Illinois Constitution of 1818

The state of Illinois adopted its first constitution in 1818 after becoming a state that same year.[7] The Illinois Constitution of 1818 was never submitted to the people of Illinois and was drafted based on constitutions from Ohio, Kentucky, and Indiana. The preamble to the constitution does not invoke God or make reference to Deity. The Declaration of Rights provides similar religious protections to that of Pennsylvania: "That all men have a natural and indefeasible right to worship Almighty God according to the dictates of conscience." It also prohibits the state from interfering with the right to worship and protects against compelled financial contribution and religious attendance. No religious test was required to hold office, and civil and political rights were not contingent on belief in God or religious affiliation.[8]

The Illinois Constitution of 1818 is similar to the Ohio Constitution of 1803 because they both protect religious worship, but the primary focus of these constitutions does not appear to be God and religious liberty.

Summary

In summary, in Pennsylvania, Liberty of Conscience was "the First Fundamental" of government.[9] This made Pennsylvania unique when compared to other colonies and other states where Joseph Smith settled. Pennsylvania's unique protections of Liberty of Conscience enabled minority and emerging religions such as The Church of Jesus Christ of Latter-day Saints to grow and flourish.

It was under these circumstances that Joseph Smith and his wife, Emma, encountered Pennsylvania—a unique enclave for minority religious beliefs and diverse opinions. Although some locals in Harmony opposed Joseph's work, he was never arrested or imprisoned for his beliefs while in Pennsylvania. Indeed, he was able to learn to translate the majority of the gold plates while there. William Penn's policies and government, especially his protections of Liberty of Conscience, prepared the way for Joseph to accomplish critical tasks in establishing the Church.

JOSEPH's ARRESTS AND IMPRISONMENT IN OHIO, MISSOURI, AND ILLINOIS

After departing Harmony, Joseph and members of the Church encountered religious prejudice under the law in states where they settled, first in Ohio and then in Missouri and Illinois. Unlike Pennsylvania, where Joseph was not arrested, imprisoned, or tried for his religious beliefs, Joseph faced significant legal battles in Ohio, Missouri, and Illinois. In fact, Joseph Smith was "a party to or a participant in at least 220 lawsuits" during his lifetime.[10] Some of the cases involved religious issues, but the majority appeared to be disputes involving "business, property, municipal, martial, and constitutional law."[11]

In February 1831 the Church moved to Kirtland, Ohio.[12] Kirtland flourished for several years as new converts joined the Church. In 1837, to raise money for the Church and boost Kirtland's struggling economy, Church leaders planned to create a bank called the Kirtland Safety Society.[13] The bank would provide loans to customers and accept deposits from investors. Investors would purchase bank notes backed by the bank's limited reserve of silver and gold coins, which could be redeemed at a later time or sold to others.

Oliver Cowdery applied for a charter from the Ohio state legislature so the bank could be officially designated a bank. Before the Ohio state legislature made a decision, the Kirkland Safety Society opened for business and issued bank notes in exchange for deposits of money from individuals, which was permitted under Ohio law. Many individuals deposited money in the bank or purchased bank notes.

But the Ohio state legislature denied the Church leader's application for a charter. This was unexpected because twenty banks had been chartered in Ohio since 1830.[14]

By the end of January 1837, the Kirkland Safety Society was in a crisis because the bank did not have a charter, and newspapers circulated articles questioning its legitimacy. Investors and depositors requested their money back en masse. By mid-April the United States had entered into a financial crisis, and fears of economic recession prevailed. Banks closed and businesses failed. The Kirtland Safety Society ultimately was forced to close its doors. The Church leaders believed that the Ohio state legislature refused to grant their charter based on religious prejudice.[15]

As a result of the Kirtland Safety Society's failure, Joseph and other Church leaders were charged with bank fraud, many lawsuits were filed against Joseph, and Joseph was arrested several times.[16] One person brought false criminal charges against Joseph, claiming that Joseph had been conspiring against him.[17] Mobs threatened members of the Church with violence, and Joseph continually faced false charges and calls to pay back debt. It may be that citizens and authorities of Ohio did not follow the Ohio Constitution because it was a relatively new and unsettled state.

Because of the persecution in Ohio, members of the Church were forced westward and relocated to Missouri. But Joseph's experience in Missouri was similar to Ohio. In November 1838 Joseph and other Church leaders were arrested and brought to Richmond, Missouri, before Judge Austin A. King for "crimes of High Treason against the State," which could include charges of treason, murder, arson, robbery, burglary, and larceny. These charges appeared to be pretext for religious persecution and holding Joseph and other Church leaders hostage to force the Church members to leave Missouri.[18] According to Joseph, he could not defend himself in court because most of his defense witnesses were arrested and put into prison without an opportunity to testify on his behalf, which was a violation of Joseph's due process rights.[19]

The trial lasted for more than two weeks. Judge King found probable cause against them—meaning that he thought there was sufficient evidence that Joseph and others had committed a crime—and imprisoned them in Liberty Jail in Clay County, Missouri. Joseph and other Church leaders were transported together to the jail. Before entering the jail, the blacksmith arrived with orders from Judge King to handcuff and chain them together. According to Hyrum Smith, the blacksmith commented that the judge "had done this that [they] might not get bail" and had "declared his intention to keep [them] in jail until all the Mormons were driven out of the state."[20] Joseph and the other Church leaders stayed in the unheated jail for four months during the winter, from December 1, 1838, until April 6, 1839.[21]

Citizens of Missouri also filed, according to Joseph, "vexatious lawsuits against" him and other Church leaders as a means of harassment.[22] The tensions between the Church and mobs in Missouri continued to escalate. Church members were driven from their homes as mobs attacked unarmed families and took prisoners. Church members fought back, which resulted in armed conflict and skirmishes with the mobs. False and exaggerated reports and rumors circulated, blaming the Church for the aggression. After hearing these false reports, the governor of Missouri, Lilburn Boggs, decided to intervene. He ordered Missouri militiamen to confront Church members and bring them into submission. In addition, in a deliberate and transparent act of persecution, Governor Boggs issued an executive order directing that "the Mormons must be treated as enemies, and *must be exterminated* or driven from the State if necessary for public peace."[23] Even though the Missouri Constitution protected freedom of religion, it was obvious that Governor Boggs did not enforce it or follow it.

Without religious protection in Missouri, and an order of extermination against them, members of the Church looked for refuge in Illinois. They moved to the banks of the Mississippi River and named their new city Nauvoo. Joseph Smith served as mayor of the city. Before long, citizens of Illinois became uneasy with the success of Nauvoo and the influence of members of the Church. In August 1842 Joseph was arrested and charged with assisting in the attempted shooting of Governor Boggs.[24] He adamantly denied such accusations and believed they lacked credible support.[25]

Later a newspaper in Nauvoo began printing slanderous news stories about Joseph and members of the Church. In June 1844 the Nauvoo City Council convened under the direction of Joseph and, after hours of meetings and deliberation, designated the newspaper a public nuisance. The city council feared that the newspaper would evoke violence against members of the Church, and it elected to suppress the printing press and destroy it.[26] This incident caused ripples through Illinois, prompting then Illinois governor Thomas Ford to intervene. Governor Ford understood that Joseph and Church members had acted in good faith, but under political pressure he sent armed militia to Nauvoo to confiscate the weapons and guns of Church members and required that Joseph submit to state officials: "If you by refusing to submit, shall make it necessary to call out the Militia I have great fears that your city will be destroyed and your people many of them exterminated."[27] Joseph, his brother Hyrum, and other Church leaders had no choice and voluntarily surrendered.[28]

They were taken before Justice of the Peace Robert F. Smith and charged with "riot" for closing and destroying the printing press, and they were released on bail while awaiting trial. But a complaint of treason was filed against Joseph and Hyrum, a capital offense under Illinois law, and they were then immediately arrested by an Illinois constable and retained in prison without a hearing.[29] Religious prejudice seemed to be the motivation behind the arrests and imprisonment and the violation of their constitutional rights. Two days following the arrest by the Illinois constable, a mob stormed the prison in Carthage, Illinois, and killed Joseph and Hyrum.[30] Joseph paid the ultimate sacrifice for his divine mandate—his life.

Harmony, Pennsylvania, Today

In Ohio, Missouri, and Illinois, Joseph encountered significant hostility from state officials and state civilians in the form of lawsuits, arrests, and trials because of his religious beliefs. The Church membership had increased significantly since Harmony, and the Church attracted much more attention from civilians and governments. Joseph was no longer in the remote hills of Harmony translating the Book of Mormon with a few others helping him. In addition, the rule of law in these relatively new states may not have evolved such that constitutional law was respected and enforced, and government officials in those states may have held religious prejudices. As William Penn famously stated, "Governments, like clocks, go from the motion men give them; and as governments are made and moved by men, so by them they are ruined too; wherefore governments rather depend upon men, then men upon governments."[31] Constitutions are only words on paper unless governments and citizens honestly uphold and obey the law.

Even in New York in his early years, Joseph faced searches, arrests, trials, and detentions, apparently motivated by religious persecution. Specifically, (1) in 1826 the state of New York brought a charge of "disorderly person" against Joseph; (2) in 1827 apparently two constables from New York stopped and searched his wagon when he was traveling to Pennsylvania; (3) in 1829 Lucy Harris brought a lawsuit against him in Lyons, New York; (4) in 1829 he was arrested, imprisoned, and tried in Chenego County, New York; and (5) in 1829 he was arrested, imprisoned, and tried in Broome County, New York.

In contrast, there is no record that Joseph was arrested, detained, imprisoned, or tried while in Harmony. The only recorded legal proceeding involving Joseph in Pennsylvania was a non-adversarial judgment by Mr. George H. Noble to transfer Joseph's debt from Mr. Hale to Mr. Noble. Pennsylvania was a unique enclave for religious liberty. William Penn's doctrines and policies were still vibrant during Joseph Smith's time, demonstrated by the Supreme Court's ruling in *Updegraph v. The Commonwealth* the year before Joseph arrived in Pennsylvania. Pennsylvania was committed to "complete" Liberty of Conscience, and the extreme persecution that accompanied the gold plates was confronted head-on by William Penn and Pennsylvania's protection of Liberty of Conscience. Isaac Hale's protection and influence in Harmony also helped safeguard the plates, but Isaac Hale may not have been able to offer this protection without the support of Pennsylvania law.

William Penn, when he was inspired by God to establish the colony of Pennsylvania, may have envisioned that almost one hundred fifty years later, his laws and policies would prepare the way for Joseph Smith to translate the majority of the Book of Mormon, receive the priesthood of God, and receive significant revelations for the Church. Pennsylvania's Liberty of Conscience fostered an environment that enabled Joseph to gain his prophetic voice and establish the foundation of the Church. William Penn envisioned that Pennsylvania would be an "example . . . to the nations" and a "holy experiment." As he predicted, Pennsylvania truly is the "seed of a nation."[32]

Today the Priesthood Restoration Site stands as a testimony that God inspires prophets to bring forth His purposes and as a symbol of religious liberty. As eloquently stated by President Russell M. Nelson almost two hundred years after Joseph resided in Harmony, "How thankful we are for these historical events and for the supernal significance of revelation, scriptures, restoration of priesthood authority, and baptism, all of which unfolded here in this relatively remote but very sacred and serene location."[33]

NOTES

1. Vincent Phillip Munoz, "Church and State in the Founding-Ear State Constitutions," *American Political Thought: A Journal of Ideas, Institutions, and Culture* 4 (Winter 2015): 10–11.

2. Ohio Constitution of 1802. The Ohio Constitution of 1802 remained in effect until September 1, 1851, when a new constitution was adopted. See Ohio Constitution of 1851.

3. Ohio Constitution of 1802, Article VIII, section 3.

4. Ohio Constitution of 1802, Article VIII, section 26.

5. Missouri Constitution of 1820. The Missouri Constitution of 1820 remained in effect until a new constitution was ratified in August 1846.

6. Missouri Constitution of 1820, Article XIII, Declaration of Rights.

7. Illinois Constitution of 1818. The Illinois Constitution of 1818 remained in effect until 1848 when a new constitution was adopted. See Illinois Constitution of 1848.

8. Illinois Constitution, Article VIII, sections 3 and 4.

9. "Fundamental Constitutions of Pennsylvania," reprinted in *William Penn and the Founding of Pennsylvania: A documentary History*, ed. Jean R. Soderlund (Philadelphia: University of Pennsylvania Press, 1983).

10. Gordon A. Madsen, Jeffrey N. Walker, and John W. Welch, eds., *Sustaining the Law: Joseph Smith's Legal Encounters* (Provo, UT: BYU Studies, 2014), xii (introduction).

11. Madsen, Walker, and Welch, *Sustaining the Law*, xvii (introduction). Joseph Smith was involved in several lawsuits in Iowa, but these lawsuits appeared purely civil in nature, and Joseph never maintained a permanent residence in Iowa or spent meaningful time there. Madsen, Walker, and Welch, *Sustaining the Law*, 461–514.

12. History, 1838–1856, volume A-1 [23 December 1805–30 August 1834], 92, josephsmithpapers.org; Richard Lyman Bushman, *Joseph Smith: Rough Stone Rolling* (New York: Alfred A. Knopf, 2005), 144.

13. *Latter Day Saints' Messenger and Advocate* (Kirtland, OH), 1836, 375; Dale W. Adams, "Chartering the Kirtland Bank," *BYU Studies* 23, no. 4 (1983): 468.

14. Bushman, *Joseph Smith: Rough Stone Rolling*, 330.

15. "Historical Address by George A. Smith," in *Journal of Discourses*, 13:107. ("The charter was denied us on the grounds that we were 'Mormons.'")

16. History, 1838–1856, volume B-1 [1 September 1834–2 November 1838], 780, josephsmithpapers.org; Adams, "Chartering the Kirtland Bank," 470. For an in-depth legal analysis of the Kirtland Safety Society, see Jeffrey N. Walker, "Looking Legally at the Kirtland Safety Society," in Madsen, Walker, and Welch, *Sustaining the Law*, 179–226.

17. Transcript of Proceedings, June 5, 1837, State of Ohio on Complaint of *Newell v. Smith*, Geauga County, Ohio, Court of Common Please Record Book T, 52–53, Geauga County Archives and Records Center, Chardon, Ohio.

18. For a detailed analysis of the Court Inquiry by Judge King, see Gordon A. Madsen, "Imprisonment by Austin King's Court of Inquiry in 1838," in Madsen, Walker, and Welch, *Sustaining the Law*, 271–295. After a thorough legal analysis of the evidence, charges, and trial, Madsen concluded that "binding over Joseph Smith and the others for treason" was without legal basis and that Judge King "was determined to put Joseph Smith and those he perceived to be principal Mormon leaders in prison on some nonbailable charge and hold them there as hostages until the Mormons left the state." Madsen, "Imprisonment by Austin King's Court," 295.

19. History, 1838–1856, volume C-1 [2 November 1838–31 July 1842], 858, josephsmithpapers.org; Madsen, "Imprisonment by Austin King's Court," 276.

20. History, 1838–1856, volume D-1 [1 August 1842–1 July 1843], 1615, josephsmithpapers.org; Kenneth L. Alford and Craig K. Manscill, "Hyrum Smith's Liberty Jail Letters," in *Foundations of the Restoration* (Provo, UT: BYU Religious Studies Center, 2016), 190.

21. History, 1838–1856, volume C-1 [2 November 1838–31 July 1842], 858, josephsmithpapers.org; Alford and Manscill, "Hyrum Smith's Liberty Jail Letters," 190.

22. Minute Book 2, 127, josephsmithpapers.org.

23. Lilburn W. Boggs, Jefferson City, MO, to John B. Clark, Fayette, MO, 27 Oct. 1838, Mormon War Papers, Missouri State Archives (emphasis added).

24. Journal, December 1841–December 1842, 129, josephsmithpapers.org.

25. Letter to Sylvester Bartlett, 22 May 1842, 2, josephsmithpapers.org.

26. President Dallin H. Oaks concluded that the decision to suppress the printing press by the Nauvoo City Council, "including its interpretation of the constitutional guarantee of free press, can be supported by reference to the law of their day." For a detailed analysis of the legality of closing the printing press, see Dallin H. Oaks, "Legally Suppressing the Nauvoo Expositor in 1844," in Madsen, Walker, and Welch, *Sustaining the Law*, 427–459.

27. History, 1838–1856, volume F-1 [1 May 1844–8 August 1844], 142, josephsmithpapers.org.

28. Thomas Ford, *History of Illinois, From Its Commencement as a State in 1818 to 1847* (New York: s.n., 1854), 336–37; History, 1838–1856, volume F-1 [1 May 1844–8 August 1844], 153–55, josephsmithpapers.org.

29. Ford, *History of Illinois*, 339–40; History, 1838–1856, volume F-1 [1 May 1844–8 August 1844], 158–160, josephsmithpapers.org.

30. Ford, 347–48; History, 1838–1856, volume F-1 [1 May 1844–8 August 1844], 182–183, josephsmithpapers.org. Notably, while Joseph Smith was named as a defendant in a lawsuit, "he was never convicted of any criminal offense." Madsen, Walker, and Welch, *Sustaining the Law*, xvii (introduction).

31. "The Frame of the Government of the Province of Pennsylvania in America [. . .]" (1682), Historical Society of Pennsylvania.

32. "To Robert Turner, 5 March 1681," in *The Papers of William Penn*, ed. Richard S. and Mary Maples Dunn (Philadelphia: University of Pennsylvania Press, 1981–1987), 2:83 (spelling modernized); "To James Harrison, 26 August 1681," in *Papers of William Penn*, 2:108.

33. "Transcript: President Russell M. Nelson Remarks and Dedicatory Prayer at Priesthood Restoration Site," *Newsroom of The Church of Jesus Christ of Latter-day Saints*, Sept. 19, 2015, https://newsroom.churchofjesuschrist.org/article/priesthood-restoration-site-dedication-transcript.

APPENDIX I

GROWTH OF THE CHURCH
IN PENNSYLVANIA

THROUGH MISSIONARY EFFORTS, THE CHURCH GREW IN PENNSYLVANIA after Joseph Smith's departure. At the end of 1830 the membership of the Church numbered 2,000 in Pennsylvania, with 126 members occupying the northern counties.[1] Church branches were first established in the counties of Bradford and Tioga.[2] By 1839 the Church established branches in southeastern Chester and Philadelphia counties. A branch was organized in Philadelphia by Joseph Smith on December 23, 1839.[3] There were forty members within sixty miles of Philadelphia. The Harmony area did not have a Church unit until the year 2000.[4] As of 2023, over 52,000 members of the Church populate the state of Pennsylvania.[5]

William Penn prepared the way for Joseph Smith to establish the Church. The deep connection between these two pioneers of religious liberty is apparent today in Philadelphia. On September 18, 2016, a Latter-day Saint temple was dedicated in Philadelphia, with a gold statue of the angel Moroni boldly standing atop one of the spires. Only six blocks away from the temple is the City of Philadelphia's city hall, where a prominent statue of William Penn marks the skyline. At the top of the steps of the Philadelphia Art Museum, where Rocky Balboa famously ran up the stairs, you can look out over Philadelphia. Among the buildings and lights stand two figures, and they are the only two figures highlighted in the skyline—William Penn and the angel Moroni.

William Penn Statue on City Hall Tower.

Philadelphia. Pa.

Statues of William Penn and the angel Moroni.

Notes

1. Curtis, V. Alan. "Missionary Activities and Church Organizations in Pennsylvania, 1830–1840" (master's thesis, Brigham Young University), 1976.

2. Brown, 2.

3. Brown, 2. Mark Twain did not think highly of the Book of Mormon. He is quoted as stating that the book was "Chloroform in print. An insipid mess of inspiration, with the Old Testament for a model, and including tedious plagiarism of the New Testament." Mark Twain, *Roughing It* (Hartford CT: American Publishing Company, 1872), 127–28. Twain objected particularly to the frequent use of "and it came to pass," stating that if those phrases were left out, the book would be reduced to a pamphlet. Twain, 128. Twain's keen interest and focus on the Book of Mormon and Joseph Smith in *Roughing It* are an indication of Joseph's success in transmitting his message to a wide audience, as even persons of prominence, such as Mark Twain, took notice and felt compelled to comment.

4. Stanley James Thayne, "In Harmony? Perceptions of Mormonism in Susquehanna, Pennsylvania," *Journal of Mormon History* (Fall 2007): 147.

5. "Facts and Statistics: Pennsylvania," *Newsroom of The Church of Jesus Christ of Latter-day Saints*, accessed Mar. 21, 2024, https://newsroom.churchofjesus-christ.org/facts-and-statistics/state/pennsylvania.

5. "Facts and Statistics: Pennsylvania," *Newsroom of The Church of Jesus Christ of Latter-day Saints*, accessed Mar. 21, 2024, https://newsroom.churchofjesus-christ.org/facts-and-statistics/state/pennsylvania.

APPENDIX II

THE SUSQUEHANNA RIVER: INSPIRATION

THE SUSQUEHANNA RIVER HAS SERVED AS A SOURCE OF INSPIRATION for generations. No one is certain as to the origin of the Susquehanna's name, or even its precise meaning. By most accounts, the suffix *hanna* is Algonquin, meaning "a stream of water" or "river."[1] And *Susque* is believed to mean "crooked."[2] Hence, "crooked river" is the Susquehanna's generally accepted meaning.[3] On his exploratory visit to the river in 1608, Captain John Smith identified the Indians that greeted him as, in the language of Algonquin, Sasquesahanocks and Sasquesahanougs. The tribe eventually became known as Susquehannockes or, in its modern form, Susquehanna.[4]

The name Susquehanna, or "crooked river," is fitting, for the Susquehanna is anything but straight. It winds its way for approximately 444 miles from its northernmost point at Lake Otsego in Cooperstown, New York, to its mouth on the Chesapeake Bay.[5] The West Branch curves east-northeast for much of its 240-mile journey before dropping southeast to rendezvous with the North Branch at Northumberland, near the center of Pennsylvania. The North Branch meanders for about 324 miles in an S-shaped curve, starting in New York, entering Pennsylvania, and then returning back to New York before finally returning to Pennsylvania. Once the branches unite, the Susquehanna flows another 111 miles south, then southeast, entering Maryland for the final twelve miles of its journey before flowing into the Atlantic Ocean at Havre De Grace—the midway point between Philadelphia and Washington, DC.[6] No other eastern United States river delivers more water to the Atlantic Ocean than the Susquehanna.[7] At some points, the Susquehanna is as much as a mile wide and is shallow and treacherous so that ships cannot navigate its waters.[8]

The Susquehanna River near Harmony, Pennsylvania. Photograph by the author.

With its countless tributaries, wondrous views, and heavenly waters, the Susquehanna leaves an indelible impression. Much of Pennsylvania's history is built around early settlements on the banks of the Susquehanna, and many people have received inspiration, economic prosperity, and opportunity from its waters.[9]

"Great Bend"

The North Branch is considered the Susquehanna's primary source.[10] It enters Susquehanna County, Pennsylvania, from the northeastern corner of New York and advances south five miles before making an abrupt turn west for ten miles, only to then return northward back into the state of New York.[11] The part of Pennsylvania carved out by the river is known as the "Great Bend," a beautiful and fertile district.[12] Herman Fairchild, a well-known geologist, labeled this area the "accident of the Susquehanna."[13] He explained that

another developing stream flowing west along New York's border captured the south-flowing Susquehanna's water and turned it into its course, which became the present North Branch running west toward Binghamton, New York. The old Susquehanna course, beheaded by the present course, became Tunkhannock Creek. The "Great Bend" is the most conspicuous physical anomaly of the Susquehanna.[14]

The "Great Bend" curves through the Appalachian Mountains of Pennsylvania, making its terrain exceedingly hilly, with endless precipices and deep and narrow gorges. So broken and irregular are the hills as to furnish scenery strikingly wild and remarkably picturesque.[15] "I have witnessed the finest scenery to be presented in the different quarters of the globe, but nowhere have I seen nature more beautiful than she appears from summits of these hills," observed one early explorer of the region.[16] The Susquehanna River will continue to serve as a source of inspiration and guidance for those who take a moment to contemplate near its waters.[17]

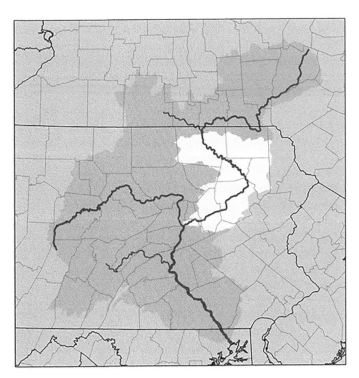

Map of Susquehanna River watershed sub-basins,
I. Karl Musser.

Notes

1. Susan Q. Stranahan, *Susquehanna, River of Dreams* (Baltimore and London: The Johns Hopkins University Press, 1993), 3. The word *Susquehanna*, derived from Sisku (mud) and hanna (a stream), was probably overheard by someone listening to the Indians speak among themselves at the time of a flood. The Indians would have said, "Juh Achsis quehanne," which means "How muddy the stream is," and this would have been taken as the proper name of the river." George P. Donehoo, *A History of the Indian Villages and Place Names in Pennsylvania* (Harrisburg, PA: The Telegraph Press, 1928), 215; Garford F. Williams, "Susquehanna County, Pennsylvania," *Susquehanna County Historical Society Journal of Genealogy and Local History* 19, no. 2 (Fall/Winter 2008): 54.

2. Williams, "Susquehanna County, Pennsylvania," 54.

3. Abner H. Baird Collection, *Harmony, Pennsylvania: Deeds, Wills, Maps, Pictures and Historical Information of the Joseph Smith and Isaac Hale Farms*, L. Tom Perry Special Collections, Harold B. Lee Library, Brigham Young University, Provo. Historian Grant Carter believes that *Susquehanna* means "crooked water." Grant E. Carter, "Along the Susquehanna," *Improvement Era*, May 1960, 3.

4. Stranahan, *Susquehanna, River of Dreams*, 3. The Susquehannocks believed that the "Great Spirit" made the earth, and all that it contains, for the common good of mankind. It was not for the benefit of a few but of all. They reverently worshipped the "Great Spirit" who created them, "who governed the world, who taught the streams to flow and the bird to build her nest, who caused the day and night and the changing seasons, who stocked the streams with fish and the forests with game." C. Hale Sipe, *The Indian Wars of Pennsylvania* (Harrisburg, PA: The Telegraph Press, 1929), 17–18; Richmond E. Myers, *The Long Crooked River: The Susquehanna* (Boston: The Christopher Publishing House, 1949), 5. All that the Susquehannocks possessed, all that they enjoyed, and all that they looked upon was considered a gift to them from the "Great Spirit," who gave them life. Myers, *Long Crooked River*, 54.

    John Smith described the Susquehannocks as follows: "Those are the strangest people of all those countries, both in language and attire." Barry C. Kent, *Susquehanna's Indians: Anthropological Series Number 6* (Harrisburg, PA: The Pennsylvania Historical and Museum Commission, 1993), 26. Susquehannocks is not the name by which the tribe elected to be called, but it was given to them by the Englishman or other tribes, and it stuck. Kent, *Susquehanna's Indians*, 28. The Susquehannocks were a mighty people and feared by other tribes. Kent, 26.

    The Susquehannocks would rather have an empty stomach than neglect their duty by not satisfying the wants of the stranger, the sick, or the needy. They paid respect to persons of old age. In both their public and private meetings, they heeded the advice and observations of their elders. Myers, *Long Crooked River*, 54.

5. Jack Brubaker, *Down The Susquehanna To The Chesapeake* (University Park, PA: The Pennsylvania State University Press, 2002), 28. The distance from Cooperstown to the Chesapeake is only 300 miles if traveled by road. Brubaker, *Down The Susquehanna*, 28.

6. Brubaker, *Down The Susquehanna*, x. The Susquehanna is shaped like a free-form "Y," with a West Branch and a North Branch, the main stream flowing from their union. Stranahan, *Susquehanna, River of Dreams*, 2. General Lafayette, a French general serving in the Continental Army in the Revolutionary War, as he crossed the Susquehanna on his way to Philadelphia to see George Washington, exclaimed, "Why it is surely like our own Havre de Grace in France." That community at the mouth of the Chesapeake Bay then came to be named after France's "harbor of mercy," which is known simply as Le Havre. R. G. Rincliffe, *"Conowingo!" The History of a Great Development on the Susquehanna* (New York, San Francisco, and Montreal: The Newcomen Society in North America, 1953), 10.

7. Stranahan, *Susquehanna, River of Dreams*, 2–3. On an average day, the Susquehanna delivers 25 billion gallons of water to the Atlantic Ocean.

8. Ruth Hoover Seitz, *Susquehanna Heartland* (Harrisburg, PA: RB Books, 1992), 1. In Dauphin County there is a stretch of river one-mile wide. Seitz, *Susquehanna Heartland*, 1; Sylvester K. Stevens, *Pennsylvania: The Keystone State* (New York: The American Historical Company, Inc., 1956), 8; Elizabeth Carmer and Carl Carmer, *The Susquehanna from New York to the Chesapeake* (Champaign, IL: Garrard Publishing Company, 1964), 75. In April 1826 the captain of the steamboat *Codorus* labored along the Susquehanna for four months but gave up and said the Susquehanna was impossible for steamboats to travel. Carmer, *The Susquehanna*, 77.

9. As expressed by one author, "If you are fond of the beautiful in nature, let me advise you to come and see a sunset on the Susquehanna, and linger long enough on its banks to learn its traditions and you will love it as truly as the writer." James Edwin Free, "The Susquehanna River," *Christian Advocate (1866–1905)*, Jan. 31, 1984, 5, 59.

10. Elsie Singmaster, *Pennsylvania's Susquehanna* (Harrisburg, PA: J. Horace McFarland Company, 1950), 13. "[The Susquehanna] dips down into the meadows of Pennsylvania and returns again to New York before it reaches the first city on its banks—Binghamton." Carmer, *The Susquehanna*, 85. Susquehanna County was formed on February 21, 1810. A. Margaretta Archambault, ed., *A Guide Book of Art, Architecture, and Historic Interests in Pennsylvania* (Philadelphia: The John C. Winston Company, 1924), 409; Brubaker, *Down The Susquehanna*, x1. The West Branch of the Susquehanna is shorter and somewhat narrower than the North Branch and provides less volume to the flow at the confluence. Brubaker, x1.

11. Rhamanthus M. Stocker, *Centennial History of Susquehanna County, Pennsylvania*, 2nd ed. (Baltimore, MD: Regional Publishing Company, 1974), 38. In 1976 the United States Army Corps of Engineers announced plans for

five dams in the Binghamton area. The largest would have loomed 125 feet above the river between the towns of Great Bend and Susquehanna. Water held behind this dam would have inundated thirteen Susquehanna towns from Oakland, Susquehanna, and Lanesboro in Pennsylvania through New York's villages, well beyond Great Bend. The plan did not pass due to the opposition of local inhabitants. Brubaker, *Down The Susquehanna*, 31. Today four dams operate in a span of 45 miles in the region. Seitz, *Susquehanna Heartland*, 1.

12. Henry Darwin Rogers, *The Geology of Pennsylvania, A Government Survey*, vol. 1. (unpublished, 1858), 48; Stranahan, *Susquehanna, River of Dreams*, 15. This small sector of Pennsylvania has been depicted in magazines and art covers. The river makes a wide curve at this point. Carmer, *The Susquehanna*, 336.

13. Brubaker, *Down The Susquehanna*, 29.

14. Brubaker, *Down The Susquehanna*, 29; Myers, *Long Crooked River*, 14. Of all the rivers in America, the Susquehanna is probably the most difficult to define due to its many tributaries and subsidiary rivers. Myers, 13.

15. Glaciers covered the area for 10,000 years before making their final retreat. Stranahan, *Susquehanna, River of Dreams*, 15.

16. Stocker, *Centennial History of Susquehanna County*, 569. The Erie Railway follows the Susquehanna River through the northern part of Susquehanna County, a distance of about fifteen miles. The railway has two stations within the county—Susquehanna and Great Bend. Stocker, 56.

17. Historian Jennifer Reeder states that the Susquehanna River "led Joseph Smith to find Emma Hale." Jennifer Reeder, *First: The Life and Faith of Emma Smith* (Salt Lake City, UT: Deseret Book, 2021), 16.

A Tribute to the Muralist Violet Oakley

"My own faith in an organized world governed by international law dates from my first study of the life of William Penn and his 'Holy Experiment,' as he called the unfortified Commonwealth of Pennsylvania in 1682." —Violet Oakley[1]

Violet Oakley was the pioneer woman in mural paintings and the first American woman to receive a public mural commission. In 1902 she was commissioned to paint murals in the United States Capitol building and the United States Supreme Court chambers. Later the state of Pennsylvania commissioned her to paint murals in the Pennsylvania State Capitol building in Harrisburg, Pennsylvania. Forty-three of her paintings now hang in the Pennsylvania State Capitol. Many of her murals present scenes from the life of William Penn and still adorn the walls of the Governor's Reception Room at the Pennsylvania State Capitol building.

Violet Oakley studied and pondered the life and teachings of William Penn. Before painting the murals of William Penn for the Governor's Reception Room in the Pennsylvania State Capitol building, she traveled to England to better understand him and Quakerism. She later stated, "In time I became so impressed by the belief or testimony of the Quakers against carnal warfare that this idea, the victory of law, or truth over force, became the central idea of my life."[2] She embraced many Quaker teachings, including the principles of pacifism, equality of the races and genders, and international government.

Violet Oakley also painted portraits of members of the League of Nations in Geneva, Switzerland, and felt a deep sense of connection between Philadelphia and Geneva. "I believe there exists, spiritually, a great suspension bridge, 'made without hands, eternal, in the heavens,' a bridge connecting Philadelphia, Penn's city of Brotherly Love,— and the city of Geneva," wrote Violet Oakley.[3] The suspension bridge may have been the cities' historical men who defended religious liberty. The leaders of the Protestant Reformation—William Farel, John Calvin, Theodore Beza, and John Knox—fled France and landed in Geneva, just like William Penn, the Quakers, and other believers who fled England for Pennsylvania.

Portrait of Violet Oakley, 1900. Photo by Bain News Service. US Library of Congress.

Violet Oakley received many honors during her lifetime. In 1905 she became the first woman to receive the Gold Medal of Honor from the Pennsylvania Academy of Fine Arts. In 1948 she received an honorary doctorate of laws degree from the Drexel Institute. Today her paintings and influence persist on the walls of the United States Capitol and the Pennsylvania State Capitol. It is evident that Violet Oakley truly understood William Penn's cause of religious liberty and tolerance of all faiths.

Notes

1. Violet Oakley, *The Holy Experiment: A Message to the World from Pennsylvania* (Philadelphia: Cogslea Studio Publications, 1950), 19.

2. Violet Oakley, *Law Triumphant: Containing the Opening of the Book of the Law and the Miracle of Geneva* (Philadelphia: privately printed, 1933), found at https://digitalcollections.graduateinstitute.ch/records/item/1149-law-triumphant; "Violet Oakley: Citizen of the World," Historical Society of Pennsylvania, July 27, 2015, https://hsp.org/blogs/fondly-pennsylvania/violet-oakley-citizen-of-the-world.

3. Oakley, *Law Triumphant*, 14 (spelling modernized). The internal quote is from 2 Corinthians 5:1.